The Godwinian Novel

The Rational Fictions of Godwin, Brockden Brown, Mary Shelley

PAMELA CLEMIT

CLARENDON PRESS · OXFORD
1993

Oxford University Press, Walton Street, Oxford OX2 6DP

Oxford New York Toronto
Delhi Bombay Calcutta Madras Karachi
Kuala Lumpur Singapore Hong Kong Tokyo
Nairobi Dar es Salaam Cape Town
Melbourne Auckland Madrid

and associated companies in
Berlin Ibadan

Oxford is a trade mark of Oxford University Press

Published in the United States
by Oxford University Press Inc., New York

British Library Cataloguing in Publication Data
Data available

Library of Congress Cataloging in Publication Data
Clemit, Pamela.
The Godwinian novel: the rational fictions of Godwin,
Brockden Brown, Mary Shelley/Pamela Clemit.
(Oxford English monographs)
Includes bibliographical references and index.
1. Godwin, William, 1756–1836—Criticism and interpretation.
2. Shelley, Mary Wollstonecraft, 1797–1851—Criticism and interpretation. 3. Brown, Charles Brockden, 1771–1810—Criticism and interpretation. 4. Godwin, William, 1756–1836—Influence.
5. Political fiction, English—History and criticism. 6. American fiction—English influences. 7. Rationalism in literature.
8. Radicalism in literature. 9. Romanticism. I. Title.
II. Series.
823'.609—dc20 PR4724.C57 1993 92–27583
ISBN 0–19–811220–3

Typeset by Cambrian Typesetters, Frimley, Surrey

Printed and bound in
Great Britain by Bookcraft Ltd.
Midsomer Norton, Bath.

For my father
and
in memory of my mother
(1923–1989)

Acknowledgements

I would like to thank several people who have provided argumentative support during the writing of this book. I am grateful to Marilyn Butler, my D.Phil. supervisor, for her generous sharing of knowledge, and to Paul Hamilton for his encouragement over many years. Mark Philp has made instructive criticisms of this study in draft; Anthony Clemit, John Creaser, Peter Garside, Stephen Gill, and Michael O'Neill have each commented on various chapters; David Julier has helped me to formulate my ideas throughout.

My thanks are due to Lord Abinger for permission to quote from the Abinger Collection in the Bodleian Library, and to the staff of the Bodleian Library. A version of Chapter 1 appeared in *Eighteenth-Century Fiction*, 3 (1991), 217–39. I am grateful to the editors for permission to reprint.

P.A.C.

Contents

Abbreviations and Conventions

A	Charles Brockden Brown, *Alcuin: A Dialogue, with Memoirs of Stephen Calvert* (1797–8), *The Novels and Related Works of Charles Brockden Brown*, ed. Sydney J. Krause *et al.* (Kent, Oh., 1977–86), vol. vi.
Ab. MSS	Abinger Manuscripts. References are by deposit number, following the coding used in the Bodleian Library.
AM	Charles Brockden Brown, *Arthur Mervyn; or, Memoirs of the Year 1793* (1799–1800), *Works*, vol. iii.
CW	William Godwin, *Things As They Are; or, The Adventures of Caleb Williams*, 3 vols. (London, 1794, 2nd edn., 1796, 3rd edn., 1797, 4th edn., 1816, 5th edn., 1831). References are by volume and page number to the edition in which they first occur, indicated in square brackets, followed by the page number of the standard critical edition, ed. David McCracken (Oxford, 1970), which incorporates later revisions and reprints the manuscript ending; where the later text differs from previous editions, this is indicated by adding '*var.*' at the end of the reference.
E	William Godwin, *The Enquirer: Reflections on Education, Manners and Literature. In a Series of Essays* (London, 1797).
EAL	*Early American Literature.*
EIC	*Essays in Criticism.*
F	Mary Wollstonecraft Shelley, *Frankenstein; or, The Modern Prometheus, the 1818 text*, ed. with variant readings, introduction, and notes by James Rieger (1974; Chicago, 1982).
Fl	William Godwin, *Fleetwood; or, The New Man of Feeling*, 3 vols. (London, 1805).
HC	William Godwin, *History of the Commonwealth of England. From its Commencement, to the Restoration of Charles the Second*, 4 vols. (London, 1824–8).

Im William Godwin, *Imogen: A Pastoral Romance. From the Ancient British* (1784), ed. Jack W. Marken (New York, 1963).

LC William Godwin, *Life of Geoffrey Chaucer, the Early English Poet ... with Sketches of the Manners, Opinions, Arts and Literature of England in the Fourteenth Century*, 2 vols. (London, 1803).

LM Mary Wollstonecraft Shelley, *The Last Man* (1826), introd. Brian Aldiss (London, 1985).

LP William Godwin, *Lives of Edward and John Philips, Nephews and Pupils of Milton; including Various Particulars of the Literary and Political History of their Times* (London, 1815).

M William Godwin, *Mandeville: A Tale of the Seventeenth Century in England*, 3 vols. (Edinburgh, 1817).

MM *Monthly Magazine, and American Review*, ed. Charles Brockden Brown (1799–1800), Microfilm USA 17, from original in Library of Congress.

MSJ *The Journals of Mary Wollstonecraft Shelley, 1814–1844*, ed. Paula R. Feldman and Diana Scott-Kilvert, 2 vols. (Oxford, 1987).

MSL *The Letters of Mary Wollstonecraft Shelley*, ed. Betty T. Bennett, 3 vols. (Baltimore, 1980–8). References are by volume and page number.

PBSL *The Letters of Percy Bysshe Shelley*, ed. Frederick L. Jones, 2 vols. (Oxford, 1964). References are by volume and page number.

PC John Robison, *Proofs of a Conspiracy against all the Governments of Europe, carried on in the Secret Meetings of Free Masons, Illuminati and Reading Societies* (Edinburgh, 1797).

PJ William Godwin, *Enquiry Concerning Political Justice, and Its Influence on Morals and Happiness*, photographic facsimile of 3rd edn. (1798), corr. and ed. with variant readings of the 1st (1793) and 2nd (1796) edns. by F. E. L. Priestley, 3 vols. (Toronto, 1946). References are to passages in the 1st edition unless otherwise stated.

PL John Milton, *Paradise Lost* (1667), ed. Alastair Fowler, Longman Annotated English Poets (London, 1968, 1971).

PMLA	*Publications of the Modern Language Association of America.*
R	Edmund Burke, *Reflections on the Revolution in France, and on the Proceedings in Certain Societies in London Relative to that Event* (1790), ed. Conor Cruise O'Brien (Harmondsworth, 1969).
RE	Constantin François Chasseboeuf, Comte de Volney, *The Ruins; or, A Survey of the Revolutions of Empires* (1791), anonymously trans. from the French (London, 1792, 1838).
RM	Thomas Paine, *Rights of Man; Being an Answer to Burke's Attack on the French Revolution* (1791–2), ed. Henry Collins (Harmondsworth, 1969).
SEL	*Studies in English Literature.*
SIR	*Studies in Romanticism.*
SL	William Godwin, *St Leon: A Tale of the Sixteenth Century*, 4 vols. (London, 1799).
STCL	*The Collected Letters of Samuel Taylor Coleridge*, ed. E. L. Griggs, 6 vols. (Oxford, 1956–71). References are by volume and page number.
Stud. N.	*Studies in the Novel.*
TP	William Godwin, *Thoughts Occasioned by the Perusal of Dr Parr's Spital Sermon* (London, 1801), reprinted in *Uncollected Writings (1785–1822)*, ed. Jack W. Marken and Burton R. Pollin (Gainesville, Fla., 1968).
UTQ	*University of Toronto Quarterly.*
V	Mary Wollstonecraft Shelley, *Valperga; or, The Life and Adventures of Castruccio, Prince of Lucca*, 3 vols. (London, 1823).
VRW	Mary Wollstonecraft, *Vindication of the Rights of Woman: with Strictures on Political and Moral Subjects* (1792), ed. Miriam Brody Kramnick (Harmondsworth, 1975, 1982).
W	Charles Brockden Brown, *Wieland; or The Transformation, together with Memoirs of Carwin the Biloquist* (1798, 1803), *Works*, vol. i.

Quotations from Spenser are from *The Faerie Queene*, ed. A. C. Hamilton, Longman Annotated English Poets (London, 1977); quotations from Milton are from *Complete Shorter Poems*, ed.

John Carey, Longman Annotated English Poets (London, 1968, 1971); quotations from Shelley's poetry are from *Shelley: Poetical Works*, ed. Thomas Hutchinson, corr. G. M. Matthews (Oxford, 1970); quotations from Byron are from *Byron: Poetical Works*, ed. Frederick Page, corr. John Jump (Oxford, 1970). In all other quotations, the original spelling and punctuation have been preserved. In references to letters and manuscripts, square brackets indicate an inferred or conjectured date or spelling and angle brackets indicate an authorial cancellation, following the respective editor or cataloguer. Otherwise all square brackets are my own.

Introduction

THIS book studies the development of an original genre of fiction in the Romantic period. It takes as its starting-point the consciously political form pioneered by William Godwin (1756–1836) in *Things As They Are; or, The Adventures of Caleb Williams* (1794) and developed in the works of his principal followers, Charles Brockden Brown (1771–1810) and Mary Wollstonecraft Shelley (1797–1851). To argue for the importance of authorial engagement with external concerns is not to deny the importance of aesthetic considerations. My study relates Godwin's political theories not only to literary themes and content but to formal and technical considerations as well. Above all, Godwin's triumph is one of technique: in *Caleb Williams* he creates an imaginatively sophisticated, economically plotted, and mythologically capacious narrative form which proved capable of 'new and startling' combinations of meaning in the works of his fictional heirs.[1] This innovative blend of philosophy and fiction proved so distinctive in its aims and methods that nineteenth-century reviewers wrote of 'the Godwin school' of novelists, who, 'by a common master, a common philosophical as well as poetical belief, common training . . . and many specific resemblances in manner and style, are proclaimed to be one'.[2] Whether there are valid grounds for proclaiming the novelists in the Godwin school to be 'one' is the subject investigated here.

Recognizing the three Godwinian writers as a group uncovers ties at all levels, starting with the familial and social ties between Godwin and Mary Shelley and extending outwards to a complex pattern of literary, philosophical, and political interchange which includes the works of Charles Brockden Brown in the new

[1] William Hazlitt, 'Mr Godwin' [1830], *The Complete Works of William Hazlitt*, ed. P. P. Howe, 21 vols. (London, 1930–4), xvi. 394; quoted in full at the start of Ch. 2.

[2] George Gilfillan, 'Mrs Shelley', *A Second Gallery of Literary Portraits* (Edinburgh, 1850), 284; cf. Gilfillan, 'William Godwin', *A Gallery of Literary Portraits* (Edinburgh, 1845), 34–5; [J. W. Croker], review of *Frankenstein*, *Quarterly Review*, 18 (Jan. 1818), 382; review of *Valperga*, *Blackwood's Edinburgh Magazine*, 13 (Mar. 1823), 284.

American republic. This pattern involves disruptions as well as parallels. Just as Percy Shelley and Byron engage in productive debate with Wordsworth and Coleridge, the major poets of the previous generation, so too Brown and Mary Shelley elaborate, reappraise, and redefine Godwin's narrative art. However, the Godwinian novelists form a more coherent group than the Romantic poets. Whatever their ideological differences and changes in historical circumstances, they adhere to the narrative model pioneered in *Caleb Williams*. In establishing a specific set of conventions for literary communication, the Godwinian novel sets up its own framework for debate. With its capacity to remember and modify its own earlier versions, the Godwinian novel permits a progressively deepening cultural revaluation, as similar situations are explored by successive writers with greater refinement and resourcefulness.

To focus on the distinctive type of intellectual fiction developed by the Godwinian writers is not to deny the existence of other narrative modes which engage with political concerns in the Romantic period. The richness and diversity of formal developments in the novel in the years from 1789 to 1830 have been shown by Gary Kelly's survey, *English Fiction of the Romantic Period, 1789–1830* (1989). Especially relevant to Godwin's early career is the revolutionary novel produced by the English Jacobin writers of the early 1790s. Godwin's subsequent experiments in historical fiction, *St Leon: A Tale of the Sixteenth Century* (1799), *Fleetwood; or, The New Man of Feeling* (1805), and *Mandeville: A Tale of the Seventeenth Century in England* (1817), need to be viewed in relation to Scott's more colourful narrative art which offers further possibilities for the representation of topical concerns. In the second half of the period, Mary Shelley develops the Godwinian narrative model at a time of general experimentation with a range of non-naturalistic fictional forms. For example, in *Anastasius; or, Memoirs of a Greek* (1819) Thomas Hope presents a blend of cultural anatomy and confessional technique that looks back to Dr John Moore's study of egotistical personality and aristocratic values in *Zeluco: Various Views of Human Nature* (1789). Hazlitt took this mixed form a stage further in *Liber Amoris; or, The New Pygmalion* (1823), where he made critical use of subjective techniques to explore contemporary aesthetic trends. At the same time Peacock's highly cerebral satires offered a major formal innovation in the analysis of social and intellectual concerns. The general growth of experimentation with non-realist forms in this period is part of the fertile background to the phenomenon of the Godwin school.

Historically informed criticism of Godwin's novels begins with two influential studies of fiction in the Romantic period, Gary Kelly's *The English Jacobin Novel, 1780–1805* (1976) and Marilyn Butler's *Jane Austen and the War of Ideas* (1975, 1987).[3] In these accounts, *Caleb Williams* is viewed as the most successful of a series of radical novels produced in the immediate aftermath of the French Revolution by a group of writers who frequented the circle of London radicals centred on the Dissenting publisher Joseph Johnson.[4] During the literary and philosophical debate which followed the publication of Edmund Burke's *Reflections on the Revolution in France* (1790), the major Jacobin novelists, Thomas Holcroft, Elizabeth Inchbald, and Godwin developed a common interest in fiction as a means of disseminating the ideas of Godwin's principal philosophical work, the *Enquiry Concerning Political Justice* (1793). What was distinctive in Jacobin fiction, according to Kelly, was its attempt to illustrate Godwin's proposition that 'the characters of men originate in their external circumstances' by means of a 'unity of design', whereby the incidents of the story would be related to the developing character of the participants.[5]

In fact few Jacobin novels achieve this unified philosophical design. The main significance of Jacobin fiction as a precursor of *Caleb Williams* lies in its use of the themes of Richardson and his followers to illustrate a growing preoccupation with social oppression. On the whole the Jacobin novelists remained suspicious of the subjective techniques of sentimental literature, based on the intuitive psychology of Shaftesbury and Hume which Godwin sought to refute in the first edition of *Political Justice*.[6] Thus they failed to develop a new form in which to embody their philosophical

[3] Gary Kelly, *The English Jacobin Novel, 1780–1805* (Oxford, 1976), 179–208; Marilyn Butler, *Jane Austen and the War of Ideas* (Oxford, 1975; 2nd edn., 1987), 29–87.

[4] G. P. Tyson, *Joseph Johnson: A Liberal Publisher* (Des Moines, 1979), 121.

[5] William Godwin, *Enquiry Concerning Political Justice* (2nd edn., 1796), chapter heading to Bk. 1, ch. 4, *PJ* i. 24; Thomas Holcroft, *Alwyn; or, the Gentleman Comedian*, 2 vols. (London, 1780), Preface, i, p. vi, quoted by Kelly as the 'manifesto' of the English Jacobin novelists, 14.

[6] See Butler, *War of Ideas*, 33–42.

concerns. Instead, the most effective Jacobin novels are modelled on *Pamela* (1740) and *Clarissa* (1747–8), with their central struggles for mastery and independence of mind within an entrenched paternalistic society.

Inchbald's economical tale of domestic oppression, *A Simple Story* (1791), is especially instructive in showing how the critical investigation of sentimental ideas in the works of Richardson could be harnessed in support of rational philosophy. The novel centres on a power-struggle between the volatile Miss Milner and her guardian, the Roman Catholic priest Dorriforth, who later inherits property, abandons his vocation, and marries his ward. The strength of Inchbald's analysis lies, in Kelly's words, in her portrayal of 'the repression and the force of powerful but natural feelings',[7] as Dorriforth subjects Miss Milner to repeated inquisitions about her social conduct. In the novel's second part, Inchbald presents the education of Miss Milner's daughter as a corrective to her mother's lack of control, but the novel's larger questions about paternal authority remain unanswered.

The theme of parental oppression has a more overt political meaning in *Anna St Ives* (1792), where Holcroft uses the eighteenth-century courtship and seduction plot to illustrate a Godwinian faith in the power of rational judgement. But in his zeal to inculcate rational values, Holcroft excludes whole areas of human experience: despite the intermittent complexity of viewpoint introduced by his choice of the epistolary form, characters are simplified for demonstrative ends even at the culmination of the story. It was this 'obtrusion' of political ideas on the reader 'when their passions were roused, & imagination was on tiptoe for events' that Godwin criticized after reading the novel in manuscript.[8] Ronald Paulson has commented of the treatment of revolutionary concerns in Jacobin fiction: 'Somewhere within all of these novels lurked the allegorical form with its simple equivalents.'[9] In foregrounding the programmatic element in Jacobin fiction, however, Paulson overlooks the more technically sophisticated mode of fiction pioneered in *Caleb Williams*.

This book offers a reassessment of Godwin's whole career as a

[7] Kelly, *English Jacobin Novel*, 79.

[8] Godwin, undated MS critique of *Anna St Ives*, Ab. MSS, b. 227/6.

[9] Ronald Paulson, *Representations of Revolution (1789–1820)* (New Haven, Conn., 1983), 239.

philosophical novelist. Its basic contentions are twofold: first, that there is a greater unity between Godwin's fiction and his philosophy than has generally been allowed; and second, that Godwin's fictional achievement is best viewed not in terms of the rapid evolution and disintegration of the Jacobin tradition, but in relation to a more imaginatively compelling group of novels which flourished throughout the Romantic period. My study is divided into two parts. The first part deals with Godwin's novels between 1784 and 1817, and the second part examines the works of his two major followers.

Although *Caleb Williams* has traditionally been seen as Godwin's first significant work, his earlier novel, *Imogen: A Pastoral Romance* (1784), shows that he is experimenting with fiction in an intellectually sophisticated way long before the Jacobin writers were brought together in the period of controversy immediately following the French Revolution. Godwin's use of Spenserian and Miltonic models in *Imogen* suggests his primary allegiance to an older tradition of politically engaged literature going back to a body of writings which flourished in opposition to court culture and values after the Restoration. According to his own account of his early years, Godwin was saturated in works dealing with the Puritan ethic of free choice.[10] Above all he responded to the symbolic modes of the Bible and *Pilgrim's Progress*, which offered a progressive narrative form, unified by a single-minded quest for spiritual truth. Godwin's early recognition of the power of allegory and fable, rather than elaborately plotted, more naturalistic modes of representation, helps to explain his unique success in writing a novel with a coherent philosophical design in the early 1790s.

To understand the degree of interaction between philosophy and imaginative techniques in *Caleb Williams*, we need to recognize Godwin's primary philosophical allegiance to the traditions and assumptions of eighteenth-century Rational Dissent. The extent to which *Political Justice* reflects Godwin's engagement with eighteenth-century Dissenting traditions has been documented most fully by Mark Philp.[11] In this reading, Godwin's case for 'the sacred and indefeasible right of private judgment' (*PJ* ii. 449), and his associated discussions concerning the nature of truth and virtue,

[10] Godwin, autobiographical fragment, [1756–1769], Ab. MSS, b. 226/1.

[11] Mark Philp, *Godwin's Political Justice* (London, 1986), 15–37; cf. F. E. L. Priestley, 'Critical Introduction', *PJ* iii. 78–81.

are deeply indebted to Dissenting theological debates. In the debates from 1770 to 1773, over compulsory subscription to the Thirty-nine Articles, and from 1787 to 1792, over the Test and Corporation Acts, discussion moved beyond the issue of freedom of conscience to broader questions of moral and political duty, divorced from their original theological context.[12] To prefer conscience before tradition is to resist attempts to marshal opinion, since, in the words of Milton's Eve, 'Our reason is our law' (*PL* ix. 654). In *Political Justice* Godwin appropriates the arguments for autonomy and self-determination which Milton puts in the mouths of Eve and Satan to support his argument for the dissolution of all legislative restraints. Godwin's vision of the gradual withering away of governmental institutions is premissed on the individual's duty to seek out truth for himself or herself through the unrestrained exercise of private judgement.

Godwin alone succeeded in creating a fictional form in which to convey these specific philosophical concerns. Rejecting the eighteenth-century courtship plot in favour of a tale based on flight and pursuit, he transforms a straightforward opposition of class stereotypes into a dynamic conflict of personalities in which the protagonists are constantly changing roles. Godwin's boldest innovation, however, lies in his use of the first-person narrative to explore his philosophical interests. By allowing his beleaguered protagonist to tell his own story, he gives scope for an analysis of the psychological effects of systematized oppression. Yet Godwin is not content with a critique, however penetrating, of social inequality. The inbuilt unreliability of his first-person account throws the burden of interpretation and decision on the reader, soliciting his or her active participation. This is not to suggest that meaning is open to indiscriminate appropriation or to advocate a plurality of critical methods: instead we need to recognize the historically specific assumptions governing Godwin's manipulation of point of view. Through appealing to the reader as judge, Godwin seeks to activate his central philosophical belief in the 'unspeakably beautiful' doctrine of private judgement (*PJ* i. 182), which is based on the assumption that we have an obligation to seek out objective truths in the moral and political realm.

[12] A. H. Lincoln, *Some Political and Social Ideas of English Dissent, 1763–1800* (Cambridge, 1938), 182–270.

Recognition of the political dimension of Godwin's use of the first-person narrative leads to a revaluation of the subjective mode of his later historical novels, which are commonly read in terms of his abandonment of radical ideals in favour of Romantic preoccupations with individual selfhood.[13] In fact, the tenacity of Godwin's political optimism demands attention. After the mid-1790s, his increased attention to the inner lives of individuals reflects the gradualist theory of political progress which is central to his influence on younger writers, not confined to those discussed here. Percy Shelley was by no means alone in his opinion that 'Godwin has been to the present age in moral philosophy what Wordsworth is in poetry'.[14] In his later historical fictions, Godwin takes as his subject the impact of revolutionary change on individual lives, and his insight into the formative power of public events invites comparison with the more celebrated historical narratives of Scott and Byron. At the same time, however, Godwin's use of the single confessional narrative makes for a less open-ended fiction than *Caleb Williams*. After *St Leon*, the initiative for technical development and self-criticism in the Godwinian novel passes to Charles Brockden Brown and Mary Shelley.

The works of Brown and Mary Shelley present a range of variants on the primary Godwinian form established in *Caleb Williams*. The recurring plot and the first-person narrative are modified and developed in response to shifting ideological pressures in the post-revolutionary period. In *Wieland* (1798), rejecting Godwin's early belief in the sanctity of private judgement, Brown turns his first-person narrative technique back on itself to dramatize the dangers of uncontrolled individualism, a concern taken further in Mary Shelley's experiments with multiple points of view. Yet, however sceptical of Godwin's political philosophy, Brown and Mary Shelley share his capacity to project theoretical concerns in extreme and totally arresting imaginative forms. Godwin's bold symbolic plot proliferates in significance in the writings of his school, achieving its most equivocal reformulation in *Frankenstein*

[13] Kelly, *English Jacobin Novel*, 223; P. N. Furbank, 'Godwin's Novels', *EIC* 5 (1955), 214–18; George Sherburn, 'Godwin's Later Novels', *SIR* 1 (1962), 65–82.

[14] P. B. Shelley, 'On Godwin's *Mandeville*' [1817], *Examiner* (28 Dec. 1817), 826, *The Complete Works of Percy Bysshe Shelley*, ed. Roger Ingpen and Walter E. Peck, Julian Edition, 10 vols. (London, 1926–30), vi. 222.

(1818). Mary Shelley's early analysis of the oppressed psyche gains its immense power because she is already writing within a genre discussing social issues and revolutionary change, but at the same time the novel's structural complexity brings to the fore the radical instability of meaning already latent in *Caleb Williams*. Mary Shelley's studies of egotistical ambition in her novels of the 1820s show a further deflection and subversion of earlier Godwinian themes, as Godwin's early analysis of social oppression gives way to a new emphasis on individual moral error, which requires the restraining power of strong government. Nevertheless, the striking formal and technical resemblances among this group of novels testify to the strength of Godwin's insight into the power of narrative to embody a 'new and startling' blend of philosophical enquiry and psychological observation.

While this book argues for a continuity of interests in the Godwinian novel between the 1790s and the 1820s, there is some distinction to be made in terms of projected audience. Although in the Preface to the second edition of *Caleb Williams* (1796), Godwin claimed to address 'persons whom books of philosophy and science are never likely to reach' (*CW* i, p. vi [2]/1), the appearance of the first edition, priced 10*s*. 6*d*., suggests that his projected readers were unlikely to be those of the second part of Paine's *Rights of Man* (1792), which appeared in a 6*d*. edition.[15] Nevertheless, there is some evidence that *Caleb Williams*, like *Political Justice*, reached all levels of society. According to Godwin's early admirer John Fenwick, pirated editions of *Political Justice* were bought by 'people of the lower class' in Ireland and Scotland and by subscription in England, and *Caleb Williams* was widely seen as its companion volume: 'the creative faculties, richness, eloquence, and passion, displayed in Political Justice, were not excelled in Caleb Williams, although the latter was a form in which they were more obvious to the vulgar'.[16] By 1797 *Caleb Williams* had been through three editions. According to James Mackintosh in 1815, it was the book that most quickly needed to be replaced in Continental circulating libraries.[17] *St Leon*, too, was widely read: the thousand

[15] Richard D. Altick, *The English Common Reader: A Social History of the Mass Reading Public, 1800–1900* (Chicago, 1957), 70.

[16] [John Fenwick], *Public Characters of 1799–1800*, ii. (London, 1799), 364, 367.

[17] James Mackintosh, review of Godwin, *Lives of Edward and John Philips, Nephews and Pupils of Milton, Edinburgh Review*, 25 (1815), 486.

copies of the first edition, priced 16s., sold out immediately, and a second edition appeared in February 1800.

Subsequent novels in the Godwin school attracted a more select audience of writers and intellectuals. The novels of Charles Brockden Brown, which began to be issued in England in 1800, were mainly read by two groups of intellectuals: the Shelley circle from 1816 onwards, and the writers and reviewers centred on *Blackwood's* in the 1820s.[18] Godwin claimed that the 1818 *Frankenstein*, priced 16*s.* 6*d.*, was 'everywhere known and admired', though he also stressed its more specialized appeal: 'it can never be a book for vulgar reading'.[19] But Mary Shelley's haunting third novel, *The Last Man* (1826), priced £1. 7*s.*, did not sell well. It was only with the cheap nineteenth-century reprints which began with Bentley's Standard Novels series in 1831 that later Godwinian novels became widely available to a mass audience.[20]

The problems of historical interpretation raised by the republication of major Godwinian novels with new Prefaces from 1831 onwards are discussed in chronological sequence at the end of this study. What should be mentioned here is the issue of textual revisions. To give as full a sense of historical specificity as possible, first editions of the novels are cited throughout and special attention is given to textual changes. The revisions introduced in successive editions of *Political Justice* and *Caleb Williams* shed further light on the interaction between fiction and philosophical statement in Godwin's thought, just as the changes between the 1818 and the 1831 *Frankenstein* show Mary Shelley's shifting purpose in response to changed historical circumstances.[21] The process of modification, development, and self-criticism which characterizes the Godwinian novel as a whole is also a feature of individual texts.

[18] S. W. Reid, 'Brockden Brown in England: Notes on Henry Colburn's 1822 Editions of his Novels', *EAL* 9 (1974), 188–95.

[19] Godwin to Mary Shelley, 14 Feb. 1823, C. Kegan Paul, *William Godwin: His Friends and Contemporaries*, 2 vols. (London, 1876), ii. 282.

[20] Michael Sadleir, *XIX Century Fiction: A Bibliographical Guide based on his own Collection*, 2 vols. (London and Los Angeles, 1951), ii. 93–5.

[21] Cf. Jerome McGann's discussion of Coleridge's revisions to *The Rime of the Ancient Mariner* (1797, 1817), *The Beauty of Inflections: Literary Investigations in Historical Method and Theory* (Oxford, 1985; 2nd edn., 1988), 135–72.

Part I

1

Imogen: Godwin's Fictional Début

Imogen: A Pastoral Romance was the last of three novels produced by Godwin in the winter of 1783 and 1784 and the one over which he took the most trouble.[1] The title alone signals Godwin's departure from the eighteenth-century fictional conventions exploited in his two earlier novels, *Damon and Delia*, a picaresque narrative, and *Italian Letters*, modelled on the epistolary form. Yet critical discussion of *Imogen* has generally been confined to Godwin's interest in eighteenth-century primitivism as reflected in the Preface. The novel's most remarkable feature, its construction out of poetic models, has gone practically unnoticed. In particular, Godwin's use of Milton's *A Masque Presented at Ludlow Castle*, or *Comus*, has not been explored.[2]

Godwin's conjunction of pastoral romance, political idealism, and topical comment makes *Imogen* the first expression of that innovative blend of philosophy and fiction to be developed in *Caleb Williams*. Though allusion to Milton is in itself a commonplace of radical fiction and polemical writings of the period, Godwin's interest in *Comus* as a model for the renovation of genre is unique. The technical inventiveness of *Imogen* shows his independence of the fictional conventions which were to be used by other Jacobin novelists in the 1790s. Godwin's indirect manner of presenting ideas in fiction establishes *Imogen* as a forerunner of the non-naturalistic, mythopoeic type of fiction which he developed in his later novels. Already, by his choice of poetic models, he seeks to

[1] Godwin, autobiographical note for 1783, Ab. MSS, b. 226/2.

[2] For discussions of 18th-cent. primitivism, see Jack W. Marken, 'Introduction', *Im* 9–18, and Burton R. Pollin, 'Primitivism in *Imogen*', *Im* 113–17; Don Locke, *A Fantasy of Reason: The Life and Thought of William Godwin* (London, 1980), 26. Critics who mention Godwin's use of *Comus* include Marken, *Im* 12; I. Primer, 'Some Implications of Irony', *Im* 118–21; B. J. Tysdahl, *William Godwin as Novelist* (London, 1981), 25; Peter Marshall, *William Godwin* (New Haven, Conn., 1984), 64. Ingrid Kuczynski, 'Pastoral Romance and *Political Justice*', in Anselm Schlösser *et al.* (eds.), *Essays in Honor of William Gallacher: Life and Literature of the Working Class* (Berlin, 1966), 101–10, presents a politicized reading of *Imogen*.

place himself in a tradition of native, Protestant literature going back to Spenser and Milton, which was widely adopted by eighteenth-century critics of aristocratic culture.

Godwin's early experiment with allegorical modes presents a displaced enactment of his developing theoretical concerns. After leaving Hoxton Dissenting Academy in August 1778, he spent several periods in London before settling there in May 1782 to earn his living as a writer.[3] During these years, the demand for parliamentary reform among the politically articulate classes excluded from power reached its height. This movement has been identified as the last phase of activity of the eighteenth-century Commonwealthmen, a group which included the prominent Dissenters Timothy Hollis and Thomas Brand Hollis, whom Godwin met in 1783 and 1784, as well as Richard Price.[4] More important to Godwin's early development is the intellectual influence of the Commonwealth tradition, which maintained the study of government in the spirit of seventeenth-century writers such as Milton, Harrington, Sidney, and Locke.[5] In keeping with his interest in speculative politics, Godwin's political imagination was first exercised by the debate on the American Revolution. 'It was auspicious for me', he later recalled, 'not that a question of finances & taxes, of customs & excises, of commercial monopolies & preferences, engaged the attention at that period, but a question involving eternal principles, a question of liberty & subjugation, & a question that seemed to embrace one half of the world.'[6] For Godwin as for other radicals who achieved greater prominence in the debate on the French Revolution, the question of the rights of the American colonists provided a catalyst for theoretical discussion of English liberty. Though the full implications of Paine's attack on the British constitution were brought home only with the publication of the *Rights of Man* (1791–2), written in response to Burke's *Reflections on the Revolution of France* (1790), Paine's principles were already set out in *Common Sense* (1776), where he argued for the founding of a republican government in America, independent of British rule. Second only to *Common Sense* in forming radical

[3] My account is indebted to Marshall, *William Godwin*, 46–61, and Albert Goodwin, *The Friends of Liberty: The English Democratic Movement in the Age of the French Revolution* (London, 1979), 32–64.

[4] Caroline Robbins, *The Eighteenth-Century Commonwealthman* (Cambridge, Mass., 1959), 320–77; Godwin, undated memorandum, Ab. MSS, b. 229/2.

[5] Robbins, *Commonwealthman*, 3–21.

[6] Ab. MSS, b. 226/2.

opinion was Price's *Observations on . . . Civil Liberty* (1776), a pamphlet offering a philosophical defence of the colonists' right to political self-determination.[7] In *Observations on the Importance of the American Revolution* (1785), Price went on to celebrate this 'revolution in favour of universal liberty' as 'a revolution by which *Britons* themselves will be the greatest gainers, if wise enough to . . . catch the flame of virtuous liberty which has saved their American brethren'.[8]

For Godwin too there was more at stake than the question of American liberties. By 1779 his political views had shifted from Toryism to the Whig Opposition, and he embraced republican principles a year later. Though he remained detached from practical movements for reform, his writings of this period show a growing preoccupation with theoretical questions involving constitutional liberties. But two early pamphlets, both published anonymously, show more direct commentary on political issues: in *A Defence of the Rockingham Party* (1783) Godwin wrote in support of Fox's tactical coalition with his former antagonist, Lord North, and in *Instructions to a Statesman* (1784), written after the defeat of the Rockingham Whigs, he made a satirical attack on unprincipled statecraft. It is Godwin's less overtly political writings, however, that are more relevant to his indirect treatment of topical concerns in *Imogen*. In *The Herald of Literature* (1784) he wrote a series of literary parodies in the guise of forthcoming works of well-established writers, then proceeded to review them as if they were genuine. Even here he is preoccupied with the American debate, for he included skilful imitations of William Robertson's *History of America*, Burke's speeches on commercial links with the colonies, and Paine's *Common Sense*.[9] In his editorial remarks he took the opportunity to praise Paine's style ('exactly that of popular oratory') while distancing himself from his polemical arguments: 'They may be the sentiments of a patriot, they are not certainly those of a philosopher.'[10]

[7] Lincoln, *English Dissent*, 133.

[8] Richard Price, *Observations on the Importance of the American Revolution, and the Means of Making it a Benefit to the World* (London, 1785), 1–2.

[9] [Godwin], *The Herald of Literature; or, A Review of the Most Considerable Publications that will be made in the Course of the Ensuing Winter: with Extracts* (London, 1784), reprinted in *Four Early Pamphlets (1783–4)*, ed. Burton R. Pollin (Gainesville, Fla., 1966), Articles II, IX, X.

[10] [Godwin], *Herald of Literature*, 106.

For a more accurate guide to Godwin's theoretical stance we must turn to *An Account of the Seminary* (1783), the prospectus for his planned school at Epsom, which shows the impact of the French *philosophes* on his thought. By the end of 1782 Godwin's reading of d'Holbach, Helvétius, and Rousseau led him to reject the notion of original sin in favour of the belief 'that human depravity originates in the vices of political constitution'.[11] In *An Account of the Seminary*, drawing selectively on Rousseau's *Discourse on the Origins of Inequality among Men* and on *Émile*, he sought to present a mode of education that would liberate the mind from institutional pressures:

> The state of society is incontestibly artificial; the power of one man over another must be always derived from convention, or from conquest; by nature we are equal. The necessary consequence is, that government must always depend upon the opinion of the governed. Let the most oppressed people under heaven once change their mode of thinking, and they are free.[12]

Godwin's turn to novel-writing at the end of 1783 should be viewed in the context of this belief in a renovation of opinion as an essential prerequisite to wider social and political change. From his earliest writings, Godwin aims to renovate 'the opinion of the governed' through imaginative fable rather than doctrinal statement. In keeping with the Commonwealthmen's concern with the training of good citizens, he is particularly concerned with remoulding the perceptions of 'the young reader'.[13] In *Imogen* Godwin remodels the exemplary action of eighteenth-century conduct books to create a proto-revolutionary narrative.

Even a brief outline of the plot shows Godwin's integration of imaginative and philosophical concerns. Two major points may be immediately noted. First, there is the novel's symbolic setting in primitive Wales: as signalled by the subtitle, *From the Ancient British*, Godwin's narrative should be read in relation to the influential radical argument that English democratic government originated before the Norman conquest.[14] Second, Godwin adopts

[11] Godwin, undated note, Ab. MSS, b. 229/9; cf. Godwin's account of his loss of faith, c. 604/1.

[12] [Godwin], *An Account of the Seminary . . . at Epsom in Surrey, for the Instruction of Twelve Pupils in the Greek, Latin, French and English Languages* (London, 1783), reprinted in *Four Early Pamphlets*, 2.

[13] Review of *Imogen*, *English Review*, 4 (Aug. 1784), 142.

[14] Christopher Hill, *Puritanism and Revolution* (1958; Harmondsworth, 1986),

the allegorical structure of quest, trial, and rescue. With its cluster of associations with romance and spiritual quests, this economical plot brings the simplicity and suggestiveness of myth to bear on contemporary issues, anticipating the multi-layered representative function of later Godwinian narratives. More precisely, Godwin evokes Spenser's 'Legend of Britomartis, or of Chastitie', in the third Book of *The Faerie Queene*, which had been used as a source of imagery for critics of court values since the early seventeenth century.[15] But it is *Comus* that provides a language for Godwin's secular enterprise. It is central to the instructive purpose of *Imogen* that Milton's phrasing, resonant with moral authority, is pervasive, but at the same time this moral authority is undercut by significant shifts of emphasis as Godwin rejects the underlying sense of humanity's imperfections which is crucial to *Comus*. Godwin rewrites Milton's exemplary theme of virtue in distress as a paradigm of revolutionary experience, highlighting the power of private judgement to dethrone hereditary vice.

The story is set in the Welsh valley of Clwyd, a native mountain republic where the undeclared lovers, Edwin and Imogen, live in perfect equality in conformity with the precepts of the Druids. On their journey home from a bardic festival, the lovers are besieged by threatening forces: a goblin of darkness, a supernatural storm, and a ferocious wolf. In a scene reminiscent of Proteus's rescue of Florimell, Roderic appears and carries Imogen off to his palace in a golden chariot.[16] When the tempest subsides, Edwin vows to rescue Imogen and defeat the false enchanter. He seeks the advice of the hermit Madoc, whose instructive rôle resembles that of Milton's Attendant Spirit.

Madoc's function is to educate Edwin into an awareness of his historical situation: 'this is your hour of trial' (*Im* 45). Godwin evokes a range of allegorical precedents to sketch the rise of government as a perversion of pastoral values. Madoc traces the origins of Roderic's tyrannical power to his mother's abuse of great talents: like Comus's mother Circe and Spenser's Radigund,

98–113; Gwyn A. Williams, *Artisans and Sans-Culottes: Popular Movements in France and Britain during the French Revolution* (1968; 2nd edn., London, 1989), 11–15.

[15] David Norbrook, *Poetry and Politics in the English Renaissance* (London, 1984), 252–3.

[16] Spenser, *The Faerie Queene* (1590–6), III. viii. 35.

Rodogune sought to enslave all men, building a stately mansion to house 'crouds of degenerate shepherds . . . in every brutal form' (*Im* 46).[17] On the principle of hereditary succession, her property passes to her only son, Roderic, who claims further affinity with Comus and the Spenserian deceivers Proteus and Cupid by virtue of his magical ability to assume different shapes.[18] Crucially, though, Roderic's power is limited by a curse, pronounced at his birth by a disaffected goblin, which prophesies the exact circumstances of his destruction:

WHEN RODERIC SHALL BE OVERREACHED IN ALL HIS SPELLS BY A SIMPLE SWAIN . . . WHEN RODERIC SHALL SUE TO A SIMPLE MAID, WHO BY HIS CHARMS SHALL BE MADE TO HATE THE SWAIN THAT ONCE SHE LOVED, AND WHO YET SHALL RESIST ALL HIS PERSONAL ATTRACTIONS AND ALL HIS POWER; THEN SHALL HIS POWER BE AT AN END. HIS PALACES SHALL BE DISSOLVED, HIS RICHES SCATTERED, AND HE HIMSELF SHALL BECOME AN UNPITIED, NECESSITOUS, MISERABLE VAGABOND. (*Im* 47)

As in Horace Walpole's Gothic romance, *The Castle of Otranto* (1764), the plot turns on the fulfilment of prophecy. Walpole's aristocratic fable depicts the overthrow of a property-owner and the restoration of the rightful heir. By contrast, Godwin predicts the dissolution of property values through the action of humble figures, a simple maid and her swain. At intervals the goblin reappears to remind Roderic of his inescapable destiny, inviting comparison with another influential representation of the supernatural Gothic, Henry Fuseli's recently exhibited painting, *Nightmare* (1782).[19] The goblin, who articulates Roderic's deepest thoughts and fears, suggests an unacknowledged aspect of the self, and travesties the heavenly wisdom offered by the supernatural Spirit in *Comus*.

To foil Roderic's hereditary power of enchantment, Madoc equips Edwin with a 'small and sordid root' (*Im* 48) which resembles the Attendant Spirit's treasured haemony.[20] But the plant's powers are superfluous to a plot which emphasizes secular

[17] Milton, *A Masque Presented at Ludlow Castle, 1634* [*Comus*] (1637), ll. 50–77; *Faerie Queene*, V. iv. 29–33.

[18] Cf. Paine: 'Aristocracy has never more than *one* child', *RM* 104; *Im* 47, cf. *Faerie Queene*, III. viii. 40–1, xi. 30–9.

[19] Fuseli's painting was exhibited at the Royal Academy in 1782 and widely available as an engraving after Jan. 1783, Nicholas Powell, *Fuseli: The Nightmare* (London, 1973), 98; Fuseli was a member of Joseph Johnson's group from the early 1780s, Tyson, *Joseph Johnson*, 66.

[20] Cf. *Comus*, ll. 628–40.

moral choice and gives the initiative to a woman of the common people. When Imogen wakes up in Roderic's palace, she is subjected to a series of temptations which reflect all the specious contrivances of advanced political society. Drawing on Spenser's elaborate settings, Godwin recasts the exemplary moral action of *Comus* as a symbolic confrontation of old and new orders. He sets the vices of a decaying constitution in opposition to pastoral values and the precepts of the Druids.

The 'grand, and simple, and commanding' architecture of Roderic's mansion, supported by 'pillars of the Ionic order' (*Im* 97), signals his role as an exemplar of aristocratic decadence, for it immediately brings to mind the classical elegance of the eighteenth-century country house. More revealing of Godwin's philosophical point of reference is the managêment of Roderic's vast estate. It is no accident that Roderic's land is an enormous 'inclosure' which prospers through 'that wondrous art, as yet unknown in the plains of Albion, of turning up the soil with a share of iron' (*Im* 61), for Rousseau had isolated ploughing as the source of the inequalities of civil society: 'for the philosopher it is iron and wheat which first civilised men and ruined the human race'.[21] Roderic's admission that he is suffocated by a life of ease and envious of pastoral simplicity further supports Rousseau's account of social progress: 'behold man, who was formerly free and independent, diminished as a consequence of a multitude of new wants into subjection'. What appals Imogen most is the 'unresisting passivity' of Roderic's household; like Rousseau's primitive man, she cannot understand the terms 'master' and 'servant' by which he maintains his authority:[22]

> The Gods have made all their rational creatures equal. If they have made one strong and another weak, it is for the purpose of mutual benevolence and assistance, and not that of despotism and oppression. Of all the shepherds of the valley, there is not one that claims dominion and command over another. (*Im* 59)

In offering Imogen a share in his prosperous estate, Roderic holds out the promise of a revolutionary transformation in her fortunes:

[21] Rousseau, *Discourse on the Origins and Foundations of Inequality among Men* (1755), trans. and ed. Maurice Cranston (Harmondsworth, 1984), 116.

[22] Ibid. 119, 106; cf. Paine: 'Submission is wholly a vassalage term . . . and an echo of the language used at the Conquest', *RM* 113.

'From this moment let a new aera and better prospects commence' (*Im* 64). However, brought up in the Druids' belief that 'the mind is the nobler part', Imogen rejects this offer in favour of rational 'freedom and independence' (*Im* 65, 64).

Imogen is then conducted into a room hung with an arras depicting heroic women of antiquity, where Roderic attempts to win her through a song in praise of the civilizing power of feminine charms. Again Godwin invokes a Spenserian frame of reference to make a contemporary point. In the mouth of the deceiver Roderic, Spenser's eulogy of female virtue is redeployed to highlight the eighteenth-century use of an idealized concept of womanhood to shore up patriarchal values.[23] In opposition to this 'mummery, dissimulation, and hypocrisy' (*Im* 73), Imogen struggles to maintain a sense of personal rectitude. The next challenge takes place in Rodogune's enchanted garden, where Roderic exploits his Protean gift by appearing disguised as Edwin. He counsels a surrender of her will to oppressive circumstances: 'it is in vain that we resolve, and in vain that we struggle' (*Im* 86). But, unlike the passive women of *Otranto* ('It is not ours to make election for ourselves; heaven, our fathers, and our husbands, must decide for us'),[24] Imogen resists being cast as a figure in someone else's plot. Instead she adopts the posture of a defiantly independent heroine: 'If the courage of Edwin fail, I will show him what he ought to be. . . . You shall see what an injured and oppressed woman can do' (*Im* 85). Armed with this enhanced rational self-reliance, she resists the final temptation of a feast of excess, which is heralded by close verbal echoes of *Comus*: 'Let the board of luxury be spread. . . . Night is the season of dissipation and luxury' (*Im* 92).[25]

At this point Edwin enters Roderic's grounds in the manner of a knightly challenger. Dazzled by the ornate splendours of the palace, Edwin is brought before Roderic, who invites him to a banquet of sensual extravagance. Roderic's seductive argument for drinking deep of the 'cup of pleasure' (*Im* 102) brings to mind all the implications of Comus's philosophy of self-indulgence, which is counterpointed by the Lady's explicitly egalitarian sentiments:[26]

[23] *Faerie Queene*, III. iv. 1–3; Jane Spencer, *The Rise of the Woman Novelist* (Oxford, 1986), 15–17; cf. Mary Wollstonecraft's attack on 'mistaken notions of female excellence', *VRW* 81–3.

[24] Horace Walpole, *The Castle of Otranto* (1764), ed. W. S. Lewis (Oxford, 1964, 1982), 88.

[25] Cf. *Comus*, ll. 122–4.

[26] Cf. *PJ* i. 15.

If every just man that now pines with want
Had but a moderate and beseeming share
Of that which lewdly-pampered Luxury
Now heaps upon some few with vast excess,
Nature's full blessings would be well-dispensed
In unsuperfluous even proportion.
(ll. 767–72)

But 'by an irresistible impulse of goodness' (*Im* 103), Edwin actively resists Roderic's plea and succeeds where the Lady's Brothers 'mistook' (l. 814): he snatches the enchanter's wand and breaks it in pieces. Like earlier architectural symbols of a corrupt ruling order (but unlike Comus's palace), Roderic's mansion collapses in ruins, and he and his train vanish 'like shadows at the rising of the sun' (*Im* 104).[27] Pastoral harmony is speedily restored, but by contrast with romance precursors such as Spenser's Pastorella, Imogen does not turn out to be a princess in disguise.[28] Instead the rural lovers are reunited and return to their haven of equality in the vale of Clwyd, where virtue is rewarded by the sense of having passed through the 'ordeal of temptation' with 'an approved fortitude' (*Im* 106).

Even in this brief account, the extent to which Godwin transforms Spenserian and Miltonic themes to reflect his own philosophical interests should be apparent. The technical sophistication of his enterprise, however, can only be appreciated by contrast with later, more polemical treatments of the *Comus* theme in the novels of Robert Bage, Thomas Holcroft, and Elizabeth Inchbald.

A Pastoral Romance

At one level, Godwin's use of the theme of virtue in distress reflects a commonplace of eighteenth-century fiction. According to E. A. Baker, popular romantic fiction found its mainstay in 'the theory that fiction should portray virtue attractively, and show it always triumphing over vice'.[29] This concept derived moral authority from Milton's precedent, where the trial of virtue reflects its Puritan definition as integrity of mind: as St Augustine

[27] Cf. the fall of Busirane's mansion, *Faerie Queene*, III. xii. 37, 42–3, and the collapse of Otranto, Walpole, *The Castle of Otranto*, 108.

[28] *Faerie Queene*, VI. xii. 15–20.

[29] E. A. Baker, *The History of the English Novel*, v. (London, 1934, 1957), 22–3.

comments, chastity 'is not a treasure that can be stolen without the mind's consent'.[30] Although the Lady is physically at risk when she is imprisoned in the magic chair, Comus remains helpless in the face of her intellectual defiance. In novels which sought to propagate a Puritan morality in opposition to the degenerate habits of the ruling class, attempted rape became a stock situation in which that 'strong siding champion Conscience' (l. 211) had to prove its worth. Desiring to emulate 'the glorious Milton', Richardson pushed this emphasis on internal resources to its limit.[31] Allowing the rape of Clarissa to take place in a minutely documented social setting, he exposed the clash between the Puritan ideal of virtuous conduct and the ethic of self-interest prevalent in eighteenth-century society.[32]

More directly relevant to Godwin's purpose is Richardson's first novel, *Pamela*, which united profoundly appealing romance themes with naturalistic social detail. Richardson's choice of a servant as heroine, persecuted by a landed proprietor who eventually marries her, establishes the proto-revolutionary plot stripped to its essentials in *Imogen*, and taken up again in the radical novels of the 1790s. In exchanges between a recognizably eighteenth-century servant and master, the egalitarian sentiments of *Comus* take on a new directness: 'my *soul* is of equal importance with the soul of a princess,' declares Pamela, 'though in quality I am but upon a foot with the meanest slave'.[33] Like Imogen, Pamela is clothed in pastoral garb for her period of temptation, and her resistance to material wealth is couched in terms of pastoral values.[34] Imogen's 'ardent desire to set out for the cottage of her father' (*Im* 59) is surely indebted to Pamela's wish to return to her parents' home, where she imagines them praying 'with hearts more pure, than are to be met with in palaces!'[35] Finally, though, Richardson's transformation of his heroine into the 'happy condition' of a gentlewoman forms no part of Godwin's scheme.[36]

[30] St Augustine, *Concerning the City of God against the Pagans*, trans. Henry Bettenson, ed. David Knowles (Harmondsworth, 1972), 40.

[31] For Richardson's admiration of Milton, see *Selected Letters of Samuel Richardson*, ed. John Carroll (Oxford, 1974), 176, 98.

[32] See Christopher Hill, 'Clarissa Harlowe and her Times', *EIC* 5 (1955), 315–40.

[33] Richardson, *Pamela; or, Virtue Rewarded* (1740), ed. Peter Sabor with introduction by Margaret Doody (Harmondsworth, 1980), 197.

[34] Ibid. 87, 112.

[35] Ibid. 199.

[36] Ibid. 337.

A more overtly radical use of *Comus*, which may have stimulated Godwin's interest, appeared in Bage's first novel, *Mount Henneth* (1782). This witty epistolary narrative tells of James Foston's education in benevolence through a series of adventures in primitive settings. In an Indian episode, suitably remote from the constraints of advanced society, Bage takes issue with Richardson's treatment of female dishonour in *Clarissa*. Foston arrives at the house of a Persian merchant just in time to rescue his daughter Caralia from being butchered by marauding soldiers, but he is too late to prevent her from being raped. Unlike Clarissa, though, Caralia does not die: instead Foston marries her and brings her to England. Caralia's fears for her good name offer a direct critique of 'the reigning manners and opinions' in English society as reflected in fictional treatments of the dishonoured woman: 'Women who have suffered it, must die, or be immured for ever. Ever after they are totally useless to all the purposes of society. . . . No author has yet been so bold as to permit a lady to live and marry, and be a woman after this stain.'[37] But Foston's travels have so enlarged his outlook that he insists that Caralia's 'mind is fit for heaven', and that a woman would be 'more dishonoured by a wanton dream' in which she willingly participated. In this way the 'test of reason' exposes the injustice of received social morality. Though Bage's ironical attitude to what he terms 'the loss of—innocence, a bagatelle' tends to defuse his radicalism,[38] his sentiments anticipate Wollstonecraft's more polemical attack on Richardson in the *Vindication of the Rights of Woman* (1792): 'When Richardson makes Clarissa tell Lovelace that he had robbed her of her honour, he must have had strange notions of honour and virtue. For, miserable beyond all names of misery is the condition of a being, who could be degraded without its own consent!' (*VRW* 166)

Several overtly didactic novels of the revolutionary decade amplify Wollstonecraft's point. In Holcroft's *Anna St Ives*, the aristocrat Clifton threatens Anna with rape in order to break her will. But Anna does not believe in the notion of female dishonour, and her exemplary fortitude owes much to the eloquent defiance of the Lady in *Comus*:

Nay, think you that . . . I would falsely take guilt to myself; or imagine I had received the smallest blemish, from impurity which never reached my

[37] Robert Bage, *Mount Henneth*, 2 vols. (London, 1782), i. 233, 230.
[38] Ibid. 147.

mind? That I would lament, or shun the world, or walk in open day oppressed by shame I did not merit? No! . . . You cannot injure me—I am above you![39]

Here Holcroft exploits 'the entire mythology of rape, the "fate worse than death" ' in the service of his larger political argument, which highlights the power of reason to transcend prejudice and prescription.[40] As Anna's suitor Frank Henley insists with disconcerting simplicity: 'No man can be degraded by another; it must be his own act.'[41] More sophisticated is Inchbald's allegorical treatment of social oppression in *Nature and Art* (1796). Following Godwin's symbolic treatment of political relations in *Imogen* and *Caleb Williams*, Inchbald blends issues of class and gender: the plight of Hannah Primrose, the servant who is sentenced to death by the aristocrat who seduced her, reflects the multiple levels at which social tyranny operates. Yet, despite this overt social criticism, the radical tendency of Jacobin fiction is limited by a final conformity to romance expectations. Holcroft's independent-minded hero and heroine resolve their dissatisfaction with the existing order by marrying and joining the privileged classes, just as the hero of Bage's *Hermsprong* (1796), brought up in the egalitarian society of the new American republic, proves to be the long-lost heir of a British aristocrat. In reaffirming the conventions they set out to question, the novels of the mid-1790s fail to carry through their radical political aims.

It is this implicit validation of the existing order that Godwin sought to avoid, ten years earlier, through the stylized genre of pastoral romance which permits a critical distance from eighteenth-century fictional assumptions. In *Italian Letters* Godwin had experimented with Richardson's epistolary style and seduction theme, the conventions used by Holcroft in *Anna St Ives*, to present a straightforward opposition between rural innocence and aristocratic depravity. As in Holcroft's novel, social criticism is simply grafted on to a derivative plot, though Godwin's choice of an Italian Renaissance setting shows his growing interest in displaced modes of social criticism. The more radically experimental character of *Imogen* is suggested by Godwin's early autobiographical

[39] Thomas Holcroft, *Anna St Ives* (1792), ed. Peter Faulkner (Oxford, 1970), 423–4.

[40] Ian Donaldson, *The Rapes of Lucretia: A Myth and its Transformations* (Oxford, 1982), 80.

[41] Holcroft, *Anna St Ives*, 140.

fragment, in which he recalled his youthful reveries: 'I made whole books as I walked, books of fictitious adventures in the mode of Richardson . . . & books of imaginary institutions in education and government, where all was to be faultless.'[42] Mary Shelley's later dismissal of *Imogen* as a 'forced & fictitious pastoral' by comparison with the 'forms of power & excellence' displayed in *Caleb Williams* has been cited with approval by most critics; but in fact the conspicuous artifice of *Imogen* is an aspect of its genre.[43] Godwin's use of pastoral romance anticipates the aims, though not the method, of his later first-person narratives. He seeks to disrupt rather than passively validate the reader's preconceptions, to persuade the reader to his own point of view rather than to consolidate 'things as they are'.

In this respect he would have found Milton's use of the masque, the artistic form developed by the early Stuarts to embody their absolutist claims, especially instructive. Though the masque was traditionally designed to affirm aristocratic power, the entire form of *Comus* scrutinizes the basis of its own rituals. Recent scholarly readings of *Comus* have shown how Milton's moral strenuousness undercuts conventional masque expectations. As 'an emergent Puritan's recuperation . . . of the masque', *Comus* argues for equality in the spiritual sphere independent of worldly rank.[44] What appealed to Godwin, though, was not Milton's piety but the political implications of his use of masque conventions. The Lady's enchantment is undone not by the presence of nobility, as the audience would have expected, but by the commoner Sabrina, the spirit of the place and the representative of true pastoral values. Towards the end of the masque Milton uses pastoral as a means of depicting an ideal order centred on an aristocracy of virtue rather than material wealth and power.

With this masterly precedent in the reformation of genre, Godwin's choice of native literary sources suggests his desire to return to the politically subversive mode of Renaissance pastoral emphasized by George Puttenham: its ability 'under the vaile of homely persons . . . to insinuate and glaunce at greater matters . . .

[42] Godwin, autobiographical fragment [1756–69], Ab. MSS, b. 228/1.

[43] Mary Shelley, 'Life of William Godwin' [1839], Ab. MSS, c. 606/1–5.

[44] John Creaser, ' "The Present Aid of this Occasion": The Setting of *Comus*', in David Lindley (ed.), *The Court Masque* (Manchester, 1984), 134; cf. Cedric C. Brown, *John Milton's Aristocratic Entertainments* (Cambridge, 1985), 78–103.

such as perchance had not bene safe to have disclosed in any other sort'.[45] Godwin seeks to liberate pastoral from the courtly associations which led Hazlitt, however mistakenly, to describe Sidney's *Arcadia* as 'a lasting monument of perverted power'.[46] Godwin's revisionary purpose has a further topical resonance in the context of the pastoral rituals favoured by Marie-Antoinette in the court of the *ancien régime*.[47] Clifton's energetic satire of the *fête-champêtre* in *Anna St Ives* provides an illuminating gloss on Godwin's juxtaposition of pastoral simplicity and courtly excess:

The simplicity of the shepherd life could not but be excellently represented, by . . . the ragouts, fricassees, spices, sauces, wines, and *liqueurs*, with which we were regaled! Not to mention being served upon plate, by an army of footmen! But then, it was in the open air; and that was prodigiously pastoral![48]

This is not to project the political concerns of the 1790s on to Godwin's early novel: although writers on both sides of the debate on the French Revolution exploit pastoral imagery to convey a sense of break with past traditions, it is questionable how far these more sophisticated metaphors of natural process, which developed in response to Burke's imagery of organic continuity in *Reflections*, are relevant to Godwin's pre-revolutionary novel.[49] Paine, however, had already used pastoral imagery in support of arguments for a simplified constitution in the period of the American War. In *Common Sense* Paine depicted the rise of government in terms of debased pastoral values: 'Government, like dress, is the badge of lost innocence: the palaces of kings are built on the ruins of the bowers of paradise.' As an alternative to the decaying British system, he posited an image of rural seclusion, 'a small number of persons settled in some sequestered part of the earth'.[50]

Mindful of the currency of pastoral ideals in radical thought,

[45] George Puttenham, *The Art of English Poesie* (1589), reprinted in *Elizabethan Critical Essays*, ed. G. Gregory Smith, 2 vols. (Oxford, 1904), ii. 40.

[46] Hazlitt, 'Lectures on the English Poets' [1818], *Works*, v. 98; on Sidney's critique of aristocratic values, see Norbrook, *Poetry and Politics*, 92–7.

[47] Norbert Elias, *The Court Society*, trans. Edmund Jephcott (Oxford, 1983), 224–5, 256–66.

[48] Holcroft, *Anna St Ives*, 116.

[49] For a survey of image patterns in the French Revolution debate, see Paulson, *Representations of Revolution*, 57–87.

[50] Thomas Paine, *Common Sense* (1776), ed. Isaac Kramnick (Harmondsworth, 1976), 65, 66.

Godwin moves beyond Paine's transformation of imagery to modify the entire system of expectations signalled by the pastoral form. Rejecting the mode of direct social commentary, he gives imaginative presence to his contemporary theme by drawing on a range of popular eighteenth-century modes which evoke a simplified past. Godwin's use of Celtic mythology is especially significant. Recent historians have provided illuminating accounts of the growth of scholarly interest in the recovery of a mythical Welsh past in the second half of the eighteenth century. Prys Morgan has documented an explosion of nationalist activity in London–Welsh circles in the early 1790s, led by Edward Williams, also known by his Welsh name, Iolo Morganwg, and William Owen Pughe, who sought to transform earlier notions of ancient Welsh culture into a secular ideology bodying forth the hopes of committed radicals.[51] In this way, Welsh ideas of a pure society paralleled radical arguments that the rights of 'free-born' Englishmen were lost under the yoke of Norman rule. Yet this imaginative defence of ancient liberties was already current among British writers in the period of the American War.[52] In *Imogen* Godwin already recognizes the potential of Celtic myth as a form of displaced national commentary.

From the Ancient British

The Preface alone signals Godwin's interest in national myth, for he presents the revised *Comus* as a recently discovered translation of great linguistic purity, thus adding his voice to those of oppositional writers already claiming a native British mythology. At the same time he maintains the teasing editorial voice of his earlier accomplished exercise in literary parody, *The Herald of Literature*. Godwin complicates the issue of *Imogen*'s authenticity by mentioning Macpherson's Ossian poems, published between 1760 and 1763 with Prefaces describing them as 'genuine remains of ancient

[51] Prys Morgan, *A New History of Wales: The Eighteenth-Century Renaissance* (Llandybie, 1981), and 'From a Death to a View: The Hunt for the Welsh Past in the Romantic Period', in Eric Hobsbawm and Terence Ranger (eds.), *The Invention of Tradition* (Cambridge, 1983), 43–100; cf. Gwyn A. Williams, *Madoc: The Making of a Myth* (1979; Oxford, 1987), 89–117, and 'Romanticism in Wales', in Roy Porter and Mikuláš Teich (eds.), *Romanticism in National Context* (Cambridge, 1988), 9–36.

[52] See above, n. 14.

Scottish poetry'.[53] Though these poems were later discovered to be forgeries, Macpherson's imaginative evocation of Scottish history had a lasting appeal for writers and intellectuals in the period.[54] In his *Critical Dissertation on the Poems of Ossian* (1763), Hugh Blair defended the Ossianic enterprise in terms that would have appealed to Godwin: 'it is the business of a poet not to be a mere annalist of Facts, but to embellish truth with beautiful, probable, and useful fictions'. Thus Ossian, 'building upon true history, has sufficiently adorned it with poetical fiction'.[55] In the epic fragments *Fingal* (1762) and *Temora* (1763), cited by Godwin in his Preface, Macpherson offers not a factual account of historical events but an imaginative evocation of the fortunes of peoples, the decline and fall of Fingal's race. With this compelling precedent for the use of myth to recuperate the past, Godwin also mentions the works of the authentic Welsh bards Taliesin and Aneirin, brought to light by the painstaking scholarship of Welsh intellectuals such as Evan Evans. In *Some Specimens of the Poetry of the Antient Welsh Bards* (1764), Evans included extracts from Aneirin's *Y Gododdin*, a genuine sixth-century fragment which he had recently discovered.[56] Taking care to dissociate himself from Macpherson, Evans made a case for further research on ancient British manuscripts which would shed light on 'a great many passages in history . . . that are now dark and dubious'.[57]

The source of Godwin's hidden manuscript remains as elusive as that of *Otranto*. He makes a series of contradictory claims: it was written in Welsh and then translated; in the absence of a classical precedent for *Comus* it may have been Milton's source; its real author is a Welshman who lived later than Milton; and, finally, the translator's own enthusiasm for *Comus* may account for 'verbal coincidencies' (*Im* 23). What is clear, however, is that Godwin insists on the non-classical origins of *Comus* in order to promote its

[53] [Hugh Blair], Preface to [James Macpherson], *Fragments of Ancient Poetry, Collected in the Highlands of Scotland, and Translated from the Galic or Erse Language* (Edinburgh, 1760), p. iii.

[54] Fiona Stafford, *The Sublime Savage: James Macpherson and the Poems of Ossian* (Edinburgh, 1988), 163–78.

[55] [Blair], *Critical Dissertation on the Poems of Ossian* (London, 1763), 29.

[56] Aneirin's *Y Gododdin* was a genuine find made by Evan Evans in August 1758; Morgan, *Eighteenth-Century Renaissance*, 80.

[57] Evan Evans, *Some Specimens of the Poetry of the Antient Welsh Bards, Translated into English* (London, 1764), pp. iii, 155.

current national resonance: 'Its fame is continually increasing, and it will be admired wherever the name of Britain is repeated, and the language of Britain is understood' (*Im* 23).

This national dimension is developed through the novel's setting in Snowdonia at the time of the Druids. Godwin is not concerned with an idealized past but with a secular myth of a future state, as he builds on the association of the Druids with independence and political liberty shared by Milton's 'Lycidas' and the work of eighteenth-century patriot poets such as James Thomson and Thomas Gray.[58] The prophetic dimension of the Welsh bardic tradition gained immense popular currency after the publication of Gray's 'The Bard' (1757), which purports to tell of the slaughter of the last of the Welsh bards by Edward I on his invasion of Wales in 1282, but is in fact dominated by the potent central image of the lone surviving bard calling down curses on Edward's troops (ll. 1–8). So charged with significance was Gray's mythical subject, the overthrow of native Welsh by English oppressors, that it was regarded as historical truth by the Welsh themselves, and it contributed greatly to the late eighteenth-century vogue for the Welsh bard as a defender of ancient liberties.[59]

Given this potent frame of reference, Godwin's Welsh mountain setting offers a return to pre-Conquest freedom and a liberation from institutional orthodoxies. Godwin draws special attention to the absence of Christianity, which is replaced by the secular precepts of the Druids (*Im* 21). Prys Morgan has described the eighteenth-century shift in the status of the Druid 'from the arcane obscurantist, who indulged in human sacrifice, to the sage or intellectual defending his people's faith and honour'.[60] Godwin exploits this shift in significance to the full, for he presents the bards as exemplary poets, priests, and statesmen, but remains mindful of their barbaric past. The full implications of his use of bardic prophecy are seen in the festival at the start of the novel, which seems to celebrate the vigour of the Druids' faith in opposition to the 'degeneracy of modern times' (*Im* 35). On closer inspection, though, Godwin criticizes the heroic past memorialized by the bards as equally degenerate.

[58] Milton, 'Lycidas' (1638), ll. 53–4; Marilyn Butler, 'Romanticism in England', in Porter and Teich (eds.), *Romanticism in National Context*, 43–4.

[59] Morgan, 'From a Death to a View', 82–3; Evans cites Gray's poem as historical truth, 45 n.

[60] Morgan, 'From a Death to a View', 63.

Through the bardic competition which concludes the festival Godwin tells us how to read the rest of the novel. As in *Sketches of History* (1784), where he presents New Testament episodes as 'philosophy teaching by example',[61] Godwin offers a series of inset narratives to instruct the reader. The first song establishes divine intervention, crucial to the failure of Comus's temptation of the Lady, as legendary and archaic. Pursued by the rapacious Modred, the daughter of Cadwallo is saved not by the intervention of an Attendant Spirit with divine powers, but by the magical ability to assume the different shapes of hare, wolf, and hind. Thus she entices Modred, intent on rape and murder, to his death by drowning: 'Let the fate of Modred be remembered for a caution to the precipitate. . . . Heaven never deserts the cause of virtue' (*Im* 32). The song thus enacts in miniature the main plot of *Imogen*, which turns on the prophecy of Roderic's downfall at the hands of a shepherdess armed with the precepts of the Druids.

Godwin's use of Ossianic subject-matter sheds further light on his instructive design, for he invokes Macpherson's stark rendering of history in terms of rape and military violence to highlight an alternative model for heroic action. Narrated in Macpherson's rhythmical prose manner, the inset tale of Cadwallo's daughter invites comparison with a specific fragment which tells of the persecution of the daughter of Cremor by 'Ullin famous in war'.[62] Similarly, the 'action and enterprise' that Roderic contemplates, in true Ossianic fashion, is the brutal rape of Imogen: 'There is something noble, royal, and independent, in the thought' (*Im* 56, 55). This debased concept of heroism further brings to mind the tyranny, fraud, and usurpation introduced by the Norman conquest, memorably described by Paine: 'A French bastard landing with an armed banditti, and establishing himself king of England against the consent of the natives, is in plain terms a very paltry rascally original.'[63] By contrast, Godwin offers a redefinition of heroic virtue which emphasizes the active mental resources of Edwin and Imogen.

Godwin pursues his redefinition of British heroism in his choice of characters' names, always significant in his novels and especially so in *Imogen* because they show a complete departure from the pastoral precedents used in his first novel, *Damon and Delia*, in

[61] Godwin, *Sketches of History, in Six Sermons* (London, 1784), 67.

[62] [Macpherson], *Fragments*, 27.

[63] Paine, *Common Sense*, 78.

favour of Welsh national heroes. Cadwallo, Llewelyn, and Roderic were native Welsh princes and kings, valiant defenders of Welsh independence against Saxon or Norman invaders, whose deeds were commemorated in ancient Welsh poetry. The name of Godwin's hero recalls Edwin, Prince of Northumberland, and ally of the Welsh against the Saxons.[64] That of the hermit Madoc alludes to the mythical twelfth-century Welsh prince who was said to have discovered America, the archetype of brave new non-hierarchical societies. However, it is hard to know whether Godwin was aware of the full topicality of the Madoc legend: Welsh interest in Madoc revived during the 1770s in the context of increased emigration from Wales to America, but it was not until the publication of a book on Madoc by Dr John Williams in 1791 that this transatlantic myth gained wider currency in London.[65]

Godwin's contemporary theme gains further imaginative presence through a range of literary allusions which establish Imogen as a representative British heroine, oppressed by a decadent aristocrat. In keeping with the preference for native as opposed to classical models expressed in much of the critical discourse of the period, Godwin draws on native sixteenth-century and seventeenth-century models, Spenser, Shakespeare, and Milton. As early as 1756, Joseph Warton had voiced the need for a return to native historical subjects in poetry, citing the examples of Shakespeare's history plays and Milton's comment in *The Reason of Church Government*: ' "I am meditating what kind of knight BEFORE THE CONQUEST might be chosen, in whom to lay the pattern of a christian hero." '[66] In *Observations on the Faerie Queene* (1756, 1762), Joseph's brother and fellow-antiquarian Thomas adopted a similar view, placing Spenser at the high point of a native romance tradition. In *The History of English Poetry* (1774–81), Thomas represented 'our national poetry' as arriving at its maturity in 1600, after which his narrative closes, thus avoiding the 'French' influences of the seventeenth and eighteenth centuries.[67]

In keeping with this polarization of literary values, Godwin

[64] Morgan, 'From a Death to a View', 81–6; Evans, *Specimens*, *passim*.

[65] Morgan, 'From a Death to a View', 83; cf. Williams, *Madoc*, 112, 117.

[66] Joseph Warton, *An Essay on the Writings and Genius of Pope*, vol. i. (London, 1756), vol. ii (London, 1782), i. 280.

[67] Thomas Warton, *The History of English Poetry, From the Close of the Eleventh to the Commencement of the Eighteenth Century*, 4 vols., final vols. never completed (London, 1774–81), Preface, i, p. v.

enriches Imogen's representative role by invoking a range of native precedents. Allusions to Spenser's 'Legend of Britomartis' introduce a powerful symbol of active femininity, for Spenser presents the Welsh-born Britomart as the source of rejuvenation of the British race.[68] Her conquests offer an exemplary blend of good deeds and chastity, the reverse of stereotypical female dependency in eighteenth-century fiction. For the name of his heroine Godwin turns to *Cymbeline*, in which courtly corruption is offset by the Welsh pastoral setting which nurtures British independence. Tempted by the Italian guile of Iachimo, Imogen's honour is closely linked with the integrity of Britain as she suffers, 'More goddess-like than wife-like, such assaults | As would take in some virtue' (II. ii. 8–9). The ultimate recognition of virtue for what it is—'not a thing for sale, and only the gift of the gods' (I. v. 7–8)—leads to the regeneration of the kingdom, a conclusion hinted at towards the end of *Comus* when the ideal action of the masque is related to its Ludlow setting.[69] Sabrina, the goddess of the Severn, rescues the Lady by offering the antithesis of Circe's magic, and her healing powers are strongly identified with the rural life of the estate administered by Bridgewater:

> For which the shepherds at their festivals
> Carol her goodness loud in rustic lays,
> And throw sweet garland wreaths into her stream
> Of pansies, pinks, and gaudy daffodils.
>
> (ll. 847–50)

By contrast, Roderic, despite his authentic Welsh name, has more in common with the 'foreign manners, customs [and] images' introduced at the Conquest.[70] He is presented through a range of exotic and conspicuously artificial devices drawn from Spenser and his eighteenth-century imitators. With its sumptuous interiors, wall-hangings depicting scenes from classical antiquity, banquet-halls, and seductive music, Roderic's mansion is especially reminiscent of Busirane's castle, the scene of Britomart's prolonged temptation at the end of Book III. As in Thomson's *The Castle of*

[68] *Faerie Queene*, III. iii. 23: 'Renowmed kings, and sacred Emperours, | Thy fruitful Ofspring, shall from thee descend; | . . . | And their decayed kingdomes shall amend: | The feeble Britons . . . | They shall upreare . . .'.

[69] On the national dimension of the pastoral resolution of *Comus*, see Cedric Brown, *Milton's Aristocratic Entertainments*, 104–31.

[70] J. Warton, *Essay on Pope*, ii. 2–3.

Indolence (1748), a highly effective Spenserian burlesque which offers an indirect commentary on contemporary values, the world to be rejected is symbolized by the pleasurable enchantments of a false magician in his richly furnished mansion. Godwin's contemporary point is especially evident in the ornate pageant illustrative of simplicity, which culminates in an attempt to crown Imogen with a jewel-laden coronet, an outright parody of monarchical ritual (*Im* 70). In this way Godwin gives a more precise topical resonance to a figure already linked in *Comus* with the forces of social and political conservatism. As an eighteenth-century voluptuary, Roderic's enthralment to the values of his class anticipates the more psychologically complex but equally 'foreign-made' Ferdinando Falkland: 'Oh impotence of power! oh mockery of state! What end can ye now serve but to teach me to be miserable?' (*CW* i. 48 [1]/20; *Im* 74)

Given this suggestive framework of literary reference, Godwin's exploration of a simplified past in *Imogen* cannot be construed as a retreat from political concerns as some critics have argued,[71] although it does show that, in the early 1780s, his primary interest lies in speculative politics. That the pastoral world remains unscathed at the end suggests that Godwin retains the high idealism of Milton's pastoral resolution, even if he does not subscribe to its piety. Godwin's pastoral ideal may be most profitably viewed in terms of the mental attitude he seeks to inculcate in the interests of gradual but irresistible political progress: 'Truth dwells with contemplation. We can seldom make much progress in the business of disentangling error and delusion, but in sequestered privacy, or in the tranquil interchange of sentiments that takes place between two persons' (*PJ* i. 290). The bard Llewelyn underlines this preference for contemplative rather than active politics when he rejects the impetuous pursuit of 'a splendour that dazzles, rather than enlightens . . . a heat that burns rather than fructifies', and advocates instead the gradual enlightening and fructifying power of 'the shadowy and unnoticed vale of obscurity' (*Im* 39). The entire plot of *Imogen* enacts this purposeful renovation of inner resources as the crucial preliminary to wider social change. As Godwin later insisted, a state of equality need not be one of stoical simplicity; on

[71] Kuczynski, 'Pastoral Romance', 108, and Kelly, *English Jacobin Novel*, 111–12.

the contrary, it offers a basis for a vision of perpetual improvements: 'The most penetrating philosophy cannot prescribe limits to them, nor the most ardent imagination adequately fill up the prospect' (*PJ* i. 451).

Further light is shed on Godwin's version of pastoral by the currency of alternative societies, often with Welsh links, among radicals in the 1790s. The best-known example is the Pantisocracy scheme, the non-hierarchical and rationally self-reliant community planned by Coleridge, Southey, and others in 1794. Based on Godwin's arguments for the abolition of property in *Political Justice*, this was originally planned as an emigration to America. From the start, however, Coleridge's desire to appropriate 'all that is good in Godwin' was offset by the sense of pervasive social oppression that Godwin explores in *Caleb Williams*. Even the children, Coleridge wrote to Southey, were 'already *deeply* tinged with the prejudices and errors of Society'.[72] By January 1795 the emigration scheme had been dropped in favour of a retreat to Wales, and six months later Coleridge admitted that the plan had failed altogether because it expected too much of its participants.[73]

Imogen plays a more significant role than has been allowed in Godwin's career as an intellectual novelist. As early as 1784, Godwin's innovative use of poetic sources demonstrates his separateness from the eighteenth-century fictional models to be used in Jacobin fiction of the 1790s. Already he is experimenting with fiction to discuss theoretical issues in an artistically resourceful and satisfying way. In reworking the genre of pastoral romance, he seeks to liberate the reader from a range of customary expectations, anticipating his bolder analysis of hierarchical structures in *Caleb Williams*. When Godwin next turns to fiction, however, he rejects the moral absolutes of pastoral romance, and dramatizes what happens when truth no longer dwells 'with contemplation', but is loosed into the world as an active political challenge.

[72] Coleridge to Robert Southey, 21 Oct. 1794, *STCL* i. 115, 119.

[73] Coleridge to Southey, 19 Jan. 1795, [early Aug. 1795], *STCL* i. 150, 158.

2

Caleb Williams: The Paradigm of the Godwinian Novel

Things As They Are

The appearance of *Things As They Are; or, The Adventures of Caleb Williams* (1794) just over a year after the *Enquiry Concerning Political Justice* (1793) made Godwin 'a sort of phenomenon in the history of letters', according to William Hazlitt, his most perceptive early critic. Looking back on Godwin's career in 1830, he recalled: 'It was a new and startling event in literary history for a metaphysician to write a popular romance. . . . Mr. Godwin was thought a man of very powerful and versatile genius; and in him the imagination and the understanding reflected a mutual and dazzling light upon each other.'[1] However, much recent criticism of Godwin's most profoundly original novel has led to a complete separation of philosophy and fiction. Several critics have denied any connection between *Political Justice* and *Caleb Williams*, guided by Godwin's retrospective account of the composition of *Caleb Williams* in the Preface to the Bentley's Standard Novels edition of *Fleetwood* (1832).[2]

[1] Hazlitt, 'On the English Novelists' [1819], 'Mr Godwin' [1830], *Works*, vi. 132, xvi. 394; cf. William Enfield, review of *Caleb Williams*, *Monthly Review*, 2nd ser. 15 (Sept. 1794), 145–9.

[2] Godwin, Preface to *Fleetwood* (1805), Standard Novels, No. 22 (London, 1832), pp. v–xiv, reprinted in CW 335–41. See Leslie Stephen, 'William Godwin's Novels', *Studies of a Biographer*, 2nd ser. (London, 1902), iii. 119–54; Furbank, 'Godwin's Novels'; Patrick Crutwell, 'On *Caleb Williams*', *Hudson Review*, 11 (1958), 87–95; Rudolf Storch, 'Metaphors of Private Guilt and Social Rebellion in Godwin's *Caleb Williams*', *English Literary History*, 34 (1966), 188–207; A. D. Harvey, 'The Nightmare of *Caleb Williams*', *EIC* 26 (1976), 236–49; Robert Uphaus, '*Caleb Williams*: Godwin's Epoch of Mind', *Stud. N* 9 (1977), 276–96. More historical approaches include Kelly, *English Jacobin Novel*, 179–208; Butler, *War of Ideas*, 57–75; Paulson, *Representations of Revolution*, 230–9; Kelvin Everest and Gavin Edwards, 'William Godwin's *Caleb Williams*: Truth and "Things As They Are" ', in Francis Barker *et al.* (eds.), *1789: Reading, Writing, Revolution: Proceedings of the Essex Conference on the Sociology of Literature* (Colchester, 1982), 129–46.

A more accurate guide to the circumstances of the novel's first publication is provided by the 1794 Preface, which was provocatively dated to coincide with the arrest on 12 May of Thomas Hardy, secretary of the London Corresponding Society and the first of twelve radicals to be charged with treason in late 1794.[3] Withheld from publication because of its radicalism, the Preface later appeared in the second edition of 1796. Here Godwin invites us to read the novel as, in the words of a later autobiographical note, 'the offspring of that temper of mind in which the composition of my Political Justice left me',[4] and as a contribution to the pamphlet debate on the French Revolution: 'The question now afloat in the world respecting THINGS AS THEY ARE, is the most interesting that can be presented to the human mind. While one party pleads for reformation and change, the other extols in the warmest terms the existing constitution of society' (*CW* i, p. v [2]/1). In keeping with the increased polarization of opinion after May 1792, Godwin presents the controversy, which has been described as 'perhaps the last real discussion of the fundamentals of politics in this country',[5] as a simple division of views. Against the plea for 'reformation and change' made most eloquently by Paine in the *Rights of Man*, he sets Burke's emotive defence of 'the existing constitution' in *Reflections on the Revolution in France*. Godwin's own aim seems straightforward enough: addressing 'persons whom books of philosophy and science are never likely to reach', he seeks to convey the 'truth' that 'the spirit and character of the government intrudes itself into every rank of society'; and he turns to fiction as an experimental 'vehicle' for this 'valuable lesson' (*CW* i, p. vi [2]/1).

Even without the Preface, the topicality of the novel was undoubtedly evident to contemporaries on its first publication on 26 May 1794.[6] The appearance of *Political Justice* in February 1793 had already established Godwin as the leading radical theorist

[3] D. Gilbert Dumas, 'Things As They Were: The Original Ending of *Caleb Williams*', *SEL* 6 (1966), 581.

[4] Godwin, autobiographical note for 1793, Ab. MSS, c. 606, Kegan Paul, *William Godwin*, i. 78.

[5] Alfred Cobban, *The Debate on the French Revolution, 1789–1800* (Oxford, 1950), 31. My account is indebted to James T. Boulton, *The Language of Politics in the Age of Wilkes and Burke* (London, 1963); Goodwin, *Friends of Liberty*; Marilyn Butler (ed.), *Burke, Paine, Godwin, and the Revolution Controversy* (Cambridge, 1984).

[6] See also Marilyn Butler, 'Godwin, Burke, and *Caleb Williams*', *EIC* 32 (1982), 237–57, and Philp, *Godwin's Political Justice*, 103–19.

of the period, but this is not to suggest that he remained a contemplative man of letters.[7] The years from 1791 to 1796 formed the period of Godwin's greatest activity in radical circles, in which he produced pamphlets and letters to newspapers as well as *Political Justice* and *Caleb Williams*. He dined with the 'French Revolutionists' on several occasions, and regularly attended debates in Parliament. During the writing of *Caleb Williams*, from February 1793 to May 1794, he offered friendship and support to those persecuted for their opinions.[8] He began the third volume only weeks after the trials for sedition of the Scottish radicals Thomas Muir and Thomas Palmer, both of whom were found guilty and savagely sentenced to transportation.[9] In January 1794 Godwin visited Joseph Gerrald in Newgate, where he was awaiting trial after his arrest at the second Edinburgh Convention of December 1793, and wrote him a long letter advising him about his defence.[10] The State trials of October 1794 brought persecution closest to Godwin himself, as he saw radical leaders such as Hardy, Tooke, Thelwall, and Holcroft being charged with high treason. Godwin was swift to intervene: within forty-eight hours he had produced the pamphlet, *Cursory Strictures on the Charge delivered by Judge Eyre to the Grand Jury*, which effectively demolished the charge of 'constructive treason' on which the men were held. Hazlitt later said that Godwin's 'legal acuteness' probably saved the lives of the twelve radicals.[11] Certainly the pamphlet gained something of a legendary status among radicals, and it marked the height of Godwin's popular reputation.

Godwin's treatment of the issue of free speech in *Caleb Williams* gives further evidence of the novel's close relation to public events. In February and March 1793 Godwin wrote a series of letters,

[7] Cf. Lamb's account of '*Philosopher* Godwin', Lamb to Thomas Manning, 8 Feb. 1800, 18 Feb. 1800, *The Letters of Charles and Mary Anne Lamb*, ed. Edwin J. Marrs, Jr., 3 vols. (Ithaca, NY, 1975–8), i. 183, 185–6.

[8] *Caleb Williams* was begun 24 Feb. 1793 and finished 8 May 1794, Ab. MSS, f. 66; Godwin's daily diary entries give details of his visits, attendance at trials, and correspondence with persecuted radicals, Ab. MSS, e. 200–1.

[9] Muir and Palmer were tried in Aug. and Sept. 1793; see Goodwin, *Friends of Liberty*, 286–91.

[10] Godwin's letter to Gerrald, 23 Jan. 1794, is reprinted in part in Kegan Paul, *William Godwin*, i. 125–8, and in *Caleb Williams*, ed. Maurice Hindle (Harmondsworth, 1988), 355–8.

[11] Hazlitt, 'William Godwin', *Works*, xi. 26; cf. Godwin's note written across his diary entries, 27 Oct.–1 Nov. 1794: 'To this pamphlet Mr Horne Tooke frequently declared that he was indebted for his life . . . Jan. 29, 1809'; Ab. MSS, e. 201.

signed 'Mucius', to the *Morning Chronicle*, in which he protested against the activities of the Association for the Preservation of Liberty and Property against Republicans and Levellers.[12] Founded in November 1792 by John Reeves, and supported by Pitt, Burke, and Windham, this Association was part of a major effort to silence radical agitation, and its major activity was the publication and distribution of loyalist pamphlets. In *Caleb Williams* Godwin invokes a specific instance of the Association's methods of persecution, its proclamations against Paine, who was tried in his absence for authorship of the *Rights of Man* in December 1792.[13] Godwin had already drawn attention to this incident in his letter to John Reeves of 8 February 1793:

> I was myself present at the trial of this man. We all know by what means a verdict was procured: by repeated proclamations, by all the force, and all the fears of the kingdom being artfully turned against one man. As I came out of court, I saw hand-bills, in the most vulgar and illiberal style distributed, entitled, The Confession of Thomas Paine. I had not walked three streets, before I was encountered by ballad singers, roaring in cadence rude, a miserable set of scurrilous stanzas upon his private life.[14]

In the novel he retells this episode from the point of view of the victim of political harassment. Walking through the streets of London, Caleb hears a hawker bawling his wares: 'Here you have the Most Wonderful and Surprising History, and Miraculous Adventures of Caleb Williams! . . . All for the price of one halfpenny' (*CW* iii. 172–3 [1]/268–9 *var.*). Panic-stricken, Caleb envisages 'a million of men, in arms against me' (*CW* iii. 175 [1]/270), and, in a paragraph added in 1796, this revelation of inescapable despotism brings him to the point of suicidal despair (*CW* iii. 177 [2]/270). The activities of the pamphlet's author, Falkland's hired man, Jones (Gines, in the second edition), closely resemble those of the Reevite persecutors, and are experienced by Caleb as an interminable Gothic nightmare: 'The employment to which this man was hired was that of following me from place to

[12] Godwin wrote the first 'Mucius' letter on 16 Jan. 1793, the second and third on 17 Jan., and the fourth on 18 Jan., Ab. MSS, e. 200.

[13] E. P. Thompson, *The Making of the English Working Class* (1963; rev. edn., Harmondsworth, 1968, 1980), 112–15.

[14] Godwin to John Reeves, *Morning Chronicle*, 8 Feb. 1793, reprinted in *Uncollected Writings (1785–1832)*, ed. Jack W. Marken and Burton R. Pollin (Gainesville, Fla. 1968), 116.

place . . . blasting my reputation. . . . It was like what has been described of the eye of omniscience pursuing the guilty sinner' (*CW* iii. 245, 249 [1]/305 *var.*).

Godwin's most lasting contribution to the debate on the French Revolution is cast in the guise of the 'valuable lesson' of *Caleb Williams*, but is more complex and challenging than the 1794 Preface suggests. Godwin rejects the simple categories of the Preface in favour of a more searching, politically ambivalent version of revolutionary change. For his division of opinion into two sides needs to be qualified by the more discriminating attitude set out in *Political Justice*. In 'Of Resistance', a chapter rewritten for the second edition, he posits a third category:

> The great cause of humanity, which is now pleading in the face of the universe, has but two enemies; those friends of antiquity, and those friends of innovation, who, impatient of suspense, are inclined violently to interrupt the calm, the incessant, the rapid and auspicious progress which thought and reflection appear to be making in the world. (*PJ* i. 256)

To understand fully Godwin's aims in *Caleb Williams*, we need to recognize his critical detachment from both sides of the Revolution debate. This is best approached through the multiple meanings assigned to the phrase he adopts as his subtitle, 'things as they are'.

First, Godwin retained a mixed attitude to Burke, the major advocate of unquestioning acceptance of 'things as they are'. Burke was clearly an inspiration during Godwin's early development: in an undated autobiographical fragment he looked back to the spring of 1773, and paid tribute to the formative influence of 'the speeches of Burke and Fox, to whom from this time I conceived an ardent attachment, which no change of circumstance or lapse of time has ever been able to shake'.[15] In the early *Defence of the Rockingham Party* he praised Burke's rise through his talents and knowledge, but deplored his 'aristocratical principles'.[16] After the publication of *Reflections*, however, Godwin's former admiration for Burke as a champion of individual liberty gave way to distrust. For many radical admirers Burke became 'the great apostate from liberty and betrayer of his species'.[17]

[15] Godwin, autobiographical fragment, Ab. MSS, b. 226.

[16] [Godwin], *A Defence of the Rockingham Party, in their Late Coalition with the Right Honourable Frederic Lord North* (London, 1783), reprinted in *Four Early Pamphlets*, 30.

[17] Hazlitt, 'Sir James Mackintosh', *Spirit of the Age*, *Works*, xi. 100.

Although Godwin shared in this general feeling of betrayal, his response to Burke remained ambivalent, and in this sense he passed Hazlitt's 'test of the sense and candour of any one belonging to the opposite party, whether he allowed Burke to be a great man'.[18] The extent to which Godwin continued to engage with Burke's ideas is reflected in the sheer volume of his reading: he studied *Reflections* several times between 1792 and 1794, and made detailed notes on Burke's *Philosophical Enquiry into the Origin of our Ideas of the Sublime and Beautiful* (1757).[19] In *Political Justice* Godwin bases the specious arguments in favour of the existing system on Burke's 'fervent admiration of the English constitution' (*PJ* iii. 273 n.), and defines his own position in opposition to Burke's case for prescription and prejudice. Discussing 'the Aristocratical Character', he criticizes those who assent to a society divided on feudal lines on the grounds that ' "We find things very well as they are" ' (*PJ* ii. 112). In addition, as several critics have noted, Godwin's address to 'the enlightened and accomplished advocates of aristocracy' (*PJ* ii. 544) at the end of the third edition of *Political Justice* provides the basis for a reading of *Caleb Williams*, especially the character of Falkland, in terms of his mixed attitude to Burke.[20] Here Godwin imitates the rhythms of Burke's celebrated eulogy of Marie-Antoinette, a favourite target of radical pastiche,[21] to evoke a sense of admiration for the talents of the aristocracy mixed with sorrow at their application: 'our hearts bleed to see such gallantry, talents and virtue employed in perpetuating the calamities of mankind' (*PJ* ii. 545). In an obituary on Burke, also added in 1798, Godwin described him as 'a memorable example, of the power of a corrupt system of government, to undermine and divert from their genuine purposes, the noblest faculties' (*PJ* ii. 545 n.). At the start of *Caleb Williams*, the same verbal echo of *Reflections* alerts the reader to resemblances between Godwin's account of Burke and Caleb's story of Falkland: 'My heart bleeds at the recollection of his misfortunes as if they were my own' (*CW* i. 18 [1]/10).

[18] Hazlitt, 'Character of Mr Burke, 1807', *Works*, vii. 305.

[19] Godwin read *Reflections* in Jan. 1792, Oct. 1793, and June 1794, Ab. MSS, e. 199–201.

[20] Boulton, *Language of Politics*, 226–32; cf. David McCracken, 'Godwin's Reading in Burke', *English Language Notes*, 7 (1970), 264–70, and 'Godwin's *Caleb Williams*: A Fictional Rebuttal of Burke', *Studies in Burke and his Time*, 11–12 (1969–71), 1442–52.

[21] See Charlotte Smith, *Desmond: A Tale*, 3 vols. (London, 1792), i. 62–4; Robert Bage, *Man As He Is*, 4 vols. (London, 1792), iv. 72–3.

Despite his opposition to Burke's case for tradition, Godwin is not to be wholeheartedly identified with the side of 'reformation and change'. This adds a further layer of complexity to his analysis of 'things as they are'. Godwin's disagreement with reformers such as Paine and Thelwall calls into question any interpretation of *Caleb Williams* as a revolutionary drama with himself in the leading role, wrenching open the chest of aristocratic secrets.[22] In addition, Godwin's central ethic of respect for individuals created a profound distaste for violent revolutionary activity. As early as 1783, he rejected externally imposed sanctions on the individual in favour of the free exercise of private judgement.[23] In *Political Justice* this antipathy to all coercive behaviour is crucial to his distrust of associations for political reform. Distinguishing between revolution based on uncontrolled passion, and the tranquil operation of reason leading to gradual improvement, he dismissed the over-zealous revolutionist in favour of 'the wise and the virtuous man' who 'ought to see things precisely as they are, and judge of the actual constitution of his country with the same impartiality, as if he had simply read of it in the remotest page of history' (*PJ* iii. 159). Here Godwin echoes earlier radical assaults on aristocratic prejudice, as in Paine's independent-minded authorial stance—'I view things as they are, without regard to place or person' (*RM* 250)—and Bage's desire to construct the reforming 'glass of truth; and see things as they are' in *Man As He Is*.[24] But Godwin's alternative vision of 'things as they are' is primarily indebted to Dissenting notions of impartial judgement. In *A Discourse on the Love of Our Country*, the sermon preached at the notorious meeting of the Revolution Society on 4 November 1789, which Godwin had attended, Price had given an early warning that the reformers might be as lacking in impartiality as their governors:

> All our attachments should be accompanied, as far as possible, with right opinions.—We are too apt to confine wisdom and virtue within the circle of our own acquaintance and party . . . A wise man will guard himself against this delusion. He will study to think of all things as they are, and not suffer any partial affections to blind his understanding.[25]

A similar moral discrimination led Godwin, in his concluding

[22] Furbank, 'Godwin's Novels', 216; on the topical associations of this episode, see Hindle, 'Introduction', p. xxiv.

[23] [Godwin], *Account of the Seminary*, 53.

[24] Bage, *Man As He Is*, i. 23.

[25] Richard Price, *A Discourse on the Love of Our Country* (London, 1789), 4.

address to the advocates of reform, added in 1798, to reaffirm the values of peaceful 'conviction and persuasion' (*PJ* i. 260) rather than revolutionary upheaval: 'What I should desire is, not by violence to change its [society's] institutions, but by discussion to change its ideas' (*PJ* ii. 539).

These two aspects of Godwin's thought, his regretful condemnation of the aristocracy and his emphasis on moral reform in advance of practical measures, make the first edition of *Caleb Williams* far more than a straightforward commentary on social abuses. No doubt it was this complexity of meaning that led to the distribution of sympathies among early readers noted by Mary Shelley: 'those in the lower classes saw their cause espoused, & their oppressors forcibly & eloquently delineated—while those of higher rank acknowledged & felt the nobleness, sensibility and errors of Falkland with deepest sympathy'.[26] Before looking at these competing views in the novel, however, we need to consider how Godwin's imaginative strategies relate to his pivotal belief in the unfettered exercise of private judgement.

One of the first critics of *Caleb Williams*, writing to the government-funded *British Critic*, alleged that Godwin's principal aim was 'to throw an odium upon the laws of his country'. Godwin's reply provides a more helpful guide to his philosophical purpose:

> But this is a mistake into which no attentive and clear-sighted reader could possibly fall. The object is of much greater magnitude. It is to expose the evils which arise out of the present system of civilized society; and, having exposed them, to lead the enquiring reader to examine whether they are, or are not, as has commonly been supposed, irremediable; in a word, to disengage the minds of men from prepossession, and launch them upon the sea of moral and political enquiry.[27]

Here Godwin redefines the 'valuable lesson' of the Preface as a moral enquiry which also poses an imaginative challenge. As he wrote in the first edition of *Political Justice*, it is the special function of imaginative literature to liberate the reader from the constraints of 'things as they are'. 'When the mind shakes off the fetters of prescription and prejudice, when it boldly takes a flight into the

[26] Mary Shelley, 'Life of William Godwin'.

[27] *British Critic*, 5 (Apr. 1795), 444, and 6 (July 1795), 94; on the funding of the *British Critic*, see Derek Roper, *Reviewing before the Edinburgh: 1788–1802* (London, 1978), 180–1.

world unknown . . . it is at such moments that the enquiring and philosophical reader may expect to be presented with the materials and rude sketches of intellectual improvement' (*PJ* iii. 270). In turning to the unfettered imaginative space he thinks fiction can provide, Godwin seeks to 'disengage the minds of men from prepossession' and thus to alert them to the possibilities of reform.

This truly radical undertaking serves to problematize, rather than simply to illustrate, many of the conclusions of the first edition of *Political Justice*, as Godwin highlights the difficulties of achieving an impartial view of 'things as they are'. Godwin's imaginative strategy needs to be seen above all in relation to his criticism of Burke. In *Reflections* Burke is concerned to impress the subject's duty of submission to hierarchical society through a range of emotive techniques: he draws on images of nature, antiquity, and the patriarchal family, as well as biblical and Miltonic allusions, to promote unquestioning obedience to institutions 'embodied . . . in persons; so as to create in us love, veneration, admiration, or attachment' (*R* 172).[28] Burke describes the French Revolution as a series of crimes against this 'natural' paternalistic order, a disruptive, potentially contagious mixture of tragedy and farce: 'Every thing seems out of nature in this strange chaos of levity and ferocity, and of all sorts of crimes jumbled together with all sorts of follies' (*R* 92). In a central passage steeped in imagery of transgression, he depicts the mob's dethronement of Louis XVI as a parricidal drama with the mob's persecution of Marie-Antoinette as its most outrageous, yet compelling, scene (*R* 164–6).

It is this sequence of false fictions that Godwin exposes and counters with a different interpretation of revolutionary change in *Caleb Williams*. For Godwin, as for Paine, Wollstonecraft, and others, it was Burke's rhetoric and imagery that 'set the terms of the whole subsequent discussion'.[29] In the *Vindication of the Rights of Men* (1790) Wollstonecraft was quick to point out that Burke's authority lay in his 'sentimental exclamations' rather than the validity of his argument,[30] a line of attack taken up by Paine, who drew attention to Burke's manipulation of 'facts' for theatrical purposes: 'Mr Burke should recollect that he is writing History, and

[28] Boulton, *Language of Politics*, 103–30.

[29] Cobban, *Debate on the French Revolution*, 5.

[30] Mary Wollstonecraft, *Vindication of the Rights of Men, in a Letter to the Right Honourable Edmund Burke* (London, 1790), 5.

not *Plays*; and that his readers will expect truth, and not the spouting rant of high-toned exclamation' (*RM* 71–2). In *Vindiciae Gallicae* (1791), a moderate defence of the French Revolution addressed to Burke's own audience, James Mackintosh recognized that Burke's formidable appeal to habit, custom, and prejudice amounted to 'the manifesto of a counter revolution'.[31]

Profiting from these earlier critiques, Godwin sought to cut through the 'decent drapery' (*R* 171) of Burkean prejudice to challenge his underlying premisses. Arguing for the necessity of strong government, Burke depicts the individual as fallible and in need of moral guidance, an attitude which is resolutely opposed by Godwin's rational arguments: 'Nothing can be more necessary for the general benefit, than that we should divest ourselves . . . of the shackles of infancy; that human life should not be one eternal childhood; but that men should judge for themselves, unfettered by the prejudices of education, or the institutions of their country' (*PJ* i. 236). Whereas Burke seeks to promote unthinking obedience by enlisting the aid of 'all the pleasing illusions, which made power gentle, and obedience liberal . . . all the super-added ideas, furnished from the wardrobe of a moral imagination' (*R* 171), Godwin insists on the need for men to be satisfied with 'the naked statement of what they really perceive' (*PJ* ii. 102). His deep distrust of Burke as a propagandist of political imposture surfaces in a direct address to the author of *Reflections*: 'Why deceive me? . . . Shall I improve while I am governed by false reasons, by imposture and artifice? . . . Why divide men into two classes, one of which is to think and reason for the whole, and the other to take the conclusions of their superiors upon trust?' (*PJ* iii. 184 n.) In the 1798 edition, drawing extensively on Paine, Godwin replaced this passage by an analysis of Burke's calculated aims in writing a book 'to persuade us that we ought to be willing to be deceived' (*PJ* ii. 140).[32] To combat this fraudulent enterprise, Godwin advocates a style of lucid simplicity: 'Is not the plain and simple truth worth all the cunning substitutions in the world?' (*PJ* ii. 102)[33]

[31] James Mackintosh, *Vindiciae Gallicae. Defence of the French Revolution and its English Admirers, against the Accusations of the Right Hon. Edmund Burke* (London, 1791), p. xi.

[32] Cf. Paine: 'They [the members of the National Assembly] have not to hold out a language which they do not themselves believe, for the fraudulent purpose of making others believe it', *RM* 114.

[33] Cf. Paine's claim to speak 'an open and disinterested language, dictated by no passion but that of humanity', *RM* 250.

Fiction alone offered the range of imaginative techniques needed to answer Burke on his own terms. In *Caleb Williams* Godwin pursues the disturbing speculation of the opening chapter of *Political Justice*: 'Perhaps it [government] insinuates itself into our personal dispositions, and insensibly communicates its own spirit to our private transactions' (*PJ* i. 4). Although this notion owes something to his early reading of Montesquieu,[34] it also provides a philosophical focus for his critique of Burkean ideology. Godwin utilizes the novel's focus on individual experience to dramatize the inner workings of hierarchical society, the psychological and linguistic strategies by which inequality is maintained. It is his first-person narrative technique, however, that offers a counter-proposition to Burke's limited view of human potential by allowing men to 'judge for themselves'.

On its most superficial level, the plot of *Caleb Williams* offers a symbolical enactment of relations between government and the governed as set out in *Political Justice*: Godwin explores the 'Moral Effects of Aristocracy' (*PJ* ii. 93) and the consequences of 'Political Imposture' (*PJ* ii. 124) through a sequence of events which has immediate relevance to the political controversy of the early 1790s.[35] But this reading does not account for the boldness of Godwin's imaginative design, in which he remoulds the eighteenth-century romance plot into a subjective nightmare of flight and pursuit. The story is told by the servant Caleb, who is impelled by an obsessive curiosity to try and discover the secret contents of his master Falkland's chest (trunk, in the second edition). But he is caught in the act by Falkland, and his quest for knowledge is replaced by a drama of persecution in which pursuer and pursued are constantly changing roles. By the time that Caleb and Falkland confront each other in a final, challenging reversal of expectations, the novel has moved irrevocably beyond straightforward political allegory. To enrich and destabilize the symbolic opposition of master and servant, Godwin adapts a range of fictional conventions. In particular, his central notion of the intrusion of government into private life requires a mode of characterization unlike anything previously existing in the novel.

[34] On the relevance of Montesquieu, see Godwin, autobiographical note for 1791, Kegan Paul, *William Godwin*, i. 67, and D. H. Monro, *Godwin's Moral Philosophy: An Interpretation of William Godwin* (Oxford, 1953), 56–85.

[35] Cf. Butler, 'Godwin, Burke, and *Caleb Williams*', 244–52; Philp, *Godwin's Political Justice*, 108–9.

Politics and Character

Godwin's need to establish a new form in English fiction to incorporate his philosophical interests is suggested by his purposeful survey of the major existing models during the composition of *Caleb Williams*. With characteristic thoroughness, he steadily worked through the novels of Smollett, Fielding, and Defoe to concentrate on works concerned with the inner life, Richardson's *Clarissa* and *Sir Charles Grandison* (1753–4), and Radcliffe's *The Romance of the Forest* (1791) and *The Mysteries of Udolpho* (1794). He was also well versed in the novels of his friends and contemporaries, such as Bage's *Man As He Is* and Charlotte Smith's *Desmond* (1792); and he criticized in manuscript Inchbald's *A Simple Story*, and Holcroft's *Anna St Ives* and *Hugh Trevor* (1794–7).[36]

Yet Godwin departed significantly from Jacobin precedents such as *Anna St Ives*. He was obviously indebted to Holcroft's novel for several plot details: like Coke Clifton, Falkland has imbibed 'high but false notions of honour and revenge',[37] while Caleb's youthful independence of mind recalls the exemplary fortitude of Anna and Frank Henley. Unlike Holcroft, though, Godwin avoids creating characters who can be used as the author's mouthpiece. 'You have repeated to me almost innumerable times the necessity of keeping characters in action, and never suffering them to sermonize', Holcroft reminded Godwin in 1800.[38] Caleb's denunciations of tyranny and celebrations of independence are not set pieces of doctrine in Holcroft's manner, but words of a fallible character in an autobiographical memoir we cannot fully trust. For example, when Caleb escapes from Falkland's house, he exclaims in delight: 'What power is able to hold in chains a mind ardent and determined? . . . I was astonished at the folly of my species, that they did not rise up as one man, and shake off chains so ignominious and misery so insupportable' (*CW* ii. 145–6 [1]/156). But this apparently unequivocal plea for collective action is immediately qualified by the adjectives used to describe it ('this

[36] Diary entries for Mar., Apr., July, Aug. 1793, and Feb. 1794, Ab. MSS, e. 200–1.

[37] Holcroft, *Anna St Ives*, 120.

[38] Holcroft to Godwin, 9 Sept. 1800, Kegan Paul, *William Godwin*, ii. 25; cf. Godwin, note dated 1800, Ab. MSS, b. 228/9.

enthusiastical state . . . [this] rapturous inebriation'), which echo Godwin's strictures against revolutionary action based on the 'frenzy of enthusiasm' (*PJ* iii. 281).[39]

Where Godwin does adopt the more transparent techniques of didactic literature, he is concerned to bring home his philosophical argument to those 'whom books of philosophy and science are never likely to reach' (*CW* i, p. vi [2]/1). In particular, he employs the same devices used in the most effective literature of loyalist reaction, Hannah More's *Cheap Repository Tracts* (1795–8), which were published by Reeves's Association from late 1792 onwards.[40] The introduction of Thomas, Falkland's servant, at key points in the action, invites direct comparison with More's *Village Politics* (1793), which was designed to refute the specious reasoning of reformers by an appeal to the common sense of ordinary working men. This was especially effective in the use of dialogue and simplified language to get across the Burkean values of loyalty to family and Church: 'My cottage is my castle,' declares Jack Anvil the blacksmith to Tom Hod the mason. 'I read my bible, go to church, and look forward to a treasure in Heaven.'[41] Godwin skilfully appropriates this technique for the opposite purpose, maintaining 'characters in action' to comment on the dehumanizing effects of institutions, as in the pared-down exchange when Thomas visits Caleb in prison:

> Lord bless us! said he [Thomas], . . . is this you?
>
> Why not, Thomas? You knew I was sent to prison, did not you?
>
> Prison! and must people in prison be shackled and bound of that fashion?—And where do you lay of nights?
>
> Here.
>
> Here? Why there is no bed!
>
> No, Thomas, I am not allowed a bed. I had straw formerly, but that is taken away.
>
> . . . .
>
> Why I thought this was a Christian country; but this usage is too bad for a dog.
>
> You must not say so, Thomas. It is what the wisdom of government has thought fit to provide.

[39] On the association of the word 'enthusiasm' with political subversion, see Susie I. Tucker, *Enthusiasm: A Study in Semantic Change* (Cambridge, 1972), 93–106.

[40] Altick, *English Common Reader*, 75–6.

[41] [Hannah More], *Village Politics, Addressed to All the Mechanics, Journeymen, and Labourers, in Great Britain. By Will Chip, a Country Carpenter* [1793], *The Works of Hannah More*, 8 vols. (London, 1801), i. 340.

Zounds, how I have been choused [deceived]! They told me what a fine thing it was to be an Englishman, and about liberty and property, and all that there; and I find it is all a flam [trick]. (*CW* ii. 274–5 [1]/202)

While Godwin adopts these simplifying devices as a means of direct social criticism, his more sophisticated use of subjective techniques gives *Caleb Williams* its distinctive power and scope as an intellectual novel. The sheer originality of Godwin's achievement was quickly recognized by his first critics. His meticulous analysis of psychological states especially appealed to Inchbald, who praised his 'most *minute*, and yet most *concise*, method of delineating human sensations', and recognized the novel's appeal to all classes: 'It is my opinion that fine ladies, milliners, mantua-makers, and boarding-school girls will love to tremble over it—and that men of taste and judgment will admire the superior talents, the *incessant* energy of mind you have evinced.'[42] Hazlitt showed the most perceptive insight into Godwin's innovation in English fiction when he praised Godwin's 'intense and patient study of the human heart' by contrast with Scott's externalized depiction of manners. He paid special tribute to Godwin's ability to make the reader share in Caleb's experience of 'things as they are': 'We conceive no one ever began *Caleb Williams* that did not read it through: no one that ever read it could possibly forget it, or speak of it after any length of time but with an impression as if the events and feelings had been personal to himself.'[43] In this way, as James Mackintosh commented of the lasting popularity of *Caleb Williams* in 1815: 'A building thrown up for a season, has become, by the skill of the builder, a durable edifice.'[44] Hazlitt's opposition of Godwin and Scott was taken further by George Gilfillan, who recognized that Godwin's adoption of a confessional narrative in *Caleb Williams* had made 'an era in the fictitious writing of the age' and created a genuine school of writers.[45]

Godwin's use of a psychological technique should not be equated with a belief in the supremacy of the psyche, as has often been assumed, since the concept of universal psychological states is altogether alien to his view of the individual as an indivisible

[42] Inchbald to Godwin, n.d., Ab. MSS, c. 509, Kegan Paul, *William Godwin*, i. 139.

[43] Hazlitt, 'On the English Novelists', 'William Godwin', *Works*, vi. 30, xi. 24.

[44] Mackintosh, review of *Lives of Edward and John Philips, Nephews and Pupils of Milton*, 486.

[45] Gilfillan, 'William Godwin', 34–5.

member of society.[46] 'The pride of philosophy has taught us to treat man as an individual,' he wrote in a passage added to *Caleb Williams* in 1797. 'He is no such thing. He holds necessarily, indispensibly, to his species' (*CW* iii. 279 [3]/303). Godwin's primary concern with the pressures of politics and society on individual lives is reflected in a blend of psychological observation and political analysis which blurs the distinction between public and private concerns. It is this move beyond the study of inner states to explore historical causes that opens up the possibility of reform. The link between analysis of inner states and political reform in Godwin's thought is set out most clearly in his unpublished essay, 'Of History & Romance' [1797], where he explains his interest in character in terms of the analysis of historical and moral causes: 'True character consists in a delineation of consistent, human character, in a display of the manner in which such a character acts under successive circumstances, in showing how character increases & assimilates new substances to its own, & how it decays, together with the catastrophe into which by its own gravity it naturally declines.'[47] It is this action of character 'under successive circumstances' that he charts in the story of Caleb and Falkland. His preceding remarks on the course of English history give a more precise sense of the pressures of 'circumstances' on 'human character', for he draws attention to the political and historical factors which mould human development:

> The period of the Stuarts is the only portion of our history interesting to the heart of man. . . . From the moment that the grand context excited under the Stuarts was quieted by the Revolution, our history assumes its most insipid & insufferable form. It is the history of negotiations & tricks . . . it is the history of corruption & political profligacy, but it is not the history of genuine, independent man.[48]

It should not be forgotten that *Caleb Williams* is set in the period after the 1688 Revolution in which 'political profligacy' undermines

[46] See above, n. 2; on historical changes in concepts of 'the individual' and 'society', see Raymond Williams, *The Long Revolution* (1961; Harmondsworth, 1965), 89–119.

[47] Godwin, 'Of History & Romance' [1797], Ab. MSS, b. 226/15; reprinted in *Caleb Williams*, ed. Hindle, 359–73.

[48] Cf. Godwin: 'The Revolution under king William was far from being characterised by any thing pre-eminently friendly to freedom in a political view, or to heroism of character', *LP* 268.

'genuine, independent man', as 'man as he is' is engulfed by 'things as they are'.

Godwin's profound sense of the intrusion of government into private life is evident even in his use of historical names, which has been generally accepted as the most straightforward aspect of his historical design. Kelly has documented links between Godwin's Falkland and the well-known royalist hero Lucius Cary, second Viscount Falkland, in terms of a shared, fatal devotion to the code of chivalry upheld by Burke.[49] According to Clarendon's *History of the Rebellion*, Cary effectively committed suicide at the battle of Newbury in 1643 by blindly charging into a hail of enemy bullets. In an effusive obituary, Clarendon praised Cary as 'a person of such prodigious parts of learning and knowledge, of that inimitable sweetness and delight in conversation, of so flowing and obliging a humanity and goodness to mankind'.[50] Similarly, when Falkland returns from the Continent, he is welcomed with a flood of compliments: 'Such dignity, such affability, so perpetual an attention to the happiness of others, such delicacy of sentiment and expression' (*CW* i. 48 [1]/20). But as the Civil War proceeded, Cary's longing for peace is said to have produced inconsistencies of character: formerly 'so exactly unreserved and affable to all men', he 'became on a sudden less communicable, and thence very sad, pale, and exceedingly affected with the spleen'.[51] This account gives a specific historical dimension to Falkland's repression of his inner feelings, which is thus inescapably linked with his aristocratic status. On first meeting Falkland, Caleb is more perceptive than he realizes: 'there was a grave and sad solemnity in his air, which for want of experience I imagined was the inheritance of the great' (*CW* i. 5 [1]/5).

As the novel proceeds, however, this historical framework proves to be alarmingly unstable. Godwin introduces more questionable parallels which show how, as Hazlitt remarked, 'heroes on paper might degenerate into vagabonds in practice'.[52] The name of Falkland's rival and victim, with whom he is progressively identified, recalls that of Sir James Tyrrel, murderer of the princes

[49] Kelly, *English Jacobin Novel*, 201–3.

[50] Edward Hyde, 1st Earl of Clarendon, *History of the Rebellion and Civil Wars in England, begun in the Year 1641* (1702–4), re-ed. W. Dunn Macray, 6 vols. (Oxford, 1888, 1969), iii. 178–9.

[51] Ibid. 188.

[52] Hazlitt, 'William Godwin', *Works*, xi. 21.

in the Tower in *Richard III* and in Prévost's *Margaret of Anjou*.[53] Tyrrel himself is described by comparison with giants of classical mythology (*CW* i. 40, 43–4 [1]/17, 18–19), while references to Alexander the Great, whom Caleb compares with the great criminal, Jonathan Wild, introduce further problems of separating heroes and villains (*CW* ii. 13 [1]/110). In addition, the outlaw Raymond alludes to the case of the scholar Eugene Aram, who killed his friend but lived an exemplary life for fourteen years before being tried and hanged, which reflects on the plight of Falkland and Caleb as well as on his own (*CW* iii. 62 [1]/228).

The ambivalence in Caleb's Christian name focuses similar problems of identity and definition in a period of 'corruption and political profligacy', for it suggests his dual role as servant and spy, victim and persecutor. According to Numbers, Caleb's biblical namesake was one of the men sent by Moses 'to spy out' the land of Canaan. On his return, Caleb is rewarded by Moses for his faithful service: 'But my servant Caleb, because he . . . hath followed me fully, him will I bring into the land wherein he went; and his seed shall possess it.'[54] The term 'spy' recurs in Caleb's description of his actions, though he also protests he has no inclination 'to turn informer' (*CW* ii. 71 [1]/130). Ian Ousby has pointed out that Godwin calls Caleb a spy at a time when internal political spying was a major issue among radicals.[55] Caleb's equivocal self-definition as both servant and spy reflects the distorting categories of a society divided on Burkean lines.

While Godwin's use of historical names defeats any notion of simple allegory, his use of novelistic conventions gives scope for an analysis of historical pressures on individual lives. Godwin's innovatory reading of character reflects his view that 'the present mixed characters of mankind' (*PJ* i. 181) are produced by men's temporary enthralment to 'things as they are', rather than an inherent sinfulness which requires the restraining power of strong government, as Burke argued.[56] Godwin's progressive concept of

[53] Godwin read *Richard III* in Dec. 1793 and Prévost's *Histoire de Marguerite d'Anjou* (1740; trans. 1755) in Sept. 1793, Ab. MSS, e. 201.

[54] Num. 13: 16, 14: 24.

[55] Ian Ousby, ' "My Servant Caleb": Godwin's *Caleb Williams* and the Political Trials of the 1790s', *UTQ* 44 (1974), 47–55.

[56] Cf. Burke: 'Society requires [that] . . . the inclinations of men should frequently be thwarted, their will controlled, and their passions brought into subjection. This can only be done by *a power out of themselves*', *R* 151.

character, which highlights man's potential for self-reform rather than inevitable tragic decline, provides the key to his departure from his eighteenth-century predecessors in the novel. From the works of Fielding and Richardson, in particular, he selects elements of plot and characterization and redeploys them for his own philosophical purpose.

Caleb Williams may thus be read as a contribution to the eighteenth-century critical debate about how fiction should accomplish its instructive purpose, either by the representation of experienced social reality, as in Fielding's novels, or by holding up examples to be imitated, as in the romances of Richardson. In his subtitle Godwin echoes the widely held distinction between these two novelists, as voiced by Clara Reeve, who complained that Fielding, unlike Richardson, 'painted human nature *as it is*, rather than *as it ought to be*'.[57] Godwin's title seems to indicate a fictional world more akin to that of Fielding than Richardson, and to some extent this is borne out by his emphasis on class stereotypes in volume one, written while he was reading Fielding and Smollett. Here the servant Caleb, educated through books but lacking experience in the world, is set in opposition to Falkland, a benevolent gentleman with a cosmopolitan education, who is in turn contrasted with Tyrrel, a boorish provincial squire. But in fact this emphasis on typical qualities underlines the breakdown of a progressive view of history. Tyrrel, the rural despot, is superseded by the aristocratic Falkland, who is challenged in turn by Caleb's egalitarian views; but all three phases collapse into violent conflict, as tyranny begets tyranny.

Godwin's revisionary attitude to Richardson's exemplary characters offers a further challenge to the reader's preconceptions. Already in *Italian Letters* Godwin had countered Richardson's idealization of character with an emphasis on mixed psychological motivation.[58] In *Caleb Williams* his plentiful allusions to *Clarissa* and *Sir Charles Grandison* suggest a systematic revision of Richardson's moral aims to convey his politicized understanding of inner states. Collins's account of Falkland's early life in volume one

[57] Clara Reeve, *The Progress of Romance, Through Times, Countries, and Manners*, 2 vols. (London, 1785), facsimile reprint (New York, 1930), i. 141; cf. C. R. Kropf, '*Caleb Williams* and the Attack on Romance', *Stud. N* 8 (1976), 81–7.

[58] [Godwin], *Italian Letters; or, The History of the Count de St Julian* (London, 1784), ed. Burton R. Pollin (Lincoln, Nebr., 1965), 31–2.

has been read as a comment on the moral ambivalence of the eighteenth-century man of honour, his apparent benevolence masking violent impulses.[59] But Godwin moves beyond this notion of innate psychological complexity to make a specific political point. Through his competing allusions to *Sir Charles Grandison* and Burke's defence of chivalric virtue, he shows that ostensibly unaccountable features of character are in fact only too explicable in terms of political corruption.

Like Richardson's well-known Christian hero, Falkland embarks on a grand tour of Italy, teaches English to a beautiful, rich Italian woman, becomes embroiled with her noble suitor, and refuses his challenge to a duel without comprising his honour. In addition, both Falkland and Grandison become involved with vulnerable wards named Emily, and both rescue a girl from a potential rapist who plans to coerce her into marriage. However, Falkland's exemplary status as a 'god-like Englishman' (*CW* i. 33 [1]/15) is undercut by his excessive regard for 'the sentiments of birth and honour' (*CW* i. 19 [1]/10). Among the Italian aristocracy this exaggerated sense of personal reputation takes precedence over respect for the lives of others, and, according to Collins, 'There is therefore scarcely any Italian that would upon some occasions scruple assassination' (*CW* i. 22 [1]/11). Back in England, when Tyrrel strikes Falkland in public, the latter resorts to the Italian method of revenge: he secretly murders Tyrrel by stabbing him from behind. After the murder, Falkland's double code of morals becomes increasingly extravagant as he is forced to take more and more extreme measures to protect his good name. Earlier he risked his life to save Emily Melvile from burning to death in a fire; but after the murder he lets two innocent men, Hawkins and his son, be executed, and nearly hounds Caleb to death, in order to preserve his reputation.

Collins's Burkean vocabulary highlights the contemporary relevance of this self-division, for it connects Falkland's internal fragmentation with his exalted sense of honour: 'His mind was fraught with all the rhapsodies of visionary honour; and in his sense

[59] Gerard A. Barker, 'Ferdinando Falkland's Fall: Grandison in Disarray', *Papers on Language and Literature*, 16 (1980), 376–86; cf. Eric Rothstein, 'Allusion and Analogy in the Romance of *Caleb Williams*', *UTQ* 37 (1967), 18–30; Donald Roemer, 'The Achievement of Godwin's *Caleb Williams*: The Proto-Byronic Squire Falkland', *Criticism*, 18 (1976), 43–56.

nothing but the grosser part, the mere shell of Falkland, was capable to survive the wound that his pride has sustained' (*CW* i. 17 [1]/9). Here Godwin directly echoes Burke's lament for the passing of the age of chivalry, which forms the rhetorical core of his defence of established institutions: 'It is gone, that sensibility of principle, that chastity of honour, which felt a stain like a wound . . . which ennobled whatever it touched, and under which vice itself lost half its evil, by losing all its grossness' (*R* 170). Godwin thus moves beyond commonplace parody of *Reflections* to present psychological division as a product of Burkean society. Falkland is portrayed not as tragically flawed, but as 'one whom the system of nature has brought down to the grave' (*CW* iii. 285 [1]/320), a type of the decadent aristocracy criticized in *Political Justice*.

While Godwin gives a selective rereading of mainstream eighteenth-century fiction, he draws more extensively on the non-realistic techniques of Gothic and sentimental fiction. These provide a mode of indirect commentary on the inner lives of individuals oppressed by institutions. The Gothic novel might seem to have an obvious appeal for the writer who wished to comment on an oppressive society, for, as Scott remarked of Radcliffe's novels, the characters 'bear the features, not of individuals, but of the class to which they belong'.[60] But, as already seen, this symbolic depiction of class roles is by no means exclusive to Gothic fiction. If Godwin adapts Walpole's Gothic fable of hereditary property in his early novels, *Imogen* and *Italian Letters*, he also reorders the feudal social groupings of major novelists such as Richardson. Moreover, what appealed to Godwin most in the 1790s was not so much Radcliffe's depiction of class roles as her psychological exploration of domestic power relations, which could be exploited for a systematized analysis of political oppression. In *The Romance of the Forest* and *The Mysteries of Udolpho*, Radcliffe utilizes the categories of the Burkean sublime to explore the same basic situation of a young woman imprisoned and tormented in a lonely place by a powerful figure of masculine authority. This adversarial plot, in which the heroine both flees from and is fascinated by a tyrannical father-figure, has often been read in terms of women's private fears of fathers, brothers, and lovers, but in fact the heroines

[60] Scott, 'Mrs Ann Radcliffe' [1824], reprinted in *Sir Walter Scott on Novelists and Fiction*, ed. Ioan Williams (London, 1968), 110.

are usually persecuted for their property, like Burke's Marie-Antoinette.[61]

In *Caleb Williams* Godwin makes explicit the political undertones of Gothic romance and brings its familial associations to bear on class relationships. But he resists the conventional pressures of the eighteenth-century romance plot, which typically leads to the affirmation of social identity through the discovery of parents and husbands. Godwin is more interested in what happens when individuals break out of their prescribed social roles: in *Caleb Williams* the pursuit between master and man cannot be resolved by familial reconciliation. In releasing the Gothic novel from the eighteenth-century courtship plot, Godwin makes it available not only to later Godwinian novelists but also to other writers who develop it as a historical form, such as James Hogg.

Godwin's exploitation of the Gothic emphasis on fear and dread is only one aspect of his critique of authority in *Caleb Williams*. In his use of the unreliable narrator, he moves beyond Walpole's and Radcliffe's disruption of narrative authority through the romance conventions of hidden manuscripts, tales-within-tales, and dream sequences, to harness other modes of confessional narrative to his philosophical design. Above all, he draws on fictional models which develop the Puritan preoccupation with the mediation of truth in narrative.[62] The structure of Caleb's narrative reflects the insistent onward pressure of spiritual autobiography, traditionally unified by an absolute notion of God-given truth,[63] but Caleb's quest for knowledge lacks the affirmative goal of the Christian life: at the end of his journey there is no prospect of spiritual reward and no benevolent maker to welcome him 'home'. Instead Godwin pursues the destabilization of authority introduced in Defoe's secular criminal memoirs, where divine judgement and institutional

[61] For a psychological interpretation of 'female Gothic', see Ellen Moers, *Literary Women* (New York, 1977), 90–110, 134–40; cf. Tania Modleski, *Loving with a Vengeance: Mass-Produced Fantasies for Women* (New York and London, 1982), 67–8; for a more historical view, see Mary Poovey, 'Ideology and *The Mysteries of Udolpho*', *Criticism*, 21 (1979), 307–30.

[62] See Michael McKeon, *The Origins of the English Novel, 1600–1740* (Baltimore, 1987), 91–100.

[63] See G. A. Starr, *Defoe and Spiritual Autobiography* (Princeton, NJ, 1965), 3–50; N. H. Keeble, *The Literary Culture of Nonconformity in Later Seventeenth-Century England* (Leicester, 1987), 227–82.

law are uneasily conflated.[64] Richardson's use of the epistolary mode in *Pamela* introduces further issues of narrative reliability: 'I long to see the particulars of your plot', Mr B. tells Pamela, registering his concern not with the facts of her letters but with 'the light [she] represent[s] things in'.[65] This declaration of exclusive faith in the subject opens up the possibility of deceptive plotting which is developed by Fielding in his counter-critique *Shamela* (1741). Here Pamela's protestations of integrity are capable of a different, socially disruptive interpretation that virtually parallels the plot of *Caleb Williams*: 'All Chambermaids are strictly enjoyned to look out after their Masters; they are . . . countenanced in Impertinence to their Superiours, and in betraying the Secrets of Families.'[66] This developing preoccupation with truth-telling in narrative establishes the background for Godwin's use of the unreliable narrator to enact his specific philosophical concerns.

'Unrecorded Despotism'

By offering several subjective accounts, of which Caleb's is the main one, Godwin appeals directly to the reader as true arbiter of political justice. When Caleb takes over from Collins as narrator at the start of volume two, he declares his aim to write 'with the same simplicity and accuracy that I would observe towards a court which was to decide in the last resort upon every thing dear to me' (*CW* ii. 1–2 [1]/106). Thus at one level Caleb's narrative appears an attempt to make the world his confessional, reflecting Godwin's early belief in the power of total frankness to erode the false opinion upon which government was established: 'If every man to-day would tell all the truth he knows, three years hence there would be scarcely a falshood of any magnitude remaining in the civilized world' (*PJ* iii. 293). The prominence of trial scenes in the novel further highlights Godwin's critique of institutional justice. 'My case is not within the reach of common remedies', says Falkland

[64] Godwin read Defoe's *Roxana* (1724) and *Colonel Jack* (1722) in July and Dec. 1793, Ab. MSS, e. 201.

[65] Richardson, *Pamela*, 268, 275.

[66] [Henry Fielding], *An Apology for the Life of Mrs Shamela Andrews. In which, the many notorious* FALSHOODS *and* MISREPRESENTATIONS *of a Book called Pamela are exposed and refuted* (1741), in *Joseph Andrews and Shamela*, ed. Douglas Brooks-Davies and Martin Battestin (Oxford, 1970, 1989), 356.

(*CW* ii. 35 [1]/117), reminding us of the arguments against legal restraints in *Political Justice*. Here Godwin presents the rule of law as a failure: since it seeks to impose a false uniformity on men's actions, it is incompatible with the claims of true justice, which takes into account individual circumstances.[67] The problems involved in bringing Falkland to justice reinforce Godwin's point that, in the realm of moral truth and justice, legal definitions of guilt and innocence are meaningless.

Yet Caleb's subjective account is more problematic than he admits, which indicates Godwin's scepticism about the authority of the self in a world dominated by institutions. As he wrote in 'Of History & Romance': 'there is something in the nature of modern government & institutions, that seems to blight in the bud every grander & more ample development of the soul'. Caleb himself is by no means exempt from the 'modes of domestic and unrecorded despotism' by which man becomes the destroyer of man (*CW* i, p. vi [2]/1). His opening lament—'I have been a mark for the vigilance of tyranny, and I could not escape' (*CW* i. 1 [1]/3)—reminds us that his tale is a retrospective construction of past events, and sets up the subjective context in which all subsequent events should be viewed. There are further indications of Caleb's unreliability as the sole witness of key episodes: of Falkland's extravagant fits of remorse, he comments, 'It must not be supposed that the whole of what I am describing was visible to the persons about him' (*CW* i. 10 [1]/7). It is this limited view of events that facilitates the crucial narrative shift from the relatively ordered, hierarchical world of Fielding and Richardson at the start of the novel to a subjective nightmare of flight and pursuit.

This destabilization of hierarchical values parodies and undermines Burke's fervent defence of the existing system. Godwin's most obvious point of reference is Burke's 'great history-piece of the massacre of innocents' (*R* 166), which presents the French royal family as the epitome of a paternalistic society based on the bonds of love, betrayed by rebellious subjects. In his *Letter to a Member of the National Assembly* (1791), Burke gave a further dramatic warning of the breakdown of the familial social model when he condemned the French leaders' propagation of Rousseauistic principles, 'by which every servant may think it, if not his duty, at

[67] Bk. 7, ch. 8: 'Of Law', *PJ* ii. 397–413.

least his privilege to betray his master'.[68] Inverting Burke's drama of filial transgression, Godwin highlights the tyrannical aspects of paternal government: although Caleb presents himself as guilt-ridden son and disloyal servant, it is Falkland who bears the secret crimes of his class. The motif of flight and pursuit reflects the irresistible power of social institutions, especially the forces of legal despotism, which Falkland mobilizes in his own defence. In opposition to Burke's imagery of safe and antiquated houses, Caleb comes to regard Falkland House as an Inquisition-like fortress and the world as a vast prison (*CW* ii. 131–2 [1]/151).

By focusing on the psychological distortions induced by political pressures, Godwin moves beyond a mere reversal of Burkean categories to cast all moral values into doubt. This exploration of the political origins of irrational states of mind gives *Caleb Williams* its uniqueness as one of the earliest explorations of dualism. Neither Caleb nor Falkland survives as a whole, and identity is in part conditioned by position in the pursuit. As one another's 'shadow' and 'plague', both experience the retarding effect of aristocratic government which reduces its victims to 'mere shadows of men' (*PJ* ii. 280). Like his master, Caleb finds himself supporting a 'counterfeit character' (*CW* iii. 142 [3]/256), as he adopts a series of disguises in which he identifies with figures on the margins of society: an Irish beggar, a young Jew, and a cripple. Meanwhile, Falkland's role as revengeful pursuer is acted out by his surrogate Jones, 'this detested adversary' (*CW* iii. 248 [1]/305), who turns Caleb's watchful eye back on himself and focuses his growing epistemological uncertainty: 'he appears to be the persecutor and I the persecuted: is not this difference the mere creature of the imagination?' (*CW* iii. 250 [1]/306) Although Caleb is mercilessly hounded through the entire country, it is on Falkland that physical marks of disintegration appear, and this prepares the way for their final exchange of roles.

It is no accident that Caleb comes to experience all social relations in terms of dependency or persecution, as Godwin adapts a central motif of Radcliffe's Gothic plot to undercut the

[68] Burke, *A Letter from Mr Burke to a Member of the National Assembly; in Answer to some Objections to his Book on French Affairs* (1791), *The Works and Correspondence of the Right Hon. Edmund Burke*, 8 vols. (London, 1852), iv. 378; read by Godwin in Nov. 1793, Ab. MSS, e. 201.

unquestioning trust in superiors inculcated in *Reflections*.[69] In contrast to the massive power of institutions, Burke depicts the individual as fallible and childlike, and the emotionally charged images of *Reflections* encourage dependency on the state as on a vast family: 'In this choice of inheritance we have given to our frame of polity the image of a relation in blood; binding up the constitution of our country with our dearest domestic ties; adopting our fundamental laws into the bosom of our family affections; keeping inseparable . . . our state, our hearths, our sepulchres, and our altars' (*R* 120). In a travesty of this vision of benevolent paternalism, Caleb experiences repeated betrayals of trust. When he is sent to the same prison that Hawkins and his son occupied, he is keen to identify with them as victims of legalized despotism. But in fact he bears a closer relation to Tyrrel's ward, Emily Melvile, in her youthful vulnerability and idolization of Falkland. In prison Caleb meets another oppressed figure, Brightwel, who examines Caleb's story with 'sincere impartiality' (*CW* ii. 245 [1]/192), and thus restores his faith in human friendship. Brightwel, however, is the last person Caleb meets on equal terms, and he dies while Caleb is still in prison. The collapse of Caleb's relationship with Falkland is repeated in his subsequent encounters with the outlaw Raymond and the watchmaker Spurrel, apparently trustworthy paternal figures who then let him down.

This cumulative pattern of expectation and reversal evokes the older revolutionary narratives in Genesis and *Paradise Lost*, used extensively by Burke in *Reflections*, where he depicts revolutionary activity in terms of the aesthetic categories of his earlier *Enquiry . . . into our Ideas of the Sublime and Beautiful*.[70] By contrast with this Old Testament drama of disobedience and punishment, Caleb's journey from or towards his master is studded with episodes from the Gospels, used for instructive purposes in the manner of *Sketches of History*. Caleb's final meeting with Collins, his early mentor, derives its peculiar emotional intensity from its ironic associations with the return of the Prodigal Son, a type of conversion-experience in Nonconformist writings:[71]

[69] Cf. Ann Radcliffe, *The Romance of the Forest* (1791), ed. Chloe Chard (Oxford, 1986), 168.

[70] Paulson, *Representations of Revolution*, 57–73.

[71] Starr, *Defoe and Spiritual Autobiography*, 45.

I was the first to recollect him. . . . In a moment the full idea of who he was rushed upon my mind; I ran; I called with an impetuous voice; I was unable to restrain the vehemence of my emotions . . . His sight was already dim; he pulled up his horse till I should overtake him; and then said, Who are you? I do not know you.

My father! exclaimed I, embracing one of his knees with fervour and delight, I am your son! once your little Caleb, whom you a thousand times loaded with your kindness! (*CW* iii. 255 [1]/309)

However, unlike Luke's account, which emphasizes the spontaneous compassion and forgiveness of the father,[72] here the erring son is rejected as Collins refuses to listen to Caleb's story.

As in many other exchanges in the novel, this meeting founders on the contradictory signals produced by emotive rhetoric. Godwin's exploration of the constraining power of social institutions pivots on issues of linguistic authority. Falkland's resolution 'to tell so well-digested a lie, as that all mankind should believe it true' (*CW* ii. 86 [1]/135) invites direct comparison with Godwin's criticism of Burke as the champion of a system of artificial distinctions which defies the 'language of truth' (*PJ* ii. 48). Linguistic deception provides the key to Falkland's authority and to Caleb's complicity with the existing system. The pursuit itself is founded on the suppression of truth. Although the contents of Falkland's chest are never disclosed, Caleb conjectures that it contains a 'faithful narrative' (*CW* iii. 273 [1]/315) of the circumstances of the murder, which he wishes to replace with his own. Yet Caleb is implicated in his master's duplicity as soon as he commits himself to guarding his secret rather than publicizing it, and this suppression of the truth colours all his subsequent actions. The full extent of Caleb's unwitting collusion with Falkland's false eminence is reflected in the erosion of his own linguistic resources, gradually replaced by the attitudes and values of his master's rhetoric.

The major source of Falkland's linguistic power lies in his use of a Burkean rhetoric of Old Testament authority, charged with the ideological notions that man is inherently sinful and in need of legislative restraints. Its impact on Caleb shows the effectiveness of religious language as an instrument of political coercion. Central to Godwin's strategy is the fact that Falkland is never presented objectively, but always through Caleb's fascinated, then fearful, perspective. In response to Falkland's repeated invocations of 'the

[72] Luke 15: 11–32.

reach of the omnipresent God', Caleb is typically 'unable to utter a word . . . irresolute, overawed and abashed' (*CW* ii. 111, 140–1 [1]/144, 154). Here Godwin draws on Burke's psychological account of the terror aroused by the 'idea of the Deity . . . whilst we contemplate so vast an object, under the arm, as it were, of almighty power, and invested upon every side with omnipresence, we shrink into the minuteness of our own nature, and are, in a manner, annihilated before him'.[73] Characteristically, though, Godwin adapts Burke's aesthetic of terror to make his own political point. For like the domestics, who regarded Falkland 'with veneration as a being of a superior order' (*CW* i. 11 [1]/7), Caleb has periods of unreserved confidence in his master in which he regresses to the passive state of mind induced by an aristocratic regime: 'I . . . implicitly surrendered my understanding for him to set it to what point he pleased' (*CW* ii. 48 [1]/122). As Godwin wrote in his early discussion 'Of Obedience', once man 'surrenders his reason', he 'becomes the partisan of implicit faith and passive obedience . . . the most mischievous of all animals' (*PJ* iii. 269). In the second edition of *Political Justice*, building on the insights gained in his novel, he gave a more extensive analysis of 'the slavish feelings that shrink up the soul in the presence of an imagined superior' (*PJ* i. 215–16) in terms that are surely indebted to Burke's analysis of the psychological effects of 'almighty power'. In this way Caleb's vocabulary of guilt, transgression, and forbidden knowledge has a political coherence, demonstrating the intrusion of government into the individual consciousness.

Given the power of hierarchical government to unsettle stable structures of perception and judgement, Caleb's self-confessed collapse into the role of passive victim needs to be closely examined in the light of earlier events. In *The Enquirer* (1797) Godwin formulated what he had already shown in *Caleb Williams* when he wrote of man's prospects in society, 'Tyranny grows up by a kind of necessity of nature' (*E* 10). The same political and social circumstances which engender Falkland's false notions of honour impel Caleb's actions. Godwin's use of the unreliable narrator makes for a highly equivocal rendering of Caleb's curiosity. At one level Caleb's conduct resembles that of the virtuous man who 'has not

[73] Edmund Burke, *A Philosophical Enquiry into the Origin of our Ideas of the Sublime and Beautiful* (1757), ed. James T. Boulton (1958; rev. edn., Oxford, 1987), 68; read by Godwin in July 1792 and June 1794, Ab. MSS, e. 200, 201.

failed to detect the imposture, that would persuade us there is a mystery in government, which uninitiated mortals must not presume to penetrate' (*PJ* i. 238).[74] But this spirit of rational enquiry quickly gives way to a thrilling compulsion: 'When one idea has got possession of the soul, it is scarcely possible to keep it from finding its way to the lips. Error, once committed, has a fascinating power, like the eyes of the rattlesnake, to draw us into a second error' (*CW* ii. 20 [1]/112–13). Although Caleb describes this compulsion as 'error' and later speaks of his curiosity as 'infantine and unreasonable' (*CW* ii. 110 [1]/144), Godwin's dramatization of other key moments in which rational judgement is suspended gives them a more ambivalent quality. For example, Caleb describes his exalted state of mind on the discovery of Falkland's secret in heightened language that recalls Burke's version of the sublime—'I was never so perfectly alive as at that moment' (*CW* ii. 70 [1]/130)[75]—and this 'state of mental elevation', by a 'mysterious fatality', leads him to try and discover the contents of Falkland's chest (*CW* ii. 75 [1]/131). Although this action proves ultimately ironic, it introduces the possibility that the mind's highest potential may be reached not in the exercise of rational thought, but in its suspension. Caleb, however, glosses this 'short-lived and passing alienation of mind' (*CW* ii. 76 [1]/132) in simpler terms as a dereliction of public duty, whereby his awareness of his own irrational motives to action leads him to suspend judgement about Falkland's (*CW* ii. 93 [1]/137–8).

The susceptibility of Caleb's activities to competing interpretations underlines the distinctive nature of Godwin's radicalism. In keeping with his rejection of violent political change, his account of Caleb's actions in the first part of the book shows the dangerous consequences of rash revolution, culminating in an assault on private property. In volume three, mindful of the recent trials of leading radicals, Godwin gives an extended critique of revolutionary activity which provides further evidence of his developing gradualist outlook.[76]

The 'enthusiasm' which overwhelms Caleb on his escape from prison—'Sacred and indescribable moment, when man regains his rights!' (*CW* iii. 10 [1]/210)—alerts the reader to Godwin's

[74] Butler, 'Godwin, Burke, and *Caleb Williams*', 254–5.
[75] Cf. Burke, *Enquiry*, 39.
[76] On Godwin's gradualism, see Philp, *Godwin's Political Justice*, 129–41.

criticism of the notion of natural rights upheld by Paine and his followers.[77] Godwin pursues his discussion of the right and wrong ways of contending for liberty in his account of the outlaws' activities. Only their leader Raymond, who is introduced by analogy with the Good Samaritan, has retained his humanity, while the others try to remove injustice by unjust means. In a statement moderated in the second edition, Raymond explains their revolutionary philosophy:

> We undertake to counteract the partiality and iniquity of public institutions. We, who are thieves without a licence, are at open war with another set of men, who are thieves according to law. If anyone disapprove our proceedings, at least we have this to say for ourselves, we act not by choice, but only as our wise governors force us to act. (*CW* iii. 27–8 [1]/216 *var.*)

Caleb's response to this justification of revolutionary defiance is mixed: while he applauds the robbers' 'uncommon energy, ingenuity and fortitude', he condemns their savage methods and their attacks on property (*CW* iii. 57–8 [1]/226). Nevertheless, while he is in their company he begins to feel indignation and resentment against Falkland for the first time. Caleb's subsequent actions dramatize Godwin's belief in the kinship between institutionalized tyranny and revolutionary violence. When Caleb resolves to denounce Falkland in public, he takes on the violent rhetoric of the novel's earlier despotical figures, Tyrrel and Falkland. He depicts his master as the modern heir of the Roman tyrants Nero and Caligula, but his own desire for retribution is couched in Falkland's 'supernaturally tremendous' tones: 'I will speak with a voice more fearful than thunder! . . . Thou hast shown no mercy; and thou shalt receive none! . . . I will be triumphant, and crush my seemingly omnipotent foe' (*CW* iii. 270–1 [1]/314). Though he claims to use no daggers, his resolution to 'tell a tale' carries the full weight of 'Revolution . . . engendered by an indignation against tyranny', which is itself 'evermore pregnant with tyranny' (*PJ* i. 267).

[77] Godwin's early chapter, 'Rights of Man', *PJ* iii. 254–60, was completely rewritten for the second edition; cf. Elie Halévy, *The Growth of Philosophic Radicalism* (1928), trans. from the French by Mary Morris, with a Preface by John Plamenatz (London, 1972), 191–203.

Godwin's Revisions

In the final meeting of Caleb and Falkland, Godwin offers a counter-proposition to this cycle of revolution and tyranny, replacing Caleb's rebellious zeal with a no less revolutionary change of heart. Godwin's immediate rewriting of this scene, prior to the novel's first publication, indicates its problematic nature. According to the date-list for the composition of *Caleb Williams*, he finished the novel on 30 April 1794, but then he composed a 'new catastrophe' between 4 and 8 May, and it is this ending that appeared in the first edition, published on 26 May.[78] While the original manuscript ending lacks an affirmative resolution, the published ending, though still unresolved in conventional terms, supports his optimistic view that the evils of the present system are not 'irremediable', but are rooted in prejudice and error.[79]

In the original manuscript ending, Caleb's mistakenly aggressive pursuit of truth leads to his defeat and final capitulation to 'things as they are'. The sight of Falkland's wasted appearance gives 'double vehemence' to his fury (*CW* 327), but his overbearing manner antagonizes his hearers, and he ends up in prison. In the first of two fragmentary postscripts, his mood changes to one of resignation: 'Alas! alas! it too plainly appears in my history that persecution and tyranny can never die!' (*CW* 332) The second postscript, addressed to Collins, is based on the disjointed papers that Clarissa writes immediately after her rape,[80] and it ends with Caleb's total defeat and withdrawal: 'It is wisest to be quiet, it seems. . . . True happiness lies in being like a stone' (*CW* 334). This unconvincing passivity suggests a brief lapse into mere commentary on social evils, which affirms and thus acquiesces in the injustice of the existing system.

By contrast, the ethical and psychological complexity of the published ending allows a glimpse of an alternative state of things,

[78] Ab. MSS, f. 66, e. 200–1.

[79] For a contrary view, see Dumas, 'Things As They Were', 584; others who argue in favour of the published ending are Mitzi Myers, 'Godwin's Changing Conception of *Caleb Williams*', *SEL* 12 (1972), 591–628; Gerard A. Barker, 'Justice to *Caleb Williams*', *Stud. N* 6 (1974), 377–88; Philp, *Godwin's Political Justice*, 114–17.

[80] Godwin reread *Clarissa* while working on the first version of his conclusion, Ab. MSS, e. 201.

fulfilling Godwin's wider aim of holding out to the reader the possibility of improvement. Equally, though, Godwin retains a full awareness of the difficult circumstances in which change must take place, and this rescues his conclusion from the charge made by Hazlitt against the first edition of *Political Justice*, that Godwin 'raised the standard of morality above the reach of humanity'.[81]

In its challenge to novel-reading expectations, the final reversal of roles between Caleb and Falkland is entirely in keeping with the ethical strenuousness of Godwin's design. The anticipation of the protagonists' reconciliation bears the multiple emotional pressures of Godwin's main narrative models, the return of the erring pilgrim to the Lord in spiritual autobiography, and the restoration of social hierarchy by marriage in the eighteenth-century romance plot. Godwin's flouting of these fictional assumptions underlines the difficulty of accommodating relationships based on equality within existing moral and social frameworks.

Caleb's dialogue with the elderly Collins reminds us of what is at stake in his final meeting with Falkland. Here Caleb resigns his claim to a fair hearing from Collins, and gains insight into the painfully hazardous operation of impartial judgement within existing society.[82] Collins defends his refusal to engage with Caleb's story in terms that spell out the tremendous cost of change in individuals governed by a lifetime of prescription and prejudice: 'If you could change all my ideas, and show me that there was no criterion by which vice might be prevented from being mistaken for virtue, what benefit would arise from that? I must part with all my interior consolation, and all my external connections. . . . And for what?' (*CW* iii. 258–9 [1]/310) Faced with this array of Burkean 'pleasing illusions', set against the dizzying possibility that there may be 'no criterion' by which vice and virtue may be seen as they really are, Caleb realizes the impotence of his demand for absolute truth, and voluntarily resigns his place in Collins's esteem.

This intimation that perceiving things as they really are may be impossible within the existing system is reinforced, only to be finally rejected, in Caleb's last meeting with Falkland. At one level Caleb's reaction to Falkland's emaciated appearance indicates a significant development from his earlier pursuit of revenge, for he is

81 Hazlitt, 'William Godwin', *Works*, xi. 18.

82 Cf. Barker's claim that Caleb's resignation shows he has achieved 'perfect disinterestedness', 'Justice to *Caleb Williams*', 383.

now emotionally overwhelmed. Having imagined his master as a demonic monster, he is confronted with the suffering individual, and this leads to a sudden change of heart: 'Shall I trample upon a man thus dreadfully reduced?' (*CW* iii. 285 [1]/320) In pursuit of 'a better and more magnanimous remedy', Caleb offers a tale of errors which highlights his and Falkland's mutual failure of 'confidence' in each other's rational potential (*CW* iii. 286 [1]/321). While Falkland failed to trust him with his secret, Caleb also failed to appeal to the better side of Falkland through 'a frank and fervent expostulation' of his grievances: 'I despaired, while it was yet time to have made the just experiment; but my despair was criminal, was treason against the sovereignty of truth' (*CW* iii. 295 [1]/323).

Godwin's dramatization of the audience's response to Caleb's 'frank and fervent expostulation' shows, crucially, that this conclusion is no 'mere piece of equity and justice' (*CW* iii. 284 [1]/319), for it also involves an undisguised appeal to the emotions. Whereas in the manuscript version Caleb relates his story to the magistrate in 'varied, perspicuous and forcible' language (*CW* 328), in the published ending he speaks in a language of heightened feeling: 'I will confess every sentiment of my heart . . . I poured them out with uncontrolable impetuosity, for my heart was pierced, and I was compelled to give vent to its anguish' (*CW* iii. 285, 288 [1]/320, 323). Furthermore, the impact of his speech is concretely shown: 'Everyone that heard me was melted into tears' (*CW* iii. 297 [1]/323). This irresistible frankness finally moves Falkland to embrace Caleb and to make his own confession of guilt, a public version of his earlier private admission to Caleb.

In a deliberately melodramatic reversal, then, Godwin shows how sincerity of utterance may triumph where revolutionary intention fails, offering a notional model for social interaction based on the operation of frankness and sympathy. Significantly, Falkland's sympathetic response to Caleb's 'artless and manly story' (*CW* iii. 298 [1]/324) echoes the central confrontation of Pamela and Mr B., where, in response to Pamela's 'very moving tale' of her sufferings, her employer exclaims: 'O my dear girl, you have touched me sensibly with your mournful tale, and your reflections upon it.'[83] Here Godwin's use of sentimental conventions shows his early recognition of the value of feeling that would

[83] Richardson, *Pamela*, 276.

not be formulated until the second edition of *Political Justice*. Godwin later placed sincerity first in the catalogue of human virtues, describing it as the 'grand fascination' by which we 'lay hold of the hearts of our neighbours, conciliate their attention, and render virtue an irresistible object of imitation' (*PJ* i. 356). Similarly, at one level, Caleb's irresistible appeal to Falkland's 'confidence' seeks to 'render virtue an irresistible object of imitation'.

But this optimistic revelation of the power of sincerity should not blind us to its extreme tenuousness. Caleb gains this insight only at a frightening personal cost. While he exonerates Falkland as a victim of the system of nature, he sees himself as morally culpable: 'a cool, deliberate, unfeeling murderer' (*CW* iii. 296 [1]/323). In this view, Caleb is left 'more desperate than ever',[84] since his change of heart is based on his acceptance of Falkland's values. His reverence for Falkland's 'godlike ambition' appears as the latest of a series of delusions about benevolent father-figures, and it recalls his earlier account of his 'most complete veneration' for his master, which involves the surrender of his own understanding (*CW* iii. 303, ii. 48 [1]/325, 122). Although Caleb predicts that he will supplant Falkland's narrative with his own, in the end he can only present himself in the character that Falkland has constructed for him, and he tells Falkland's story instead of his own.

Thus Godwin presents a notional ideal of reformed social relations, but he also shows how the mind may be forced to breaking-point under the constraints of the existing system or the pressures of sudden change. The collapse of Caleb's enquiring spirit suggests the seemingly inexorable process by which hereditary assumptions are internalized. But by showing the inner workings of prescription and prejudice, Godwin seeks to alert the reader to his or her own habitual observance of artificial distinctions, the false opinion which maintains society as it is. In this way he lays bare the artificial construction of political compliance, which is 'not founded in the nature of things', as he insisted in his early note on Burke's *Reflections*: 'there is no such inherent difference between man and man as it thinks proper to suppose' (*PJ* iii. 184 n.).

To see Caleb's remorse as the whole of the story, then, is to deny the possibility of 'a better and more magnanimous remedy' (*CW* iii.

[84] Everest and Edwards, 'William Godwin's *Caleb Williams*', 135.

286 [1]/330) modelled on the sympathetic community created by his eloquence. Caleb's truth-telling holds out the possibility, albeit a precarious one, of emancipation from institutions and the distorted postures they provoke. The final effect of a conclusion in which nothing is concluded is to present the reader with a choice: do we collude with Caleb's version of events, or learn from his tale? By encouraging the reader to live up to his or her own rational potential, Godwin seeks to activate his belief in the gradual reform of social institutions through individual renovation: 'Every change of sentiment, from moral delusion to truth . . . is itself . . . an unquestionable acquisition' (*PJ* i. 277–8).

This searching reappraisal of earlier, more optimistic statements is the first and finest instance of Godwin's revaluation of his ideas through the medium of fiction, which is taken further in successive revisions to *Caleb Williams* and *Political Justice*.[85] Over the next two years, Godwin's additions to *Caleb Williams* show what he has learned from the use of sentimental conventions in his rewritten ending. Significantly, most of these changes do not appear until the third edition of 1797, when Godwin was revising his account of moral action for the second time in preparation for the third edition of *Political Justice*.

Following Caleb's rejection of 'fine-spun reasonings' (*CW* iii. 285 [1]/319), Godwin adds several passages which further question the rational self-sufficiency promoted in the first edition of *Political Justice*, and point to the development of a concept of virtue based on feeling and sympathy. For Caleb's later experiences show the inability of man to stand alone.[86] In the text of the first two editions, his review of his situation after arriving in London is confined to a brief meditation on rural solitude. But in 1797 Godwin attributes Caleb's loneliness to the debilitating absence of social affections:

> I was shut up a deserted, solitary wretch in the midst of my species. I dared not look for the consolations of friendship; but, instead of seeking to identify myself with the joys and sorrows of others, and exchanging the delicious gifts of confidence and sympathy, was compelled to centre my thoughts and my vigilance in myself. (*CW* iii. 141 [3]/255)

Godwin's heightened emphasis on the need for human warmth and responsiveness effectively reinforces the bond of 'magnetical

[85] See Butler, 'Godwin, Burke, and *Caleb Williams*', 253–5; Philp, *Godwin's Political Justice*, 120–67.

[86] Cf. *PJ* iii. 322.

sympathy' (*CW* ii. 19 [1]/112) between Caleb and Falkland. Cut off from each other, neither is able to function properly; but, at the same time, Falkland deprives Caleb of all other opportunities to fulfil his craving for human relationships. Isolated in this way, Caleb finds his self-esteem dangerously weakened. This cumulative experience of deprivation underlies his self-divided and emotionally overwrought response to Falkland in the final scene.

The subtle shift of focus in these additions confirms the interdependency of philosophical and imaginative concerns which makes *Caleb Williams* 'a striking . . . example, of the purpose of the writer being swallowed up by the interest of the work'.[87] Uniquely among the radical novelists of the period, Godwin seizes on the narrative potential of Burke's emotive defence of hierarchical society and turns it into a psychologically complex fable. Stripping away the external documentation of Fielding and the naturalistic social detail of Richardson, he exposes the power relations at the heart of late eighteenth-century society. In foregrounding the political undercurrents of Gothic romance, he projects on to this starkly representative opposition of master and servant the contradictory pressures of all human relationships. Through his use of the first-person narrative, he restores to the reader the responsibility for seeing things as they really are, and this openness to new possibilities of meaning empowers the progressive enrichment of the Godwinian narrative throughout the Romantic period.

Over the next fifteen years, Godwin's development and diversification as an imaginative writer shows him in pursuit of his own 'better remedy'. In his later experiments in 'fictitious history', he presents an increasingly internalized treatment of his political and philosophical concerns. But at the same time he extends the paradigm established in *Caleb Williams* to include a more comprehensive historical analysis.

[87] Mackintosh, review of Godwin, *Lives of Edward and John Philips*, 486–7.

3

Godwin's Historical Novels: Theory and Practice

The Enquiring Reader

Indeed we have always been of opinion, that Mr. Godwin's *forte* is polite literature. . . . As a novellist, as a critic in the belles lettres, probably as a dramatic writer, Mr. Godwin will excel; and if he regards his own reputation, and rightly estimates his own talents, he will quit the barren track of polemics, and cultivate an imagination which is certainly capable of great and vigorous exertions.[1]

Godwin might have been pleased with this largely favourable review of *The Enquirer*,[2] but he did not heed the advice to keep politics out of polite literature in his later writings. His gesture towards political reform through the agency of feeling in the published ending of *Caleb Williams*, however notional, should warn us against viewing his later emphasis on imaginative sympathy as a retreat from political issues, as some critics have done.[3] Even Kelly, who makes a strong case for the topicality of *Caleb Williams*, argues that Godwin's novels after the mid-1790s show 'an outlook characteristic of a depoliticized Romantic liberalism', thus assimilating Godwin's post-revolutionary career to a model of literary development associated with the poets Wordsworth, Coleridge, and Southey, in which the failure of revolutionary hopes leads to a shift to private and domestic concerns.[4] But, in defiance of this general trend, Godwin maintains a radical political optimism, as he pursues the major concerns of *Political Justice* in essays, in biography, and, above all, in fiction.

[1] Review of *The Enquirer*, *Critical Review*, 2nd ser. 20 (May 1797), 64.

[2] *The Enquirer* was written between 1 Aug. 1796 and 28 Jan. 1797, and published 27 Feb. 1797.

[3] See Introduction, n. 13.

[4] Kelly, *English Jacobin Novel*, 223; see Marilyn Butler, *Romantics, Rebels, and Reactionaries: English Literature and its Background, 1760–1830* (Oxford, 1981), 65–7; Kelvin Everest, *Coleridge's Secret Ministry: The Context of the Conversation Poems, 1795–1798* (Hassocks, 1979).

Godwin's tenacity of purpose forms a central aspect of his magnetic, almost mythical appeal for the next generation of Romantic writers, especially Percy Shelley.[5] Disillusion at the excesses of the French Revolution undoubtedly bred a vogue for literary introspection, as Shelley pointed out in the Preface to *The Revolt of Islam* (1818):

> many of the most ardent and tender-hearted of the worshippers of public good have been morally ruined by what a partial glimpse of the events they deplored appeared to show as the melancholy desolation of all their cherished hopes. Hence gloom and misanthropy have become the characteristics of the age in which we live. . . . This influence has tainted the literature of the age with the hopelessness of the minds from which it flows.[6]

Seeking to combat this sense of moral desolation, Shelley presented *The Revolt of Islam* as 'an experiment on the temper of the public mind, as to how far a thirst for a happier condition of moral and political society survives . . . the tempests which have shaken the age in which we live'. Such a reconstruction of hope is based on Godwin's gradualist theory of political progress. As Godwin wrote to Shelley in March 1812, seeking to dissuade him from direct political action on behalf of the Irish: 'He that would benefit mankind on a comprehensive scale, by changing the elements and principles of society, must learn the hard lesson, to put off self, and to contribute by a quiet but incessant activity, like a rill of water, to irrigate and fertilise the intellectual soil.'[7]

Implicit in the rewritten ending of *Caleb Williams*, this line of thought is formulated for the first time in *The Enquirer*. In the Preface to these *Reflections on Education, Manners and Literature*, Godwin announces a significant redirection of political energy. Speaking of himself in the third person, he presents himself as an exemplary 'enquirer' who has turned to intellectual cultivation after the failure of his extravagant hopes for rapid political transformation: 'With as ardent a passion for innovation as ever, he feels himself more patient and tranquil. He is desirous of assisting others, if possible, in perfecting the melioration of their temper' (*E*,

[5] See Shelley to Elizabeth Hitchener, 7 Jan. 1811 [for 1812], 16 Jan. 1812; *PBSL* i. 221, 231.

[6] Shelley, Preface to *The Revolt of Islam* (1818), *Poetical Works*, 33.

[7] Godwin to Shelley, 14 Mar. 1812, Kegan Paul, *William Godwin*, ii. 207.

p. x). This activity is based on the firm persuasion that 'the cause of political reform, and the cause of intellectual and literary refinement, are inseparably connected'.

Godwin's declared shift of interest may be instructively compared with that of Milton, his principal model of a revolutionary man of letters who remained undaunted by the apparent failure of his political hopes. Just as Godwin modelled his pre-revolutionary novel, *Imogen*, on Milton's early poetry, so too after the mid-1790s his heightened interest in 'literary refinement' brings to mind his praise for *Paradise Lost* as an example of literary achievement in a period of political defeat, 'under calamities that would have broken the heart of any ordinary man' (*LP* 129). In *Paradise Lost* the defeat of apocalyptic political hopes leads to an internalized scheme of values which highlights the morally redemptive possibilities of everyday life: 'by small | Accomplishing great things, by things deemed weak | Subverting worldly strong . . .' (*PL* xii. 566–8). A similar indirect political purpose is evident in Godwin's secular pastoral ministration, which begins with a collection of essays demonstrating 'the perpetual attention we owe to experience' (*E*, p. vi). In *Thoughts Occasioned by the Perusal of Dr Parr's Spital Sermon* (1801), where he reviews the reaction against *Political Justice* at the end of the decade, he explicitly rejects the temptation of passive resignation to 'things as they are' in favour of a sustained millennial optimism: 'Let us not, from the vain fastidiousness of misanthropy, be led to blaspheme against the cause of virtue. For myself I firmly believe that days of greater virtue and more ample justice will descend upon the earth' (*TP* 82). It is questionable how far he ever departs from this view in his subsequent writings.

Godwin's heightened interest in imagination and feeling after the mid-1790s owes more to his awareness of the internal level at which reform must operate than to political disillusion. His recognition of the value of the social affections gained further impetus from his relationship with Mary Wollstonecraft. They met for the first time in 1792, but it was only after they met again in April 1796 that they started to see each other regularly.[8] They were

[8] William Godwin, *Memoirs of the Author of A Vindication of the Rights of Woman* (1798), reprinted with Mary Wollstonecraft, *Letters Written During a Short Residence in Sweden, Norway, and Denmark* (1796), ed. Richard Holmes (Harmondsworth, 1987), 235–6, 256–73; Claire Tomalin, *The Life and Death of Mary Wollstonecraft* (1974; Harmondsworth, 1977), 243–81.

married in March 1797, but on 10 September Wollstonecraft died after giving birth to a daughter, Mary. During the period of their relationship, Godwin's reading of literature influenced by the tradition of sensibility prepared the way for his increased attention to the mental lives of individuals in his next two novels, *St Leon* (1799) and *Fleetwood* (1805). At the time of Wollstonecraft's pregnancy and death, he was reading Goethe's *Sorrows of Young Werther* (1774), Rousseau's *La Nouvelle Héloïse* (1761), and Mackenzie's *Julia de Roubigné* (1777). Saturated in Wollstonecraft's own writings, Godwin also established closer contacts than previously with other women novelists such as Inchbald, Mary Robinson, Mary Hays, and Eliza Fenwick, whose works offered further autobiographical models.[9] In 1796 Godwin began the first of a long series of autobiographical fragments written in the manner of Rousseau's *Confessions* (1781).[10]

After Wollstonecraft's death Godwin reread all her writings and immediately started work on his first major testimony to the domestic affections, *Memoirs of the Author of A Vindication of the Rights of Woman* (1798), which validated private attachment both in its form, a personal memoir of an individual 'formed for domestic affection', and in its presentation of a relationship based on equality.[11] It was in *St Leon*, however, that Godwin sought to publicize his changes to *Political Justice* in the light of Wollstonecraft's thought. He declared in the Preface:

> Not that I see cause to make any change respecting the principle of justice, or any thing else fundamental to the system there delivered, but that I apprehend domestic and private affections inseparable from the nature of man, and from what may be styled the culture of the heart, and am fully persuaded that they are not incompatible with a profound and active sense of justice in the mind of him that cherishes them. (*SL* i, p. x)

To some extent this statement offers a rejoinder to the flood of recent attacks on the excessive rationalism of *Political Justice*,[12] but

[9] Godwin's diary lists his reading and social contacts in this period, Ab. MSS, e. 202–3.

[10] Ab. MSS, b. 227, b. 226/1; cf. Godwin's unpublished note of 1805: 'I sat down with the intention of being nearly as explicit as Rousseau in the composition of his Confessions', Kegan Paul, *William Godwin*, i. 13; the first six books of *The Confessions* appeared in England in 1782, the second six in 1789.

[11] Godwin, *Memoirs of [Wollstonecraft]*, 237.

[12] See B. Sprague Allen, 'The Reaction against William Godwin', *Modern Philology*, 16 (1918), 57–75; Butler, *War of Ideas*, 88–123; Philp, *Godwin's Political Justice*, 220–4.

it should be noted that Godwin does not abandon his central contentious belief in the duty of private judgement: feeling is not seen in opposition to reason, but is brought in to support man's 'profound and active sense of justice'. In the novel itself, Godwin's portrayal of St Leon's wife Marguerite, modelled in part on Mary Wollstonecraft, reflects the same desire to yoke together the private affections and rational philosophy. From the outset, St Leon's 'proud and restless desire of distinction' (*SL* i. 72) in military action is set in opposition to domestic values. Whereas St Leon's obsession with fame is based on dissatisfaction with the self—'I did not suffice to myself' (*SL* i. 111)—the exemplary Marguerite nurtures in her children 'a mind, that should find resources within itself', and this concept of independence is allied with the social affections rather than external 'rank, and affluence, and indulgence' (*SL* i. 201, 200).

If Godwin's relationship with Wollstonecraft led to major changes in his thought after 1796, it does not account for his exploration of feeling in his revisions to *Caleb Williams*, begun a year before he met her again. That he recognized the inadequacy of the first edition of *Political Justice* on the private affections almost as soon as it was completed is implicit in the emotive tone at the end of the novel, where sympathy holds out the promise of unfettered communication. In this sense Godwin's subsequent writings unfold rather than depart from the principles of *Political Justice*, as his closest friends and contemporaries realized. Inchbald commented on his statement of his revised philosophy in the Preface to *St Leon*, 'Let them [the public] not suppose your principles changed, but that [they] never knew what those principles were'; while Henry Crabb Robinson paid tribute to *Political Justice* for precisely those qualities that hostile critics said it lacked: 'No book ever made me feel more generously. I never before felt so strongly . . . the duty of not living to one's self and that of having for one's sole object the welfare of the community.'[13] Nevertheless, Godwin himself repeatedly admitted the errors of the first edition of *Political Justice*. In an unpublished schedule of literary projects for 1798 he planned a book to be called 'First Principles of Morals', which would correct the mistaken emphasis in the first part of *Political Justice*: 'The part to which I allude is essentially defective, in the

[13] Inchbald to Godwin, n.d., Ab. MSS, b. 229/8; diary extract, 1795, *Henry Crabb Robinson on Books and their Writers*, ed. Edith J. Morley, 3 vols. (Oxford, 1938), i. 3.

circumstance of not yielding a proper attention to the empire of feeling. The voluntary actions of men are under the direction of their feelings.'[14] In a more specific account of changes between the first and second editions, he attributed his recognition of the emotional springs of action to a reading of Hume's *Treatise of Human Nature* in 1795.[15] But in fact his debt to Hume remains ambiguous and difficult to separate from his general assimilation of the ideas of the other British moralists, Shaftesbury, Butler, Smith, and Hutcheson, which led him to declare in 1797: 'Not only the passions of men, but their very judgments, are to a great degree the creatures of sympathy' (*E* 57). Godwin continues to reject Hume's notion of the operation of sympathy through an endless flow of passions and sentiments in which reason is virtually powerless.[16] Instead, crucially for his theory of fiction, he retains his primary commitment to private judgement. Thus he describes the child as an individual with active powers of moral discrimination, to whom we owe 'reverence': 'he has a claim upon his little sphere of empire and discretion; and he is entitled to his appropriate portion of independence' (*E* 88–9).

This primary commitment to private judgement, validated rather than superseded by feeling, underpins Godwin's comments on the workings of imaginative fiction in several essays written for *The Enquirer*. At a time when there was little formal theorizing on literature, apart from Prefaces and reviews, Godwin's originality in producing an intellectual role for the novel demands attention. Formulated for the first time in 1797, his notion of the renovative power of fiction sheds further light on his imaginative strategies in *Caleb Williams* as well as prefiguring his later novels. As noted earlier, in the first edition of *Political Justice* Godwin values works of imagination for their power to liberate the mind from the 'fetters of prescription and prejudice' through 'flight into the world unknown' (*PJ* iii. 270). In thus presenting the 'materials and rude sketches of intellectual improvement', fiction opens the way for the 'enquiring and philosophical reader' to combat his or her enthralment to 'things as they are'. Godwin's desire to disinter the reader's positive potential underlies the provisional ending to *Caleb Williams*. Characteristically he presents no more than the 'materials

14 Ab. MSS, b. 228/9.

15 Godwin's note of 1796–7, Ab. MSS, b. 228/9.

16 Cf. Philp, *Godwin's Political Justice*, 142–9.

and rude sketches' of improvement, just as he presents the contents of *The Enquirer* 'not as *dicta*, but as the materials of thinking' (*E*, p. viii), for this open-endedness is central to his concept of truth that is not externally imposed but arises from within.

The same desire to cultivate the reader's rational potential underlies 'Of Choice in Reading', an essay published in *The Enquirer*, where Godwin appropriates Milton's arguments in *Areopagitica: A Speech . . . for the Liberty of Unlicenc'd Printing* to make a case for the freedom of children to choose their own reading-matter. Just as, according to Milton, licensing argues a mistrust of the capacities of the English people,[17] so too authoritarian censorship of the child's reading retards his or her development as a rational being (*E* 144). By contrast, Godwin highlights the need for confidence in the child's inherent powers of discrimination, which will lead him or her beyond 'the prejudices of the nursery' perpetuated by explicit moralizing (*E* 139).[18] However, Godwin devotes the rest of his essay to the problems of free choice in reading, for he admits that it is impossible to predict how the reader will interpret a work of literature. This uncertainty hinges on the discrepancy between a work's explicit moral, or the meaning intended by the author, and its more elusive 'genuine tendency', or the 'actual effect it is calculated to produce upon the reader', which 'cannot be completely ascertained but by the experiment' (*E* 133, 136), and is thus open to historical interpretation. Godwin's discrimination between these terms supports his argument for a mode of instructive literature which avoids the imposition of a direct moral, and invites the reader to play an active role in determining meaning. As Holcroft put it in more direct terms: 'The most essential feature of every work is its moral tendency. The good writer teaches the child to become a man; the bad and the indifferent best understand the reverse art of making a man a child.'[19]

Godwin is especially concerned to rehabilitate existing works in which 'the true moral and fair inference . . . has often laid

[17] Milton, *Areopagitica: A Speech of Mr John Milton for the Liberty of Unlicenc'd Printing to the Parliament of England* [1644], *The Complete Prose Works of John Milton*, ed. Don M. Wolfe *et al.*, 8 vols. (New Haven, Conn.) 1953–82), ii. 536–7.

[18] Cf. Milton, *Prose*, ii. 513–14.

[19] [Holcroft], review of *The Castle of St Vallery*, *Monthly Review*, NS 9 (Nov. 1792), 337.

concealed for ages from [their] most diligent readers' (*E* 135). His conviction that authorial intention may be at odds with a work's 'genuine tendency' provides the rationale for his own appropriation of literary works in support of his philosophical concerns. While he acknowledges the power of imaginative literature to liberate the mind from prejudice, he also seeks to ensure that the nature of this liberation will conform to his own programme for improvement. To explain this more fully, Godwin turns to Milton again, pointing out that generations of readers have remembered *Paradise Lost* for its portrait of a tyrannical God, in contrast with the author's stated intention, ' "to justify the ways of God to men" ' (*E* 135). In *Political Justice* Godwin exploits the 'genuine tendency' of *Paradise Lost* by presenting Satan as 'a being of considerable virtue' oppressed by tyrannical government:

> It must be admitted that his energies centered too much in personal regards. But why did he rebel against his maker? It was, as he himself informs us, because he saw no sufficient reason, for that extreme inequality of rank and power, which the creator assumed. It was because prescription and precedent form no adequate ground for implicit faith . . .
>
> (*PJ* i. 323–4)

By contrast with Burke's identification of revolutionary action with satanic transgression, Godwin emphasizes Satan's assertion of rational independence against brute authority. As in other radical readings of *Paradise Lost* in the 1790s, notably Blake's *The Marriage of Heaven and Hell* (1790), he praises Satan's exemplary energy of character, divorced from its original theological setting.[20] This conviction that a present-day author may recognize truths unacknowledged or repressed by his or her predecessors is central to Godwin's rewriting of Miltonic themes in *Imogen* and *Caleb Williams*. In showing that literary meaning is open to historical interpretation, Godwin establishes a mode of enquiry to be developed not only in the later novels of his school, but also in the poetic revisions of myth by Percy Shelley and Byron.

Yet Godwin is not prepared to allow that a work of imagination is open to indiscriminate appropriation. In 'Of Choice in Reading' he sets out specific criteria for interpretation that will uncover

[20] See also Roger Sharrock, 'Godwin and Milton's Satan', *Notes and Queries*, 207 (1962), 463–5; cf. Shelley, 'On the Devil, and Devils' [?1820–1], *Works*, vii. 91–2.

distinctively Godwinian truths. He particularly admires those writers whose 'genuine tendency' works to unfold the capacities of the reader's spirit: 'The principal praise is certainly due to those authors, who have a talent to "create a soul under the ribs of death*;" . . . who furnish me with "food for contemplation even to madness*;" who raise my ambition, expand my faculties, invigorate my resolutions, and seem to double my existence' (*E* 139–40).[21] In this way great literature has the capacity to liberate the individual from the constraints of 'things as they are'. Of his own development, Godwin comments, 'I cannot tell what I should have been, if Shakespear or Milton had not written' (*E* 140), and he sees the progressive tendency inherent in these authors as contributing to the gradual improvement of whole societies:

> The poorest peasant in the remotest corner of England, is probably a different man from what he would have been but for these authors. Every man who is changed from what he was by the perusal of their works, communicates a portion of the inspiration all around him. It passes from man to man, till it influences the whole mass. (*E* 140)

In *Thoughts Occasioned by . . . Dr Parr* this link between literary and political improvement has a direct contemporary application, for Godwin invokes the language of Milton and Shakespeare as an instance of human potential for improvement which transcends the deterministic views of his opponents:

> Are vice and misery, as my antagonists so earnestly maintain . . . entailed on us for ever; or may we hope ultimately to throw off, or greatly diminish, the burthen? In other cases of an eminent nature, what the heart of man is able to conceive, the hand of man is strong enough to perform. There is no beauty of literary and poetical composition which we can so much as guess at, that excels what we find executed in the divinest passages of Milton or Shakespear. (*TP* 81)

In this way, as Godwin had written of the poet Mr Clare in *Caleb Williams*, literature affords 'a kind of specimen of what the human mind is capable of performing' (*CW* i. 59 [1]/24).

It is this heightened sense of human potential that Godwin sought to create in the reader through his own fictive blend of 'interest and passion' (*CW* i, p. vi [2]/1). Already he recognized as

[21] Godwin's asterisks refer to his own notes, which identify the first quotation as 'Milton', and the second as 'Rowe' [*Comus*, ll. 560–1; *The Fair Penitent*, v. i. 21].

he was to write in a 1798 addition to *Political Justice*, that reason alone cannot 'excite us to action' (*PJ* i, p. xxvi), and this provides the philosophical justification for his use of compelling imaginative techniques. Passion, in the sense of the ardour with which an object is pursued, he came to consider as inseparable from reason, since 'Virtue, sincerity, justice, and all those principles which are begotten and cherished in us by a due exercise of reason, will never be very strenuously espoused, till they are ardently loved' (*PJ* i. 81). In his novels Godwin seeks to create this passionate disposition in the reader as the first step towards the extension of civil liberty. In March 1793, while writing *Caleb Williams*, he recorded a debate with George Dyson on the instructive potential of narrative: 'Which is the most powerful, the moral tendency fairly deducible from an interesting story, or its tendency to rouse?'[22] This 'rousing' quality removes the film of familiarity from 'things as they are' and has the same capacity to 'change' the reader that Godwin found in Milton and Shakespeare. As Godwin wrote in his 1832 account of the composition of *Caleb Williams*: 'no one, after he has read it, shall ever be exactly the same man that he was before' (*CW* 338).

History and Romance

In the unpublished essay, 'Of History & Romance' [1797], written 'while *The Enquirer* was in the press',[23] Godwin extends his claims for the educative power of fiction into the realm of history, arguing that imaginative study of the past liberates the mind from prescription and prejudice and stimulates ethical enquiry. In formulating the politicized concept of character already explored in *Caleb Williams*, Godwin also sets out the theoretical assumptions underlying his use of the first-person narrative in his major historical novels, *St Leon* and *Mandeville* (1817).

In keeping with his preoccupation with the internal structure of political relationships, Godwin declares that only imaginative study of the lives of historical individuals can educate the reader by offering models for improvement. Thus he recommends the works of classical biographers and historians such as Plutarch and Livy rather than the historians of his own day, Hume, Voltaire, and

[22] Ab. MSS, e. 273.
[23] 'Of History & Romance' [1797], Ab. MSS, b. 226/15.

Robertson, who focus on large-scale historical movements. Yet Godwin's interest in history as a vehicle to train the capacities of the imagination equally shows his use of Hume's concept of sympathy in connection with his own moral aims. As Godwin wrote in a later essay, 'Of Religion', imagination offers 'the basis of a sound morality. It is by dint of feeling, & of putting ourselves in fancy into the place of other men, that we can learn how we ought to treat them, & be moved to treat them as we ought.'[24] In the realm of history, study of individual 'passions & peculiarities' alone permits this ethical enquiry. Godwin claims that 'contemplation of illustrious men' will foster the potential for improvement latent within all men: 'While we admire the poet & the hero . . . we insensibly imbibe the same spirit, and burn with kindred fires.'[25] It is no accident that he selects the ancients, 'men of a free & undaunted spirit', as uniquely worthy of detailed study, since they are free of the blighting effects of modern government and institutions studied in *Caleb Williams*. Indeed, with the exception of the Commonwealth period, Godwin depicts the whole of English history in terms of the tyranny of a corrupt system over individual rights and liberties.

Godwin's speculations on the use of history as a vehicle for moral improvement lead him to propound a new definition of history writing which bears directly on his later fiction. Rejecting factual accounts of dates, places, and events in modern works of history, Godwin emphasizes the different kind of truth offered by an imaginative rendering of the past, as suggested by Rousseau's definition of ancient history as 'a tissue of such fables as have a moral perfectly adapted to the human heart. . . . My first enquiry is, Can I derive instruction from it? Is it a genuine praxis upon the nature of man? Is it pregnant with the most generous motives & the most fascinating examples?' To convey this insight into the workings of the human mind, the 'mere skeleton' of historical facts must be fleshed out by 'a number of happy, ingenious & instructive inventions', as in Prévost's historical novels, cast in the form of biographical narrative.[26] Godwin concludes:

[24] 'Of Religion' [1818], Ab. MSS, b. 227/1.

[25] 'Of History & Romance.'

[26] Godwin read Prévost's *The Life and Entertaining Adventures of Mr Cleveland, Natural Son of Oliver Cromwell, Written by Himself* (1732–9, trans. 1734–5) and *Margaret of Anjou* (1740, trans. 1755), in Sept. and Oct. 1793, Ab. MSS, e. 201.

> The writer of romance then is to be considered as the writer of real history; while he who was formerly called the historian, must be contented to step down into the place of his rival, with this disadvantage, that he is a romance writer, without the ardour, the enthusiasm, & the sublime licence of imagination, that belong to that species of composition.[27]

It is this 'sublime licence of imagination' that makes the delineation of human character the only true form of history, and the romance writer the only true historian.

Godwin's experiments in philosophical biography equally support his contention that readers would be 'better employed in this studying one man, than in perusing the abridgement of Universal History in sixty volumes'. During his period of friendship with Coleridge, the last of his 'four principal oral instructors' who visited him for the first time in November 1799, he planned biographies on Shakespeare and Bolingbroke and began some biographical notes on Coleridge himself, but his major completed project was the *Life of Chaucer* (1803).[28]

In this massive work Godwin's depiction of his subject as a product of his age marks a new stage in his exploration of the links between public concerns and individual states of mind, as well as between past and present. Coleridge recognized the educative potential of biography in this respect when he wrote to Godwin in 1811 with typically ambitious plans for a school-book modelled on Plutarch's *Parallel Lives*, which would place

> ancient and modern together . . . or what might perhaps be at once more interesting & more instructive, a series of Lives from Moses to Buonaparte of all those great Men, who in states or in the mind of man had produced great revolutions, the effects of which still remain, & are . . . causes of the present state of the World.[29]

In the *Life of Chaucer* Godwin sets out to produce a complete analysis of Chaucer's development in terms of the external causes acting upon him. He combines a sensitive account of the poet's private life, a scholarly commentary on his works,[30] and a

27 'Of History & Romance.'

28 Godwin identified his other three principal oral instructors as Joseph Fawcett, Thomas Holcroft, and George Dyson, Ab. MSS, c. 605; Ab. MSS, b. 226/11, c. 604/3; for Coleridge's reaction to the proposed life of Bolingbroke, see *STCL* i. 652.

29 Coleridge to Godwin, 26 Mar. 1811, *STCL* iii. 314.

30 Cf. Coleridge's tribute to Godwin as 'the Critic who in the life of Chaucer has given us if not principles of *Aesthetic*, or Taste, yet more & better Data for Principles than had hitherto existed in our Language', ibid.

panoramic survey of fourteenth-century arts, religion, and politics. As he explains in the Preface: 'We must observe what Chaucer felt and saw, how he was educated, what species of learning he pursued, and what were the objects, the events and the persons, successively presented to his view, before we can strictly and philosophically understand his biography' (*LC* i, p. viii). In creating a 'new species' of biographical study which will 'carry the workings of fancy and the spirit of philosophy into the investigation of ages past', he claims to rescue the 'science' of biography from 'men of cold tempers and sterile imaginations' who have failed to recognize its potential as an agency of improvement (*LC* i, pp. x–xi).

In the event Godwin's scrutiny of 'the causes which made [Chaucer] what he was' (*LC* i, p. viii) sheds as much light on his own historical circumstances as on Chaucer's. Godwin's comments on the decline of feudalism bear directly on his own internalized rendering of public concerns in the era of the French Revolution, for he depicts Chaucer's poetic understanding of the world as the product of a particular moment in the development of political society which led to the Peasants' Revolt of 1381: 'The causes which produced the excesses of Wat Tyler and his associates were the causes to which Chaucer owed his being as a poet' (*LC* ii. 317). This period of auspicious public events heralds an expansion of intellectual powers which parallels the increased self-consciousness said to be brought about by the French Revolution:[31]

> When did England first produce a man . . . worthy to be called a poet? When the enormous and cumbersome mass of the feudal system was more than half crumbled away, when the popular part of our constitution began to raise its head, and man in a collective sense learned to look inward upon himself. (*LC* ii. 317)

In this passage the individual's growing capacity for self-analysis, which is linked with freedom from political and social inequality, leads to the development of a specialized poetic insight: the liberating public context of Chaucer's time enables him to perceive the world around him 'with senses such as never belonged to the man . . . who was bred a slave' (*LC* ii. 317).[32] It is this exemplary human sympathy that makes him a type of the true poet 'who is the

[31] Cf. Wollstonecraft, *Short Residence*, 103.

[32] But cf. Godwin's later statement: 'the master geniuses, a Homer, a Shakespear and a Milton, seem to belong to no age, but to be the property of the world', *LC* i. 224.

legislator of mankind and the moral instructor of the world' (*LC* i. 370).[33]

However, the 'illustrious men' of another period have the most lasting importance in Godwin's historical writings, as he returns throughout his career to the productive interaction between character and external circumstances in the period of the English Commonwealth, 'the only portion of our history interesting to the heart of man'.[34] By contrast with the present-day constraints of 'things as they are', this period provided Godwin with an inspiring ideal of man's unshackled potential, and he viewed all subsequent historical developments in terms of loss and decline: 'it is probable that the nation has never recovered that tone of independence, strong thinking, and generosity, which the Restoration so powerfully operated to destroy' (*LP* 267).

Typically, Godwin invokes the age in terms of its personalities. In the Preface to the *Lives of Edward and John Philips, Nephews and Pupils of Milton* (1815), his second major biography, he explains that his subject is chosen for the light it sheds on Milton, who in his dual role of poet and patriot formed 'the most advantageous specimen that can be produced of the English nation' (*LP*, p. v). But Milton is only one hero in a period dominated by 'examples of what Englishmen were, and hostages and assurances, in appearance, of what they would be' (*LP* 266). Similarly, in *Fleetwood* the narrator mourns the passing of the great age of civil and intellectual liberty in terms of its memorable characters, 'Pym and Hampden, and Falkland and Selden, and Cromwel and Vane' (*Fl* i. 143), by contrast with the degeneration of English public spirit in the age of George II: 'I perceived that we were grown a commercial and arithmetical nation; and that, as we extended the superficies of our empire, we lost its moral sinews and its strength' (*Fl* ii. 133). The title of *Fleetwood*, along with its early working title, 'Lambert', further highlights Godwin's preoccupation with the English Civil War and its aftermath, for both names allude to prominent generals under Cromwell, who unsuccessfully opposed the Stuart Restoration.[35] In his four-volume *History of the Commonwealth* (1824–8)

[33] Cf. Shelley: 'Poets are the unacknowledged legislators of the world', *A Defence of Poetry* [1821], *Works*, vii. 140.

[34] 'Of History & Romance.'

[35] John Lambert (1619–83) and Charles Fleetwood (d. 1692) were both barred from office for life at the Restoration, and Lambert was imprisoned from 1664 until his death; on possible links between *Fleetwood* and Prévost's *Life of Cleveland*, see Kelly, *English Jacobin Novel*, 254.

Godwin depicts the interregnum in even more glowing terms. Assuming Milton's prophetic tone, he describes the men of the parliamentary armies in terms of the independence of spirit and conscious rectitude advocated in *Political Justice*: 'each individual in the most honourable sense a priest and a prophet for himself' (*HC* i. 355).[36] Godwin's sense of the close interaction between character and external circumstance is evident in the prominence he gives to the lives of individuals in the course of his narrative. In the last volume, a biographical study of Cromwell—'one of the greatest geniuses of the time in which he lived' (*HC* ii. 200)—supersedes analysis of events, and this confirms the inseparability of what Coleridge termed 'great revolutions . . . in states or in the mind of man'.[37]

Godwin's fascination with Cromwell shows the peculiarly intense nature of his biographical commitment in his later writings. This is partly due to his interest in illustrious men whose historical situation has affinities with his own. Of the *Life of Chaucer*, Scott drily remarked: 'Mr Godwin's dukes and knights hold . . . the language, we had almost said the cant, of his soi disant philosophy.'[38] While this has some truth it does not do justice to Godwin's larger aims of intellectual cultivation through historical research, nor to his desire to reconstitute the minds of illustrious historical figures: 'to make them pass in review before me, to question their spirits and record their answers' (*LC* i, p. x). In this spirit of active enquiry, he confronts his literary and historical subjects as a series of possible selves with whom he wishes to become 'personally acquainted' (*LC* ii. 572). Thus 'the reader of soul proceeds, from esteem of the work, to friendship, sympathy and correspondence with the author' (*LC* ii. 581), a comment which seems to support Jean de Palacio's observation: 'Chez Godwin, l'engagement de l'écrivain est total. Il est avec son sujet dans un rapport quasi intime, dont le JE exprime encore toute intensité.'[39] Godwin's use of the chameleon image in his account of his reading of great authors—'when I read Milton, I become Milton' (*E* 33)—further

[36] Cf. Milton's vision of the English people as 'a Nation of Prophets, of Sages, and of Worthies', *Prose*, ii. 554.

[37] See above, n. 29.

[38] Scott, 'Godwin's *Life of Chaucer*', *Edinburgh Review*, 3 (1804), 473–52, reprinted in *The Miscellaneous Prose Works of Sir Walter Scott, Bart*, ed. J. G. Lockhart, 28 vols. (Edinburgh, 1834–6), xvii. 72.

[39] Jean de Palacio, 'Godwin et la tentation de l'autobiographie (William Godwin et J. J. Rousseau)', *Études Anglaises*, 27 (1974), 153.

suggests the collapse of sympathy into self-expression that he would have found in Rousseau's writings.[40] But, in Godwin's case, this mode of self-knowledge is harnessed to his theory of human potential for improvement through rational enquiry, discussion, and reading.

Godwin's capacity for thoughtful entry into the feelings of another person is central to his development of the first-person narrative in his later novels. His choice of an autobiographical mode reflects his consistent linking of introspective analysis and political improvement, which blurs any distinction between private and public concerns. In *Mandeville* Godwin openly acknowledged the autobiographical potential of fiction: 'every historian puts much of his own character into his work; and a skilful anatomist of the soul, before he reaches the perusal of the last page, will have formed a very tolerable notion of the dispositions of the writer' (*M* ii. 282). Yet he also claimed that his first-person narrative had a wider instructive aim, defending his lengthy account of Mandeville's early years as an innovative 'task of general utility', which put a previously unrecorded 'stage in the history of man . . . into a legible and a permanent form' (*M* i. 163). In his review of *Mandeville* for the *Examiner*, Percy Shelley corroborated Godwin's radical intent when he described his explorations of character and motive as 'those useful occasions for pleading in favour of universal kindness and toleration'.[41] It was this tendentious inwardness that appealed to a reviewer of his later novel, *Cloudesley* (1830): 'The writer dives into the recesses of our minds, and makes the analysis of our inmost thoughts the *materiel* for melioration of the human species.'[42]

The full significance of Godwin's development of an internalized mode of historical fiction is best illustrated by comparison with Scott's more colourful narrative art. Scott's *Waverley; or, 'Tis Sixty Years Since* (1805–14) has been almost unanimously recognized as 'the first really historical novel', following Lukács's influential claim: 'What is lacking from the so-called historical novel before Sir

[40] Cf. Rousseau's comment on his reading of Plutarch's *Parallel Lives*: 'I became indeed that character whose life I was reading'; *The Confessions* (1781), trans. J. M. Cohen (Harmondsworth, 1953), 21.

[41] Shelley, 'On Godwin's *Mandeville*', *Examiner* (28 Dec. 1817), 826–7; *Works*, vi. 221.

[42] Review of *Cloudesley. A Tale*, *New Monthly Magazine*, 28 (1830), 368.

Walter Scott is precisely the specifically historical, that is, derivation of the individuality of characters from the historical peculiarity of their age.'[43] Yet this notion is already central to Godwin's use of symbolic Gothic themes to express the blighting effects of political despotism in *Caleb Williams* and *St Leon*, and it is explicitly formulated in his theory of historical fiction, where he describes individual character as moulded by historical circumstances. Godwin's fictional method, however, seems to offer a radical divergence from Scott's more naturalistic mode. In his best-known works Scott specializes in the externalized treatment of character in relation to history, and thus tends towards what Lukács calls 'typical' characters.[44] By contrast, although Godwin also recommends exemplary portraits of 'illustrious men',[45] his subjective narrative technique allows him to present historical pressures on the individual with an unparalleled intensity. For Hazlitt, Godwin's 'intense and patient study of the human heart' completely outshone Scott's documentary art: 'It is the beauty and the charm of Mr. Godwin's descriptions that the reader identifies himself with the author; and the secret of this is, that the author has identified himself with his personages.' Unlike Scott, he is not 'an indifferent, callous spectator of the scenes which he himself portrays, but without seeming to feel them'.[46]

Though he was not alone in preferring Godwin to Scott, Hazlitt's account of Scott's apparent limitations bears the imprint of his polemical hostility towards a writer who 'props the actual throne by the shadow of rebellion'.[47] The very contemporariness that provoked Hazlitt suggests that in one respect at least Scott's mode of historical fiction has more in common with Godwin's than is at first apparent. Despite Scott's insistent claims for the preservation of the manners of a bygone age, Coleridge clearly found in the Waverley novels a lesson for all ages:

[43] Georg Lukács, *The Historical Novel* (1937), trans. from the German by Hannah and Stanley Mitchell (1962; *Harmondsworth*, 1981), 15; cf. Avrom Fleishman, *The English Historical Novel: Walter Scott to Virginia Woolf* (Baltimore, 1971), David Brown, *Sir Walter Scott and the Historical Imagination* (London, 1979); for a critical view of Lukács, see Harry E. Shaw, *The Forms of Historical Fiction: Sir Walter Scott and his Successors* (Ithaca, NY, 1983).

[44] Lukács, *Historical Novel*, 34–6.

[45] 'Of History & Romance.'

[46] Hazlitt, 'On the English Novelists', 'William Godwin', *Works*, vi. 30, xi. 24–5.

[47] Hazlitt, 'Sir Walter Scott', *Spirit of the Age*, *Works*, xi. 65.

the essential wisdom & happiness of the Subject consists in this: that the contest between the Loyalists & their opponents can never be *obsolete*, for it is the contest between the two great moving Principles of social Humanity—religious adherence to the Past and the Ancient, the Desire & the admiration of Permanence, on the one hand; and Passion for increase of Knowlege, for Truth as the offspring of Reason, in short, the mighty Instincts of *Progression* and *Free-agency*, on the other.[48]

To some extent this assessment reflects Coleridge's concept of a mysteriously evolving, organic society modelled on Burke's *Reflections*, anticipating his polarization of the forces of permanence and progression in *On the Constitution of the Church and State* (1830).[49] But it also illuminates Scott's use of the past to enact contemporary concerns. Though much of his fiction proclaims a desire to present the past as past and hence irrecoverable, Scott was undoubtedly intrigued by the potential which historical fiction offered for comment on the present, as his observation to Southey in a letter of September 1824 suggests: 'By the way, did you ever observe how easy it would be for a good historian to run a par[a]lell betwixt the Great Rebellion and the French Revolution, just substituting the spirit of fanaticism for that of soi disant philosophy?'[50] While this comment may bear directly on *Redgauntlet* (1824), Scott's third and final study of Jacobite rebellion, it is also hard to avoid associating it with *Old Mortality* (1816), the novel closest in time and subject-matter to *Mandeville*.[51] Here Scott's depiction of the fanatical Covenanters invokes the spectre most feared by a generation saturated in the imagery of Burke's *Reflections*, that of disorganized but temporarily successful lower-class rebellion.[52] Nowhere is Scott's affinity with Godwin's later theme of the indifference of historical processes to individuals more evident than in *Old Mortality*, where the hero is swiftly drawn into events beyond his control, and his life is threatened first by one side, then by the other.

[48] Coleridge to Thomas Allsop, 8 Apr. 1820, *STCL* v. 35.

[49] See Coleridge, *On the Constitution of the Church and State* (1830), ed. John Colmer (Princeton, NJ, 1977), 24–5.

[50] Scott to Robert Southey, 26 Sept. 1824, *The Letters of Sir Walter Scott*, Centenary Edition, ed. H. J. C. Grierson *et al.*, 12 vols. (London, 1932–7), viii. 376.

[51] Godwin read *Tales of My Landlord: The Black Dwarf/Old Mortality* (1816), while revising *Mandeville* for publication, Ab. MSS, e. 214–15; see below, n. 76.

[52] On Scott's treatment of contemporary issues, see Peter D. Garside, '*Old Mortality*'s Silent Minority', *Scottish Literary Journal*, 7 (1980), 127–44.

Beginning with *St Leon* in 1799, Godwin's historical novels enact their contemporary concerns in a more ostentatious and uncompromising manner than Scott's. Though, like Scott, Godwin is concerned to relate individuals to historical events, he diverges from Scott's presentation of an ideal of coherent social evolution. Through his subjective narrative mode, Godwin presents a view of the society, and of the individual, as irredeemably fractured. Typically his protagonists experience breaking free from 'the Past and the Ancient' as a nightmare of guilt and persecution, but they find even less security in the opposing 'mighty instincts of *Progression* and *Free-agency*'.[53]

St Leon: A Tale of the Sixteenth Century

Although for most modern critics *St Leon* fails to live up to the expectations aroused by *Caleb Williams*, earlier readers did not register any falling-off in Godwin's inventive power in his second major novel, which appeared in December 1799.[54] Hazlitt classed *Caleb Williams* and *St Leon* together as 'two of the most splendid and impressive works of the imagination that have appeared in our times', while Gilfillan placed *St Leon* as second only to Scott's *Ivanhoe* (1819) as an 'ideal, sustained and poetical romance'.[55] It is certainly true that the novel contains a survey of different value-systems in the manner of Scott, but Godwin's distinctive mode of historical fiction is best understood as an extension of the narrative model developed in *Caleb Williams*. Godwin exploits the increased range of historical narrative for a figurative rendering of contemporary concerns, expanding his earlier blend of confessional narrative and symbolic Gothic themes to include a sweeping survey of European history that bears directly on the situation of beleaguered radicals in the mid-1790s. The way he uses the first-person narrative, however, suggests his increased scepticism about the unfettered exercise of private judgement after *Caleb Williams*. St

[53] See above, n. 48.

[54] Godwin wrote *St Leon* between 31 Dec. 1797 and 23 Nov. 1799; it first appears in his diary under the titles, 'The Adept', 'Opus Magnum', and 'Natural Magic', then, in July 1798, 'St Leon', Ab. MSS, e. 203; cf. Godwin's list of 'Works projected in or before the year 1795', dated Jan. 1796, Ab. MSS, b. 229/9.

[55] Hazlitt, 'William Godwin', *Works*, xi. 24; Gilfillan, 'William Godwin', 33.

Leon's systematic unreliability makes for an ambivalent, bipartisan account of revolutionary change which looks ahead to the more profoundly sceptical narratives of Charles Brockden Brown and Mary Shelley.

The scope of historical fiction for an encoded treatment of topical concerns is evident from the start. Kelly's observation that 'the practice of using history of the past to comment on the politics of the present was a well-established one in an age when governments exercised strict control over opposition', is amply supported by Godwin's use of eighteenth-century studies of sixteenth-century Europe, mainly Robertson's *History of . . . Charles V* and Robert Watson's *History of . . . Philip II*.[56] His focus on a disorientated individual in an era of political and religious turmoil brings to mind the current break-up of European society in the wars of the French Republic, notably Napoleon's Italian campaigns of 1796 and 1797. After fighting for his native France in the wars of Francis I and Charles V, St Leon's travels take him through the main centres of European religious controversy: republican Switzerland and the city-states of Germany, associated with the Protestant Reformation; and Roman Catholic Italy and Spain, dominated by the Spanish Inquisition. In keeping with the political debate of the 1790s, this period of upheaval is seen in polarized terms: institutional authority, symbolized by the Inquisition, is set against the demand of the 'heretical followers of Luther and Calvin' that 'every man should be defended in the exercise of his private judgment' (*SL* iii. 185). Godwin's depiction of European history in terms of unremitting despotism reflects his view that systematized inequality is pervasive in modern political society, and is not simply a feature of the French revolutionary period.

To further the critique of institutions begun in *Caleb Williams*, he draws on the exotic, historically distanced representation of religious persecution in Gothic and German novels—Lewis's *The Monk* (1796), Radcliffe's *The Italian* (1797), and Schiller's *The Ghost-Seer* (1789).[57] Thus St Leon is repeatedly brought before unjust tribunals and inquisitorial father-figures, and his sense of

[56] Kelly, *English Jacobin Novel*, 221; Godwin read William Robertson, *The History of the Reign of the Emperor Charles V* (1769), in July 1798, and Robert Watson, *The History of the Reign of Philip II* (1777), in July 1799, Ab. MSS, e. 204.

[57] Godwin read *The Ghost-Seer* (trans. 1795), *The Monk*, and *The Italian*, in May, Sept., and Dec. 1796, Ab. MSS, e. 203.

victimization gives rise to a cyclical view of history with obvious topical relevance:

> human affairs, like the waves of the ocean, are merely in a state of ebb and flow: "there is nothing new under the sun:" two centuries perhaps after Philip the Second shall be gathered to his ancestors . . . men shall learn over again to persecute each other for conscience sake; other anabaptists or levellers shall furnish pretexts for new persecutions; other inquisitors shall arise in the most enlightened tracts of Europe . . . (*SL* iii. 246–7)

The immediate relevance of this emphasis on political and religious tyranny was not lost on the novel's first readers: the reviewer in the *British Critic* went so far as to list examples of Godwin's 'open and offensive profaneness', drawing special attention to his description of orthodox Christianity as the invention of 'designing priests'.[58]

More sophisticated is Godwin's internalized treatment of historical issues through the character of his aristocratic hero, who declares that his country's 'national manners and temper were twined with the fibres of [his] constitution' (*SL* ii. 118). At the start of the novel St Leon presents himself as the product of an old chivalric order which is giving way before a modern tide of 'craft, dissimulation, corruption, and commerce' (*SL* i. 67). Already he is a bystander on history: the colourful opening sequence depicts the meeting between Francis I and Henry VIII in 1520 at the Field of the Cloth of Gold, where the youthful St Leon is a dazzled spectator. This theatrical display seems like the last fling of a decadent feudal order, and St Leon's fascination with military glory seems to support Holcroft's complaint that Godwin was merely repeating his earlier study of Burkean chivalry: 'your Count de St Leon is but the counterpart of your Ferdinando Count Falkland'.[59] But in the later novel Godwin's depiction of chivalrous fellowship offers a paradigm of revolutionary experience: 'the heart of man expanded itself with generosity and confidence. It burst the fetters of ages; and . . . seemed to revel in its new-found liberty' (*SL* i. 15). St Leon's misfortunes begin when he shares in the defeat of the French at the battle of Pavia, which relegates the apocalyptic hopes of the French nobility to a future epoch: 'The illustrious career which they had in fancy already traversed, was now postponed to a distant period' (*SL* i. 70). After this disappointment, St Leon's aristocratic

58 Review of *St Leon, British Critic*, 15 (Jan. 1800), 52.

59 Holcroft to Godwin, 9 Sept. 1800, Ab. MSS, b. 229/9.

values disintegrate under the pressures of a commercial society, reflecting the moral degeneration of humanity in the post-revolutionary period. His 'suppressed ambition' (*SL* i. 70) finds an outlet in gaming, recalling Burke's criticism of the legislators of the new French constitution as 'the very first who have founded a commonwealth upon gaming' (*R* 310). But Godwin's emphasis on St Leon's retreat from domestic obligations equally suggests Wollstonecraft's analysis of the socially destructive effects of financial speculation: 'A man ceases to love humanity, and then individuals, as he advances in the chase after wealth; as one clashes with his interest, the other with his pleasures . . . all the endearing charities of citizen, husband, father, brother, become empty names.'[60] Similarly, St Leon's obsessive craving for wealth leads him to squander his entire fortune and leave his family penniless. The deterioration of his high-minded ideals into a petty desire for show reflects the problem of maintaining moral integrity in a society which offers no scope for the fulfilment of ideals.

To convey the unprecedented nature of St Leon's historical dilemma, Godwin turns to the supernatural themes of Gothic fiction. St Leon's wealth is restored by chance when a mysterious stranger arrives at his house bearing the secrets of the philosopher's stone and the elixir of life, which promise a revolutionary transformation of his fortunes. At this point it seems that St Leon has got caught up in a different historical plot, for the alchemical theme links him with the figure of the revolutionary extremist in conservative propaganda. The notion that the French Revolution was the result of a vast secret society called the Illuminati had been popularized in two works of the mid-1790s, the Abbé Barruel's *Memoirs, Illustrating the History of Jacobinism* (1797–8) and John Robison's *Proofs of a Conspiracy* (1797).[61] According to these works, which also provided a potent source of imagery for Brown

[60] Wollstonecraft, *Short Residence*, 193; cf. Michel Foucault, *Madness and Civilisation: A History of Insanity in the Age of Reason* (1961), trans. from the French by Richard Howard (London, 1967), 212–14.

[61] L'Abbé Augustin Barruel, *Memoirs, Illustrating the History of Jacobinism* (1797), trans. Robert Clifford, 4 vols. (London, 1797–8); John Robison, *Proofs of a Conspiracy against all the Governments of Europe, Carried on in the Secret Meetings of Free Masons, Illuminati and Reading Societies* (Edinburgh, 1797); read by Godwin in July, Nov., and Dec. 1798, and Jan. 1799, Ab. MSS, e. 204; my account is indebted to J. M. Roberts, *The Mythology of the Secret Societies* (London, 1972), 118–202.

and Mary Shelley, a select band of intellectuals called the Illuminati aimed at the destruction of all family ties in the name of universal philanthropy. Similarly, St Leon's desire to benefit the species through his scientific powers leaves a trail of human devastation. The deaths of his wife and children lead to a guilt-stricken alienation from his species which prefigures Frankenstein's dilemma: 'I felt as truly haunted with the ghosts of those I had murdered, as Nero or Caligula might have been. . . . I possessed the gift of eternal life; but I looked on myself as a monster that did not deserve to exist' (*SL* iv. 27).

In this perspective St Leon's isolation registers the catastrophic effects of trying to break free from the past. When he aspires to the condition of eternal youth, he imagines that he is freeing himself from disabling personal ties and historical pressures. Thus he resembles the possessor of the philosopher's stone in *Hermippus Redivivus* (1744), the German tale cited in the Preface, who has 'no Sort of Tie to the World, he sees all Things die and revive without Concern'.[62] It may have been this quality of speculative detachment that later prompted Hazlitt to compare 'the character and feelings of the hermetic philosopher St. Leon' with 'those of a speculative philosophical Recluse', since St Leon's freedom from compulsive involvements suggestively prefigures the outlook of the Wanderer in *The Excursion* (1814), published as a portion of Wordsworth's planned long philosophical poem, *The Recluse*:

> unclouded by the cares
> Of ordinary life: unvexed, unwarped
> By partial bondage.[63]

The price of St Leon's release from social obligations, however, is total enthralment to the stranger's history. Like the Wandering Jew of Gothic convention: 'I found that I was only acting over again what he had experienced before me' (*SL* iii. 248).

This account may imply that Godwin is primarily concerned with

[62] Johann Heinrich Cohausen, *Hermippus Redivivus; or, The Sage's Triumph over Old Age and the Grave. Wherein, a Method is laid down for Prolonging the Life and Vigour of Man*, trans. Dr John Campbell (London, 1744), 134–5; read by Godwin in May 1795 and July 1798, Ab. MSS, e. 202, 204.

[63] Hazlitt, 'On the English Novelists', *Works*, vi. 132; Wordsworth, *The Excursion, Being a Portion of The Recluse, a Poem* (1814), i. 356–8; *The Poetical Works of William Wordsworth*, ed. Ernest de Selincourt and Helen Darbishire, 5 vols. (Oxford, 1942–9).

a Romantic drama of 'alienated selfhood' which involves a retreat from public issues.[64] But it should be remembered that the stranger's history is one of institutional persecution, repeated in St Leon's experiences of ideological oppression. After his imprisonment by the Inquisition, St Leon is literally reborn through his use of the elixir of life, but he throws off the old order only to meet a new incarnation of repressive power in Turkish domination of Hungary.[65] In keeping with his increased political gradualism in the late 1790s, Godwin offers a cautionary tale of the errors 'so common to projectors, of looking only to ultimate objects and great resting-places, and neglecting to consider the steps between' (*SL* ii. 123). Above all, St Leon's benevolent plans are defeated by entrenched human prejudices. The incident when his house is burnt to the ground by a superstitious Italian mob recalls the sacking of Joseph Priestley's house in the Birmingham riots of 1791,[66] and introduces the possibility of 'a principle in the human mind . . . eternally at war with improvement and science' (*SL* iii. 116).

The problem of maintaining radical ideals without discredit is confronted most directly through the novel's confessional form. St Leon's systematic withholding of information foregrounds issues of unreliability in a more problematic manner than Caleb's narrative, reflecting Godwin's reduced claims for private judgement after 1797. In *The Enquirer* he declares, 'Alas! impartiality is a virtue hung too high, to be almost ever within the reach of man!' (*E* 305–6), and in the third edition of *Political Justice*, he cautions against presumption in our understanding of the world and of each other.[67] St Leon can only dispel suspicions about his sudden prosperity by telling the tale of the philosopher's stone, but he has been given this source of wealth on condition that he keep it secret. The legacy of the stranger thus involves layers of dissimulation: 'I am bound, as far as possible, not only to hide my secrets, but to conceal that I have any to hide' (*SL* ii. 103). St Leon's refusal to divulge his secret shatters his idyllic relationship with Marguerite, previously based on confidence and sincerity, and blights his reputation in the public

[64] Gary Kelly, *English Fiction of the Romantic Period, 1789–1830* (London, 1989), 37.

[65] For the fourth volume Godwin consulted Robert Townson's *Travels in Hungary . . . in 1793* (1797) and l'Abbé Brenner, *Histoire des Révolutions de Hongrie* (1739), Ab. MSS, e. 204.

[66] On the Birmingham riots, see Goodwin, *Friends of Liberty*, 180–2.

[67] Philp, *Godwin's Political Justice*, 202–9.

sphere. When he is arrested on suspicion of the stranger's murder and called to account for the source of his wealth, his reply indicates that sincerity itself has become an outmoded ideal in a mercantile age:

> the only return a man of honour should make to loose conjectures and random calumnies is silence. . . . I know my innocence, and I rest upon it with confidence. Your vulgar citizens, habituated to none but the grovelling notions of traffic and barter, are not the peers of St. Leon, nor able to comprehend the views and sentiments by which he is guided.
> (*SL* ii. 261–2)

This statement has wider implications for Godwin's imagined community of enquiring readers. Although at the start of the narrative St Leon protests his sincerity, he later dismisses the possibility of openness with his audience: 'the pivot upon which the history I am composing turns, is a mystery. If they will not accept of my communication upon my own terms, they must lay aside my book' (*SL* ii. 243). His emphasis on unspoken knowledge is thus written into the tale, subverting all claims to frank communication between equals. As his son Charles protests: 'You have given utterance to different fictions on the subject, fictions that you now confess to be such; how am I to be convinced . . . ?' (*SL* ii. 188) This question is shared by the reader, for the plentiful instances of St Leon's deceptiveness hold out the possibility that his entire confession is yet another 'artful and fictitious tale' (*SL* ii. 182). While this does not deprive the reader of the active interpretative role enjoined in *Caleb Williams*, it does suggest he will never arrive at an objectively true understanding of events. St Leon's secret knowledge will always place him apart from the rest of men, as he finally admits: 'The creature does not exist with whom I have any common language, or any genuine sympathies' (*SL* iv. 8–9). His equivocations and uncertainties create the opposite effect to that of Caleb's 'artless and manly story' (*CW* iii. 298 [1]/324), with its aspiration towards unfettered communication.

Godwin's commitment to radical concerns in *St Leon* is thus fraught with problems: the increased range of his historical analysis gives rise to a heightened scepticism about the fulfilment of progressive ideals, which are viewed either as hopelessly nostalgic, or as open to distortion. Despite this cautionary message, his bold imaginative conception seized the attention of other writers who were also preoccupied with the individual casualties of historical change. Byron in particular admired Godwin's later novels, singling out *St Leon* for special praise.[68] However, Godwin's next novel, *Fleetwood* (1805), which presents a fuller exploration of a personality turned in on itself by historical pressures, bears more directly on Byron's early works, notably *Childe Harold* (1812–18). The novel's subtitle, *The New Man of Feeling*, points to Godwin's revisionist purpose in a mode which is 'apparently autobiographical but in spirit critical, itself introverted in pursuit of a critique of introversion'.[69] As in *St Leon*, the hero's egotism is presented not as an irrational instinct, but as the product of an aristocratic education, which gives rise to illusory expectations and the inability to relate to others. Both Fleetwood and St Leon envisage personal fulfilment in terms of public fame, and their inbuilt sense of a heroic past breeds dissatisfaction with the present state of society. It is this 'uneasy and aching void within' that drives Fleetwood from fashionable London and Paris to 'the craggy and inhospitable Alps' (*Fl* ii. 125, i. 159), a favourite haunt of Byron's disillusioned idealists. After a further period of dissipation Fleetwood concludes that he has 'nothing left, for the moment, to desire' (*Fl* ii. 136), and sets out on twenty years of Continental travels which prefigure Childe Harold's wanderings. In an 1813 addition to the Preface to *Childe Harold* I and II, first published in 1812, Byron described his hero as following a similar course, which was intended to show that 'early perversion of mind and morals leads to satiety of past pleasures and disappointment in new ones'.[70] Like Godwin's disenchanted heroes, the central questing figure in Byron's early poems presents a view of man as broken off from the richest possibilities of the past, and this sense of radical displacement is explicitly linked with recent political upheavals.

Godwin evidently recognized his kinship with Byron, for his next fictional study of the psychological pressures of revolutionary change, *Mandeville*, draws heavily on the misanthropic, guilt-

[68] William Maginn, 'William Godwin', 'A Gallery of Illustrious Literary Characters, No. 53', *Fraser's Magazine*, 10 (Oct. 1834), 463.

[69] Marilyn Butler, 'Satire and the Images of Self in the Romantic Period: The Long Tradition of Hazlitt's *Liber Amoris*,' *Yearbook of English Studies*, 14 (1984), 220.

[70] Byron, Addition (1813) to Preface to *Childe Harold's Pilgrimage*, Cantos I and II (1812), *Poetical Works*, 180.

stricken heroes of Byron's Turkish Tales.[71] Percy Shelley sent Byron a copy of *Mandeville* in the month of its publication, describing the central character as 'a Satanic likeness of Childe Harold the first'.[72] Godwin's fourth major novel is more ambitious than this account suggests, however, for in it he pursues his notion of true history as the study of character to its logical conclusion.

Mandeville: A Tale of the Seventeeth Century

Godwin had high hopes for *Mandeville*, writing to Percy Shelley in August 1816: 'I think it will be better than St Leon, and will take next place after Caleb Williams.'[73] Certainly it is his most unified work after *Caleb Williams*. Although it lacks the dynamic interaction of characters crucial to the success of the earlier novel, its single-minded focus on the psychology of the hero makes for a penetrating study of the pressures of politics and history on the individual. Though largely dismissed by twentieth-century critics,[74] it received high praise from Shelley. In his letter to the *Examiner* he described *Mandeville* as superior to Godwin's other works of fiction in its style and its boldness of moral speculations. Above all, he paid tribute to Godwin's imaginative energy, manifested in the overwhelming 'interest' at the core of the story:

> The events of the tale flow on like the stream of fate, regular and irresistible, and growing at once darker and swifter in their progress:—there is no surprise, there is no shock; we are prepared for the worst from the very opening scene, though we wonder whence the author drew the shadows which render the moral darkness every instant more profound, and, at last, so appaling and complete.[75]

In his first novel for more than ten years, Godwin develops his characteristic confessional form and analytical manner to a new extreme.

Godwin's return to the historical novel should also be seen in

[71] Godwin read *The Bride of Abydos* (1813), *The Giaour* (1813), *The Corsair* (1814), and *Lara* (1814) while writing the opening pages of *Mandeville* in June 1816; Ab. MSS, e. 214.

[72] Shelley to Byron, 17 Dec. 1817, *PBSL* i. 584.

[73] Godwin to Shelley, Aug. 1816, *PBSL* i. 492 n.

[74] Stephen, 'William Godwin's Novels', 149; Marshall, *William Godwin*, 339.

[75] Shelley, *Works*, vi. 222–3.

relation to Scott's more expansive treatment of historical issues. Godwin read each of the Waverley novels as they were published, and he met their anonymous author at Abbotsford during his Scottish tour of April 1816.[76] Although *Old Mortality* appeared too late to have significantly influenced Godwin's conception, which is indebted to his reading in memoirs of the Civil War period for the *Lives of Edward and John Philips*, he would have found congenial Scott's emphasis on the hero's lack of initiative in his earlier novels. Godwin had already developed his own politicized reading of character in the 1790s, but, encouraged by the popularity of the Waverley novels, he also drew on Scott's depiction of character in historical terms. Like *Waverley*, *Mandeville* deals with the political education of a young aristocrat who is haunted by visions of past violence and carried along by events he cannot control. More in keeping with Godwin's narrative mode, however, was the personalized point of view in *Guy Mannering* (1815), which Scott described as 'a tale of private life' in contrast to *Waverley*.[77] Here political struggle is domesticated and finds expression through the attitudes and prejudices of individual characters. The central opposition of Harry Bertram and Glossin, the rightful and usurping heirs to the ancient property of Ellangowan, reflects the class conflict in the novel as a whole.

Drawing on Scott's theme of an aristocratic family tricked out of its inheritance, Godwin similarly highlights the historical identities of his major characters,[78] often with the aid of footnotes in Scott's manner. As a Presbyterian landowner, Mandeville represents the progressive aristocracy at the time of the Revolution and starts out as a spokesman for the 'middle and temperate course' of the Presbyterians (*M* i. 229), by contrast with the revolutionary fanaticism of his tutor Hilkiah Bradford and the political opportunism of his rival Clifford. Initially 'a royalist to the core' who is introduced by analogy with Milton's Comus (*M* i. 269, 255),

[76] Godwin read *Waverley* in Sept. 1815, *Guy Mannering* and *The Antiquary* (1816) in May 1816, started work on *Mandeville* in June 1816, and read *Old Mortality* while revising *Mandeville* for publication in Dec. 1817, Ab. MSS, e. 214–15; cf. Godwin to Mrs Godwin, 30 Apr. 1816, Kegan Paul, *William Godwin*, ii. 236–7.

[77] Scott to John B. S. Morritt, 19 Jan. 1815, *Letters*, iv. 13.

[78] Cf. Marion Omar Farouk, '*Mandeville: A Tale of the Seventeenth Century*—Historical Novel or Psychological Study?', in Schlösser *et al.* (eds.), *Essays in Honor of William Gallacher*, 111–17.

Clifford quickly comes to terms with Cromwell's regime, but eventually turns Papist, giving Mandeville all the more reason to despise him. Historical allegiances equally colour the novel's settings. Mandeville is sent to Winchester School, 'a species of Commonwealth' (*M* i. 195), where his inability to win the respect of his fellow-pupils anticipates his later failure to distinguish himself in the royalist uprising of 1655. Mandeville's sister bears the first name of Henrietta Maria, Catholic queen consort of the recently executed Charles I, and lives under the care of Mrs Willis, another 'perfect royalist' (*M* i. 204). Their cottage, appropriately named Beaulieu, provides an other-worldly retreat from political controversy, and is idealized by Mandeville as 'the society of "just men made perfect" ' (*M* i. 210).

However, this externalized opposition of value-systems does not adequately convey Godwin's notion of the construction of character in historical terms. As Mandeville explains, it is the express purpose of his narrative 'to show how the concurrence of a variety of causes operate to form a character' (*M* i. 220), and this theme can only be fully developed through Godwin's characteristic interiorized mode. This exclusive subjective focus underscores Godwin's divergence from Scott's final emphasis on moderation and social compromise. In his review of *Fleetwood* Scott made it clear that he considered introspection a dangerous pastime, and he was especially critical of the anti-social tendencies of Fleetwood's actions: 'uniformly directed by the narrow principle of self-gratification; there is no aspiration towards promoting the public advantage, or the happiness of individuals'.[79] Though Scott accords Henry Morton, the hero of *Old Mortality*, an unusual degree of interiority, Morton's ethical stance corroborates this suspicion of an uncontrolled inner life: he rejects the Covenanters' rule of action based on 'inward light', and argues instead for the 'rational prospect' of redressing their wrongs.[80] When Morton does join forces with the Covenanters, his life is threatened by their most extreme faction, and Scott finally emphasizes his hard-won 'virtuous resolution and manly disinterestedness' by contrast with Burley's destructive fanaticism.[81]

[79] Scott, 'Godwin's *Fleetwood*', *Edinburgh Review*, 6 (Apr. 1805), reprinted in *Miscellaneous Prose*, xviii. 136–7.

[80] Scott, *Old Mortality*, *Waverley Novels*, New Edition with the Author's Notes, 48 vols. (Edinburgh, 1829–33), ix. 317, 323 (ch. 6).

[81] Scott, *Waverley Novels*, xi. 57 (ch. 3).

Godwin, however, enters into Mandeville's irrational perspective so thoroughly that the novel still tends to be read in terms of his own obsessions. His uncomfortably intense study of religious obsession surely has more in common with Hogg's exploration of Calvinist extremism in *The Private Memoirs and Confessions of a Justified Sinner* (1824), itself in part a response to Scott's omniscient point of view.[82]

The heightened psychological interest in *Mandeville* derives in part from Godwin's reading of two works acknowledged in the Preface, Joanna Baillie's play, *De Monfort* (1798), and Charles Brockden Brown's first completed novel, *Wieland* (1798).[83] Both are concerned with the passion of fraternal jealousy, but Brown's *Wieland*, a critical reworking of *Caleb Williams*, is of particular interest in terms of the development of the Godwin school of fiction. Several editions of *Wieland* appeared in England between 1800 and 1811, and this American tale was especially popular with Shelley and his friends.[84] What is especially significant here is Godwin's receptiveness to Brown's use of a psychological technique to convey a suspicion of individual judgement. In contrast to his earlier use of eighteenth-century Gothic themes to convey the pressures of institutions on individuals, notably the focus on Roman Catholicism in *St Leon*, Godwin follows Brown in adopting a Protestant setting to explore the dangers of extremism. In highlighting Mandeville's possessive relationship with his sister, he further draws on Brown's harrowing portrayal of familial bonds. With this relatively conservative precedent, Godwin's study of fanaticism from the point of view of the fanatic explores the doubts about man's rational capacities already registered in his revisions to *Political Justice*. As he wrote in a post-1830 fragment: 'It requires too much—expects more of man than man can perform—what then? . . . man is a fluctuating & variable animal, & . . . we need every assistance to hold us to the sticking-place.'[85]

In *Mandeville* Godwin exploits the first-person narrative to present a dual theory of the growth of the mind. In keeping with his

[82] For Hogg's and Scott's discussion of narrative point of view, see James Hogg, *Memoirs of the Author's Life and Familiar Anecdotes of Sir Walter Scott* (1832, 1834), ed. Douglas S. Mack (Edinburgh, 1972), 106–7.

[83] Joanna Baillie, *De Monfort*, in *A Series of Plays . . . [on] the Stronger Passions of the Mind*, vol. i (London, 1798), read by Godwin along with *Wieland* in May 1816, Ab. MSS, e. 214.

[84] See Introduction, n. 18.

[85] Ab. MSS, c. 604/2.

earlier views on the formation of character by external circumstances, he records the impact of historical events on private life from Mandeville's earliest childhood; but Mandeville's long passages of self-analysis emphasize the unaccountable origin of his irrational passions. The novel's opening sequence, which may have been drafted as early as 1809,[86] presents a cautionary tale of revolutionary excesses, plunging the reader into an account of the rebellion of Irish Catholic landowners in October 1641. Mandeville gives a deceptively impersonal account of the capture of the English garrison at Kinard in County Tyrone, and the massacre of English soldiers and their families. It is only gradually revealed that Mandeville's parents were among the massacred, and that he writes as the sole survivor of this atrocity. His subsequent narrative explores the psychological impact of civil unrest. Brought to England as a child, he dreams nightly of 'a perpetual succession of flight, and pursuit, and anguish, and murder. . . . I had hardly a notion of any more than two species of creatures on the earth—the persecutor and his victim, the Papist and the Protestant' (*M* i. 114–15). Knowledge of past violence, like Falkland's 'secret wound' (*CW* ii. 10 [1]/109), becomes a source of criminal guilt, and further contributes to his isolation from his species. Growing up in the period of the Civil War and the Protectorate, he continues to imagine that 'every thing around me was engaged in a conspiracy against me' (*M* i. 160), and attributes his suspicious temperament to 'an original taint in [his] nature' (*M* ii. 294). But these apparent fantasies of persecution have a historical basis in a public context where 'Bigotry was lord paramount on every side' (*M* i. 42). Mandeville's envious hostility towards Clifford only highlights his own complicity with the prejudiced temper of the age, and is offset by the loving companionship of his sister Henrietta, which offers the possibility of social integration. But when Clifford falls in love with Henrietta and they plan to marry, Mandeville collapses in insane jealousy, and expresses downright confusion about the source of his overwhelming feelings: 'My nature, or my circumstances, seemed to have made hatred my ruling passion' (*M* ii. 301).

The disturbing power of this tortured, fragmentary narrative lies in Godwin's analysis of the traumatic effects of revolutionary

[86] See Burton R. Pollin, 'William Godwin's "Fragment of a Romance" ', *Comparative Literature*, 16 (1964), 40–54.

upheaval. By contrast with Scott's focus on the possibilities of human greatness liberated by moments of historical crisis, Godwin explores the disabling pressures of politics and history on the individual psyche. In *Old Mortality* Morton's active pursuit of a moderate solution to religious conflict is attributed to his 'extraordinary qualities . . . hidden even from himself, until circumstances called them forth'.[87] But Mandeville's early saturation in extremist doctrines leads to a dangerous detachment from external circumstances and a sense of the futility of all action: 'Invisible things are the only realities' (*M* iii. 48). Godwin's insight into the sense of permanent exclusion engendered by political change forms the antithesis of Scott's predominantly reassuring vision of order and coherence, in which leading characters are integrated into society in terms of the public categories of nation, party, rank, and wealth.[88] Instead Godwin comes to share Brown's scepticism about the possibility of resolving internal conflicts engendered by revolutionary change.

Godwin's later scepticism about man's ability to control historical events is formulated most directly in his assessment of Cromwell in the *History of the Commonwealth*. To some extent Godwin subscribes to the popular republican view that Cromwell started out with the best of intentions, but was corrupted by personal ambition as his genuine religious zeal degenerated into fanaticism.[89] Finally, though, Godwin concludes that Cromwell was not responsible for his own downfall. As in St Leon's high-minded efforts to aid the victims of Turkish despotism in Hungary, Cromwell was at the mercy of other men's prejudices:

> But he was not free. He governed a people that was hostile to him. His reign therefore was a reign of experiments. He perpetually did the thing he desired not to do, and was driven from one inconsistent mode of proceeding to another, as the necessity of the situation in which he was placed impelled him. (*HC* iv. 597)

As another victim of private passions and public prejudice, Mandeville is forced to surrender his freedom of will and becomes more and more dependent on others. His signing away of his father's estate into the hands of unscrupulous lawyers suggestively

[87] Scott, *Waverley Novels*, x. 313 (ch. 21).
[88] Scott's *The Bride of Lammermoor* (1819) offers a more Godwinian view.
[89] 'Oliver Cromwell', *DNB* xiii. 155–85, 183.

parallels Cromwell's later dependency on the lawyer allies who helped to separate him from his original high purpose.

The scepticism of Godwin's later studies of character in history both extends and undercuts his early conviction of the intrusion of government into private life. By contrast with the liberating claims for history in 'Of History & Romance', Godwin's post-revolutionary novels confront the psychic damage wrought by impersonal historical processes. Godwin presents a view of historical change as decided not by the individual abilities of great men, but by an accumulation of external circumstances and overwhelming impulse. At the level of rational argument, then, there is all the more need to stress the profound internal level at which political reform must begin. Godwin's 'Prospectus for a New Edition of Political Justice', written in 1832, displays this increased, insistent gradualism: 'The prepossessions of mankind ought to be consulted; & they are not to be abruptly intruded on with matters for which they are in no wise prepared.'[90]

This insight exacts a price in terms of Godwin's imaginative development. The power of Godwin's primary insight into the scope of fiction to convey historical pressures on the individual should be reaffirmed: well in advance of the Waverley novels, and later in debate with them, Godwin's historical fictions adumbrate the central theme of post-revolutionary narrative art. Yet while Godwin's use of the single first-person narrative permits an unprecedented analysis of character held in thrall by external circumstances, it also fails to fulfil the promise of renewed debate at the end of *Caleb Williams*. Although St Leon's equivocations register the epistemological difficulty glimpsed in *Caleb Williams*, that there might be 'no criterion by which vice might be prevented from being mistaken for virtue' (*CW* iii. 258 [1]/310), Godwin's later novels lack the formal innovation needed to explore this issue to the full. Godwin's openly acknowledged debt to *Wieland* in *Mandeville* suggests a recognition that he has been overtaken by his followers in the development of a 'new and startling' blend of philosophy and fiction. To find the technical development that Godwin's later novels lack, along with a revaluation of Godwin's philosophy that goes beyond his own self-criticism, we must turn first to the novels of Charles Brockden Brown.

[90] Godwin, 'Prospectus of a New Edition of the Enquiry Concerning Political Justice, Oct. 9, 1832', Ab. MSS, b. 226/4, p. 4.

Part II

4

Wieland: Charles Brockden Brown's American Tale

The Godwinian Context

> Another 'wanderer o'er eternity' was Brockden Brown, the Godwin of America. . . . His name, after his untimely death . . . was returned upon his ungrateful country—from Britain, where his writings first attained eminent distinction, while even yet Americans, generally, prefer the adventure and bustle of Cooper to the stern Dante-like simplicity, the philosophical spirit, and the harrowing and ghost-like interest of Brown.[1]

While Gilfillan lamented that Charles Brockden Brown had been neglected by his countrymen, he took for granted Brown's centrality in the 'Godwin school'.[2] Twentieth-century criticism shows a reversal of these priorities: as the first professional man of letters in the new republic, Brown has been studied extensively in the context of American literary traditions,[3] but there has been little discussion of his links with Godwin. Even those critics who have recognized common elements between the two authors have tended to regard Brown as a mere imitator of Godwin. In his own time his fellow-American John Neal, writing in *Blackwood's*, pronounced him 'an imitator of Godwin, whose "Caleb Williams" made him. . . . He was the Godwin of America.'[4] The general tenor of recent American opinion may be summed up by Leslie Fiedler's undiscriminating comment that the form that best suited Brown's political aspirations was 'the gothic romance in its doctrinaire Godwinian

[1] Gilfillan, 'Mrs Shelley', 287–8.

[2] Ibid. 284.

[3] See David Brion Davis, *Homicide in American Fiction, 1789–1860: A Study in Social Values* (Ithaca, NY, 1957); Larzer Ziff, 'A Reading of *Wieland*', *PMLA* 77 (1962), 51–7; William L. Hedges, 'Charles Brockden Brown and the Culture of Contradictions', *EAL* 9 (1974), 107–42; Emory Elliott, *Revolutionary Writers: Literature and Authority in the New Republic, 1725–1810* (New York, 1982), 224–70; Jane Tompkins, *Sensational Designs: The Cultural Work of American Fiction, 1790–1860* (New York, 1985), 40–61.

[4] John Neal, 'American Writers, No. II', *Blackwood's*, 16 (1824), 415–28, reprinted in *American Writers: A Series of Papers Contributed to Blackwood's Magazine (1824–5)*, ed. Fred Lewis Pattee (Durham, NC, 1937), 57, 65.

form. "To equal Caleb Williams" was the best Brown could hope for himself.'[5] Such a view only highlights the extent to which modern critics have failed to engage with the self-conscious intellectuality and imaginative resourcefulness of the Godwinian novel.

The contrast with earlier responses to Brown's independent achievement could not be more striking. Margaret Fuller was the first American critic to note the mutually enriching affinity between Brown and Godwin: 'there was no imitation, no second-hand in the matter. They were congenial natures, and whichever had come first might have lent an impulse to the other.'[6] When Brown's novels were first published in England,[7] the group of writers centred on Godwin and the Shelleys read them with enthusiasm and were swift to claim him as one of their own. He was admired by Percy Shelley, Peacock, Keats, Hazlitt, and Mary Shelley, who read *Wieland* (1798) just before starting work on *Frankenstein* in 1816.[8] Peacock later claimed that Percy Shelley's favourite works included Schiller's *Robbers*, Goethe's *Faust*, and Brown's four Gothic novels, *Wieland*, *Ormond* (1799), *Arthur Mervyn* (1799–1800), and *Edgar Huntly* (1799), and that 'nothing so blended itself with the structure of his interior mind as the novels of Brown'.[9] Peacock himself praised

[5] Leslie A. Fiedler, *Love and Death in the American Novel* (rev. edn., Harmondsworth, 1960, 1982), 147; cf. Harry R. Warfel, *Charles Brockden Brown: American Gothic Novelist* (Gainesville, Fla., 1949), 112–43; David Lee Clark, *Charles Brockden Brown: Pioneer Voice of America* (Durham, NC, 1952), 162–77; David H. Hirsch, 'Charles Brockden Brown as a Novelist of Ideas', *Books at Brown*, 20 (1965), 165–84. For a more discerning view, see Lillie Deming Loshe, *The Early American Novel, 1789–1830* (New York, 1907), and David Punter, *The Literature of Terror: A History of Gothic Fictions from 1765 to the Present Day* (London, 1980), 190–7.

[6] Margaret Fuller, 'Papers on Literature and Art' [1846], *The Writings of Margaret Fuller*, ed. Mason Wade (New York, 1941, 1973), 378; cf. William Dunlap, *Memoirs of Charles Brockden Brown, the American Novelist; with Selections from his Original Letters, and Miscellaneous Writings* (Philadelphia, 1815; London, 1822), 74–141; [Anon.], 'On the Writings of Charles Brockden Brown and Washington Irving', *Blackwood's*, 6 (Feb. 1820), 544–61.

[7] Brown's novels were issued separately in England in 1800, 1803, 1804, 1807, 1811, and 1821, then all six were reprinted in 1821–2; Reid, 'Brockden Brown in England', 188.

[8] Mary Shelley read Brown's novels between 1814 and 1817, *MSJ* i. 89, cf. *MSJ* i. 45, 86, 91, 100.

[9] Peacock, 'Memoirs of Shelley' [1860], *The Works of Thomas Love Peacock*, Halliford Edition, ed. H. F. B. Brett-Smith and C. E. Jones, 10 vols. (London, 1924–34), viii. 77–9; cf. Eleanor Sickels, 'Shelley and Charles Brockden Brown', *PMLA* 45 (1930), 1116–28.

Wieland in terms of the author's ability to 'carry the principle of terror to its utmost limits', a quality which also appealed to Keats when he made these fine discriminations: 'very powerful—something like Godwin—Between Schiller and Godwin. . . . More clever in plot and incident than Godwin—A strange american scion of the German trunk. Powerful genius—accomplish'd horrors.'[10] In this context, Godwin's acknowledgement of *Wieland* in the Preface to *Mandeville* only confirms Brown's centrality in carrying on the Godwinian debate.

Certainly there is much evidence for Godwin's early impact on Brown. It is likely that Brown first became acquainted with *Political Justice* when selected chapters were published in one of his favourite journals, the *New-York Magazine*, in July 1793.[11] *Caleb Williams* was reprinted in Philadelphia in January 1795, and Brown's own *Monthly Magazine* contains reviews of *The Enquirer* and *St Leon*.[12] Brown's first biographer, William Dunlap, himself an early admirer of *Political Justice*, accounted for Brown's questioning of received opinions in terms of Godwin's attribution of defects in the existing system 'to some inherent ineffectiveness in the system itself, and not to the depravity of our common nature'.[13] Moreover, Brown's friend Elihu Hubbard Smith thought that Godwin's rationalism had rescued him from his early subjective tendencies, reflected in his fictive explorations of a Rousseauistic sensibility.[14] As Smith wrote to Brown in May 1796: 'You wandered in a world of your own creation. Now and then a ray of truth broke in upon you, but with an influence too feeble to dissipate the phantoms which errors had conjured up around you. *Godwin came, and all was light!*'[15]

[10] Peacock, *Gryll Grange* [1860], *Works,* v. 358; Keats to Richard Woodhouse, 21, 22 Sept. 1819, *The Letters of John Keats, 1814–1821*, ed. Hyder E. Rollins, 2 vols. (Cambridge, Mass., 1958), ii. 173; cf. Hazlitt, 'American Literature—Dr Channing' [1829], *Works*, xiv. 319–20.

[11] D. Clark, *Pioneer Voice*, 109.

[12] The *Monthly Magazine, and American Review*, ed. C. B. Brown, ran from Apr. 1799 to Dec. 1800; Dunlap, *Memoirs*, 152. *MM* 1/5 (Aug. 1799), 321; 2/6 (June 1800), 404.

[13] Dunlap, *Memoirs*, 68; Dunlap wrote to Godwin on 1 Oct. 1795 offering to edit *Political Justice* for publication in America, Ab. MSS, b. 227/2.

[14] Brown's first attempt at fiction, begun in 1790, consists of a series of extravagantly emotional letters; reprinted in D. Clark, *Pioneer Voice*, 55–107.

[15] Elihu Hubbard Smith to Brown, 27 May 1796, Warfel, *American Gothic Novelist*, 44–5.

Brown's reading of *Caleb Williams* provided an immediate stimulus to his own literary ambitions. According to Dunlap, Brown's journals for 1796 were 'interspersed with plans and scraps of Utopias', while a year later he planned a work 'equal in extent to *Caleb Williams*' which would also encompass a perfect 'system of morality'.[16] It is likely that this alludes to his early novel, *Sky-Walk; or, The Man Unknown to Himself*, which was mysteriously lost before publication. Certainly he later compared this work unfavourably with 'the transcendent merits of *Caleb Williams*'.[17] Announcing the forthcoming publication of *Sky-Walk* in a letter to the *Weekly Magazine* in 1798, Brown presented the novel in terms of Godwin's innovative blend of social analysis and psychological method, and claimed the uniqueness of this intellectual genre in American writing. Describing himself as a 'story-telling moralist' who sought to combine the ordinary pleasures of narrative with a specific 'moral tendency', he went on to align himself with Godwin's thoughtful exploration of psychological states.[18] What would grip the reader's attention, he argued, is the 'exhibition of powerful motives, and a sort of audaciousness of character'. Like the older writer, he moves beyond mere discussion of ideas in fiction to explore philosophical issues through the dynamic interaction of 'men of soaring passions and intellectual energy'. Yet his subtitle already suggests that he lacks Godwin's early optimistic faith in the knowable intentions of the revolutionary enquirer, for he will use Godwin's psychological method to display the baffling actions of a 'Man Unknown to Himself'.[19]

The development of Godwinian methods in pursuit of a critique of Godwin is Brown's distinctive achievement in *Wieland; or, The Transformation*, his first completed novel, published 14 September 1798. [20] Brown's use of subjective narrative techniques to convey conservative political fears makes *Wieland* a pivotal text between

[16] Dunlap, *Memoirs*, 46; Brown's journal entry for Sept. 1795, D. Clark, *Pioneer Voice*, 157.

[17] Brown on his unfinished romance, Dunlap, *Memoirs*, 74.

[18] Brown, Prospectus to *Sky-Walk*, *Weekly Magazine of Original Essays*, ed. James Watters, 1 (17 Mar. 1798), 202, quoted in Fred Lewis Pattee, 'Introduction' to Charles Brockden Brown, *Wieland; or, The Transformation; together with Memoirs of Carwin the Biloquist* (New York, 1926), p. xx.

[19] Brown took up the theme of unknowable motives in *Edgar Huntly; or, Memoirs of a Sleep-Walker* (1799).

[20] *Wieland; or, The Transformation: An American Tale* was first published 14 Sept. 1798, *W* 349.

Godwin's essentially optimistic critique of society in *Caleb Williams* and Mary Shelley's uncompromising pessimism in *Frankenstein.* Though much of the novel's immediate appeal lay in its qualities as a terror novel, Brown himself put great emphasis on its moral utility. In December 1798 he firmly placed *Wieland* in the realm of public debate by sending a copy to the Republican leader Thomas Jefferson, then Vice-President.[21] In the text itself he is more circumspect. In the Preface he outlines his aim as 'the illustration of some important branches of the moral constitution of man' (*W* 3), while the narrator, Clara Wieland, also highlights the educative purpose of her autobiographical narrative: 'It will exemplify the force of early impressions, and show the immeasurable evils that flow from an erroneous or imperfect discipline' (*W* 5). More unobtrusive but equally revealing is the guide to the plot offered in one of the Wielands' enlightened discussions, which centres on Cicero's defence of Cluentius, accused of having murdered his stepfather, and introduces the key proposition: 'to make the picture of a single family a model from which to sketch the condition of a nation' (*W* 30).[22]

With this proposition in mind, the selective and critical nature of Brown's reworking of the Godwinian plot becomes evident. Brown's internalized treatment of the predominantly political relationships in *Caleb Williams* is reflected in the setting of the action within the Wieland family, where the emotional tensions left implicit in Godwin's novel surface in a claustrophobic interaction between brother and sister. Told by Clara Wieland, the story turns on the family's reaction to mysterious, apparently supernatural voices. As in *Caleb Williams*, unbridled curiosity forms the mainspring of the action. But in opposition to Godwin's exploration of the intrusion of government into private life, Brown is preoccupied with how people might behave in a world without institutional restraints. What the story highlights is a series of breaks with past traditions, which forces characters into a dangerous self-reliance.

It all begins in Europe. Clara recounts the family's history,

[21] D. Clark, *Pioneer Voice*, 163.

[22] Cicero, *Pro Cluentio* (66 BC); cf. D. Davis, *Homicide*, 89, and Jane Tompkins, *Sensational Designs*, 60, but neither critic discusses the Godwinian context. My argument challenges Warner Berthoff, 'Brockden Brown: The Politics of the Man of Letters', *Serif* 3/4 (Dec. 1966), 3–11, which places Brown's shift to conservatism as late as 1801.

beginning with the rebellion of her aristocratic Saxon grandfather against his family, in order to marry the daughter of a Hamburg merchant. Completely 'disowned and rejected' (*W* 6) by his relations, he and his wife have one son, Clara's father, and die young. This first rejection of an inherited order breeds a lack of direction in the son, who spends his youth in solitary 'mercantile servitude' (*W* 7) in England.[23] When he alights on the doctrines of the Camissards, a group of French Protestants noted for their fierce independence, he falls an easy prey to their extremist creed, based on solitary worship and total obedience to an avenging God of terror. In fact his sense of persecution becomes so acute that he is unable to remain in England, so he moves to America, following in the steps of the New World settlers. In this second break with tradition, Wieland sets out to convert the North American Indians, but he only gets as far as Philadelphia, where he makes an unexpected fortune as a farmer and marries. Despite this seduction by Jefferson's agrarian ideals,[24] some years later he is inspired by the return of his tyrannical God to build a summer-house for his solitary devotions. Here he meets an inexplicable and violent death by spontaneous combustion.

This mysterious event overshadows the novel's main action, which centres on the eminently rational community created by Wieland's children, Clara and Theodore. In keeping with the American democratic ideal, they have been brought up to honour a personal sense of rectitude over traditional restraints. Of their religious training, Clara comments: 'We were left to the guidance of our own understanding. . . . We sought not a basis for our faith, in the weighing of proofs, and the dissection of creeds' (*W* 22). They transform the temple of their father's fearful deity into the seat of 'social affections' and 'delicious sympathy' (*W* 24), where they retire for enlightened conversations on the arts. The exclusiveness of this intellectual retreat is reinforced when Theodore marries his childhood sweetheart, Catharine Pleyel, and they have a family. Later Catharine's brother Henry returns from an education in

[23] On contemporary links between madness and mercantile pursuits, see Ch. 3, n. 60.

[24] For an idealized vision of Jefferson's decentralized agrarian nation, see Michel-Guillaume Jean de Crèvecoeur, *Letters from an American Farmer* (London, 1782), reprinted in Larzer Ziff (ed.), *The Literature of America: Colonial Period* (New York, 1970), 368–9.

Europe to display a modern equivalent to Theodore's inherited enthusiasm: 'Moral necessity, and calvinistic inspiration, were the props on which my brother thought proper to repose. Pleyel was the champion of intellectual liberty, and rejected all guidance but that of his reason' (*W* 25).

Six years pass in this secluded haven, closeted from cities and wars alike, and Brown introduces a sub-plot. Clara tells the story of a stray addition to the family, Louisa Conway, who is later revealed to have been abandoned by her mother, who had previously deserted her husband for another man. This sounds like the beginning of another novel, but in fact it repeats the central theme of rebellion against social or parental expectations.

The Wielands' rational idyll is further disrupted by the arrival of a European stranger called Carwin, an unstable compound of insatiable enquirer, scientific meddler, and satanic deceiver. Shortly afterwards the main characters start hearing mysterious voices warning of imaginary dangers, and their apparently well-balanced society is transformed into a nightmare of epistemological uncertainty. Convinced of a genuine supernatural presence, Theodore reverts to the fanatical behaviour of his father. Pleyel, the apparent Godwinian rationalist, views all things 'through the mists of prejudice and passion' (*W* 109) and is repeatedly led into errors of judgement. Hesitating between these responses, Clara re-enacts Caleb's curiosity about his master's secret, and becomes obsessed with the origins of the voices and with Carwin. But Falkland's chest is replaced by her private closet, which yields psychological rather than political secrets. Hearing voices from the closet at midnight, she thinks she will find her brother waiting to kill her; instead she discovers Carwin, who is planning to seduce her. Later Carwin confesses that his uncontrollable curiosity led him to create the voices through the art of ventriloquism. But this unexpected twist to the plot does not explain the final catastrophe when Theodore, in obedience to divine commands, murders his wife and children. After witnessing her brother's remorse and suicide, Clara herself becomes temporarily insane, and only survives through the care of her uncle, a doctor, who prescribes a return to Europe.

The intricate way that Brown presents the 'condition of a nation' is best illustrated by a brief comparison with *Caleb Williams*. As in Godwin's novel, the escalating violence of the plot presents variants on a single ideological proposition. Brown depicts the history of the republic as a series of rebellions and disastrous transformations, just as Godwin presents English society in terms of an inescapable climate of despotism. In *Caleb Williams* the pivotal relationship between Caleb and Falkland is anticipated in the opposition of Tyrrel and Falkland, and in Tyrrel's harassment of his tenants. Godwin highlights the wider implications of this pattern in the scene where Falkland, as justice of the peace, has to judge a virtuous peasant accused of murder. Watching the trial, Caleb feels as if 'my own life, that of my master, or almost of a whole nation had been at stake' (*CW* ii. 61 [1]/126). It is this treatment of public issues through private drama that Brown develops in his commentary on the fate of the nation through family romance.

At the same time Brown's dramatization of the fall of the house of Wieland shows a radical departure from Godwin's values, for the qualities of impartiality and independence advocated in *Caleb Williams* prove to be unequivocally destructive. In the interaction of Caleb and Falkland, Godwin is primarily concerned to expose the corrupt basis of the aristocratic system of government defended by Burke in *Reflections*. It is central to Godwin's critique of institutions that he shows Caleb to be defeated more by the intrusion of government into private life than by his own compulsive inquisitiveness. Brown, however, finds as much imposture in the new system as in the old, and he rewrites the fate of Godwin's impartial enquirer to point up the dangers of extreme individualism. His exploration of the destructive energies of Theodore and Clara, who have based their hopes of happiness solely on the conviction of their own rectitude, suggests a call for the very social controls that Godwin sought to abolish.

Crucial to Brown's formal contribution to the Godwinian novel is his sophisticated development of the first-person narrative, which enacts his critique of Godwin in an arresting and highly charged manner. Clara's limited perspective involves the reader in a chaotic and unexpectedly violent sequence of events, in which characters constantly mistake one another's identity and intentions. This narrative complexity is designed to alert the reader, as in *Caleb Williams*, but Brown inverts Godwin's rational aims. It is essential to Godwin's wider purpose that the narrative stimulates the reader into active participation, challenging him to fulfil his potential as impartial enquirer. Although Brown also invites the reader to piece together contradictory bits of information, he turns the provisional quality of the narrative to a radically different end, aiming to shock the reader by successive revelations of the limits of rational knowledge. Thus we are confronted with the transformation of benign farmer into homicidal maniac, while the conventional villain, Carwin, proves to be relatively harmless.

Before looking at these imaginative strategies in more detail, we need to account for Brown's rapid shift from enthusiastic welcome of Godwin's fiction to distrust of revolutionary aspirations. Brown's mixed allegiance to Godwin should be seen in the light of American conservative reaction against revolutionary ideas.

The Conservative Context

That Brown intended *Wieland* as a commentary on public issues is indicated by his sending a copy to Jefferson in December 1798, along with a letter pointing out the 'artful display of incidents, the powerful delineation of characters and the train of eloquent and judicious reasoning which may be combined in a fictitious work'.[25] This action invites us to read *Wieland* as a contribution to the political debate 'respecting THINGS AS THEY ARE' (*CW* i, p. v [2]/1) in the aftermath of the French Revolution. As seen in Chapter 2, after the publication of Burke's *Reflections* and Paine's reply in the *Rights of Man*, British reaction to events in France became increasingly polarized. But in post-revolutionary America, the political debate was given all the more urgency by greater social instability and closer links with France.[26] Although the French Revolution had been welcomed initially as an affirmation and extension of the American struggle for freedom, the French declaration of war on England in February 1793 posed a threat to American security. As news of atrocities in France filtered through, many feared a repetition of these events in America, and opinion became bitterly divided.

By the mid-1790s, the dispute about the direction which the new republic was to take had led to the formation of national parties.

[25] D. Clark, *Pioneer Voice*, 163–4.

[26] My account is indebted to Samuel Eliot Morison, Henry Steele Commager, and William E. Leuchtenburg, *The Growth of the American Republic*, 2 vols. (6th edn., New York, 1969), i. 299–330.

The Republicans retained the high ideal of man's innate integrity and wanted to see an agrarian nation based on this principle, with minimal government interference in private affairs. By contrast the Federalists, led by John Adams, were more pessimistic. They argued for the need for external controls to maintain law and order and to regulate the economy, and they favoured a stratified society on the English model. By 1798, party feeling was at its height.[27] Moreover, Federalist fears of French designs on the neighbouring territories had given rise to conspiracy theories, which cast Jefferson as the agent of a vast secret society plotting to subvert American society. These fears seemed to be corroborated by the fact that leading British radicals such as Joseph Priestley had indeed emigrated to America.[28]

In this atmosphere of panic and suspicion, Brown's treatment of the dangers of 'enthusiasm' invites direct comparison with conservative attacks on revolutionary extremists. The most influential work on this subject was Robison's *Proofs of a Conspiracy*, also being read by Godwin in preparation for *St Leon*, although *St Leon* did not appear until almost a year after *Wieland*.[29] Robison argued that the French Revolution had begun with the activities of the Illuminati, a secret society founded at the University of Ingolstadt in 1775, which maintained links with the French *philosophes*, freemasonry, and various religious sects and corresponding societies. Dedicated to universal benevolence, the Illuminati sought to insinuate its members into positions of power and influence, where they could work for the transformation of society through clandestine acts of violence. Robison gave a vivid account of their meetings, in which 'continuous declamations were made on liberty and equality as the unalienable rights of man. . . . Nothing was so frequently discoursed as the propriety of employing, for a good purpose, the means which the wicked employed for evil purposes' (*PC* 107). The Federalist Timothy Dwight, author of *The Conquest of Canaan* (1787), America's first epic poem and an allegory of the Revolution, was more obviously concerned to rouse public outrage against this atheistical conspiracy: 'ADULTERY, assassination,

[27] Ibid. 318–19; cf. Eric Foner, *Tom Paine and Revolutionary America* (New York, 1976), 253–5.

[28] Goodwin, *Friends of Liberty*, 487.

[29] See Ch. 3, n. 61.

poisoning, and other crimes of the like infernal nature, were taught as lawful, and even as virtuous actions.'[30] This popular conservative myth of the revolutionary intellectual as an unscrupulous plotter provides the imaginative framework for Brown's exploration of the defeat of benevolent ideals.

Brown's reading of German terror novels highlights a second major source for his dramatization of conservative political fears.[31] For his distinctive blend of politics and psychology he may have been indebted to the rational fictions of C. M. Wieland,[32] whom Clara claims as a distant relative (*W* 7), as well as to Godwin. In addition, both Schiller's *The Ghost-Seer* and its most successful imitation by Cajetan Tschink, translated in 1795 as *The Victim of Magical Delusion*, mixed apparent supernatural delusion with political intrigue, exploiting the symbolism and rituals of European secret societies.[33] The title of Tschink's novel alone points to its heady subject-matter: *The Victim of Magical Delusion; or, The Mystery of the Revolution of P - - - - - - l: A Magico-Political Tale.* Between 1795 and 1796 Brown read both novels, and the way that he utilized their public argument was picked up by Keats when he described *Wieland* as 'a Domestic prototype of Schiller's Armenian'.[34] However, one of Brown's biographers has also argued that the plot of *Wieland* is based on *The Victim of Magical Delusion*, and in fact Tschink gives a strikingly apt description of Wieland's religious delusion:

> If we . . . are not satisfied with what the contemplation of nature, and the gospel teach us of God, but desire to have an immediate, and physical communion with the invisible, we then cannot avoid the deviations of fanaticism, and are easily led to confound our *feelings* and *ideas* with external effects . . . we stray from ourselves and from the objects around

[30] On Dwight's epic poems, see Elliott, *Revolutionary Writers*, 55–91; Timothy Dwight, *The Duty of Americans, at the Present Crisis* (New Haven, Conn., 1798), quoted in Michael Davitt Bell, ' "The Double-Tongued Deceiver": Sincerity and Duplicity in the Novels of Charles Brockden Brown', *EAL* 9 (Fall 1974), 144.

[31] Harry R. Warfel, 'Charles Brockden Brown's German Sources', *Modern Language Quarterly*, 1 (1940), 357–65.

[32] Christoph Martin Wieland (1733–1813) made his name with *The History of Agathon* (1766–7; trans. J. Richardson, 1773).

[33] J. M. S. Tompkins, *The Popular Novel in England, 1770–1800* (London, 1932), 278–80.

[34] Both novels were serialized in the *New-York Weekly Magazine* between 1795 and 1797, Warfel, 'German Sources', 362; see above, n. 10.

us, to a world of ideas which is the workmanship of our fancy, and . . . mistake for *reality*, what is merely *ideal*.[35]

The general currency of hysterical portraits of intellectuals in conservative propaganda should not blind us to the thoroughgoing nature of Brown's scepticism. Tschink's account of the dangers of private religious worship, unmediated by institutions, highlights the contemporary displacement of political fears of the spread of revolutionary ideas into widespread suspicion of autonomous imaginative activity. In particular, it echoes warnings of the delusory potential of the imagination made by the Scottish exponents of Common Sense philosophy. Brown's treatment of the Wielands' dangerous self-reliance derives its philosophical rationale from the ideas of the Scottish Enlightenment, in which he was saturated from an early age. As Andrew Hook has shown, from the mid-1780s onwards the works of Reid, Beattie, and Stewart were brought to the colleges of Philadelphia, New Haven, and New Jersey.[36] By the end of the eighteenth century, Common Sense ideas had been largely assimilated into the whole range of American cultural and intellectual life. As a reaction against Humean scepticism, the theories of Reid and his followers had a special appeal for conservative upholders of religious orthodoxy. By the mid-1790s, the publication of Paine's *Age of Reason* (1794–5) had provoked a further moral backlash, and the philosophical outlook of many of the Scottish writers had been appropriated by conservative critics of revolutionary theory.[37]

Central aspects of the Scottish tradition were reflected in Brown's education, in which he profited from an immensely stimulating and self-critical environment based on two thriving centres of ideas, Philadelphia and New York City.[38] He was brought up in a Quaker household in Philadelphia, where his father's diary shows that books available for discussion included Bage's *Man As He Is*,

[35] Cajetan Tschink, *The Victim of Magical Delusion; or, The Mystery of the Revolution of P - - - - - - l: A Magico-Political Tale*, trans. Peter Will, 3 vols. (London, 1795), Preface, i. pp. i–iv, quoted in Warfel, 'German Sources', 365.

[36] Andrew Hook, *Scotland and America: A Study of Cultural Relations, 1750–1835* (Glasgow, 1975), 73–115.

[37] Paine, *The Age of Reason; Being an Investigation of True and Fabulous Theology* (London, 1794–5), went through seventeen editions in America in the mid-1790s; Foner, *Tom Paine*, 256.

[38] My account is indebted to Dunlap, *Memoirs*, 6–46; Warfel, *American Gothic Novelist*, 17–48; D. Clark, *Pioneer Voice*, 11–22.

Wollstonecraft's *Historical and Moral View of the French Revolution* (1794), and *Political Justice*. However, this open-mindedness does not necessarily indicate a radical political stance, as some critics have argued,[39] but rather points up the Quaker values of independent enquiry and intellectual curiosity. Brown was educated at Robert Proud's eminently conservative Friends' Latin School, and his subsequent choice of a legal career shows his conformity to the Quaker ethic of social usefulness. Philadelphia itself, described by John Neal in *Blackwood's* as the ' "ATHENS OF AMERICA" ',[40] was a busy publishing centre and a powerhouse of European ideas of all persuasions. In Philadelphia the books that had influenced Godwin in the formation of his philosophy were directly available to Brown, but so too were the works of the Common Sense philosophers beloved of American conservatives.[41] In this period Brown's interest in amassing and disseminating information reflects the characteristics of Scottish Enlightenment thought rather than Godwin's faith in man's potential for unlimited improvement through education. At the age of 16, for example, Brown joined several of his contemporaries in founding a Belles Lettres Club which aimed to bind together the 'whole circle of human knowledge', since 'the traits of resemblance . . . between moral and physical science are so many, so various, and so complex, that it is a task of no little labor and ingenuity properly to separate them'.[42] At the Club's first meeting, Brown made a firm distinction between intellectual improvement and progressive political theories: 'The idea of a perfect commonwealth is not the same extravagant thing in education as in politics. The settled depravity of mankind will never yield to the gentle admonitions of the wise.'[43]

Brown's career reached something of a turning-point in 1790 when he met Elihu Hubbard Smith, a brilliant medical student who

[39] Cf. Punter, *Literature of Terror*, 190.

[40] Neal, 'American Writers, No. II', 58.

[41] Hook notes the republication in Philadelphia of Robertson, *History [of] Charles V* in 1770; James Beattie, *Elements of Moral Science*, vol. i. (1790), vol. ii (1793), in 1794; Thomas Reid, *Essays on the Intellectual Powers of Man* (1785), in 1792; and Dugald Stewart, *Elements of the Philosophy of the Human Mind*, vol. i (1792), in 1793; *Scotland and America*, 78–9.

[42] Brown's inaugural address at Belles Lettres Club, quoted in D. Clark, *Pioneer Voice*, 43; cf. Hume, *A Treatise of Human Nature: Being an Attempt to Introduce the Experimental Method of Reasoning into Moral Subjects* (1739–40), ed. L. A. Selby-Bigge, 2nd edn., rev. P. H. Nidditch (Oxford, 1978), p. xix.

[43] D. Clark, *Pioneer Voice*, 44.

had imbibed the ideas of the Scottish Enlightenment from his teacher Benjamin Rush.[44] After completing his medical training in Edinburgh, Rush sought to give Common Sense theories of the mind a practical application in his pioneering work on mental illness, on which Brown drew heavily in *Wieland*. From 1793 onwards Smith introduced Brown to a wealth of new associates at the New York Friendly Club. In the same year Brown abandoned his legal studies to devote himself fully to literature. In New York he met some of the most talented men on the Federalist side, such as Timothy Dwight and John Adams's son Charles.[45] In their moral earnestness and political conservatism—Smith is said to have described Jefferson as 'Jacobinical almost to lunacy'—this talented group turned to Scotland as a centre of learning.[46] Smith kept a diary which indicates the remarkable breadth of their discussions, and his list of topics debated on 30 September 1797 shows their familiarity with leading Scottish thinkers: 'criticism on the political works of Harrington, Al: Sidney, Sir T. More, Hobbes, Locke, Hume, Adam Smith, Sir James Stuart . . . Godwin—on the metaphysics of Locke, Reid, Beattie, A. Smith, D. Stuart, Hume, Godwin . . .'.[47] When it came to discussion of 'novels and novel writing', Smith's notes from a meeting in late 1796 suggest a similar inclusiveness, ranging from Smollett, Fielding, and Richardson to the radical novelists Charlotte Smith, Holcroft, and Godwin.[48]

Given this predominantly conservative environment, it is hardly surprising that Brown's first published work reflects a divided response to the early optimism of British radicals. In *Alcuin: A Dialogue* (1797–8) he seems to present a relatively pure vision of a democratic society based on the writings of Godwin and Wollstonecraft. Parts I and II were originally printed as a book in 1798, then serialized in the *Philadelphia Weekly Magazine* with the subtitle 'The Rights of Woman'.[49] Although the publication of

[44] Benjamin Rush (1745–1813) was Professor of the Theory and Practice of Medicine at Pennsylvania University from 1789; see D. Davis, *Homicide*, 70–5.

[45] Dunlap, *Memoirs*, 46.

[46] Smith, unpublished diary, quoted in James E. Cronin, 'Elihu Hubbard Smith and the New York Friendly Club, 1795–8', *PMLA* 64 (1949), 477.

[47] Ibid. 474; the list includes Sir James Stewart, *Inquiry into the Principles of Political Oeconomy* (1767).

[48] Ibid. 476; Brown's journal shows his reading of Richardson, and French and German novels in translation, D. Clark, *Pioneer Voice*, 105, Warfel, *American Gothic Novelist*, 225.

[49] Robert D. Arner, 'Historical Essay', *A* 273–4; on *Alcuin* and the Quaker belief in sexual equality, see D. Clark, *Pioneer Voice*, 110–25.

Parts III and IV was announced in 1798, they never appeared in print until after Brown's death, which suggests the rapidity of his change of views in this period. The first section is made up of conversations between the revolutionary 'enthusiast' Alcuin and Mrs Carter, a moderate supporter of female equality. Its conclusions are imaginatively enacted in the second section, where Alcuin recounts his Utopian vision of complete sexual equality in the 'paradise of women' (*A* 34).

Considered as a whole, the dialogue illustrates the problems of containing revolutionary progress once it has begun. On the one hand it offers a straightforward Godwinian analysis of social despotism. But at the same time Alcuin's vision of a transformed society alarms Mrs Carter, even though it is largely her own invention. When Alcuin speaks of the absence of marriage, she takes refuge in a stereotyped conservative response: 'A class of reasoners has lately arisen, who aim at the deepest foundation of civil society. . . . The journey that you have lately made, I merely regard as an excursion into their visionary world' (*A* 52). Already Brown is aware of the disjunction between the ideal theories and practical achievement of the progressive thinker. While he acknowledges the usefulness of Alcuin's imaginative vision, he stresses the need for caution and external controls, since 'the worst judge of the nature of his own conceptions is the enthusiast' (*A* 36).

As in Tschink's warning of the 'deviations of fanaticism', this distrust of unregulated imaginative activity agrees in essentials with Common Sense warnings of the delusive power of the imagination. What is of special interest here is the support that the philosophical outlook of the Scottish writers gave to moral criticism of novel-writing, for a distinction should be made between the original doctrines and the way they were appropriated in America.[50] Responding to Hume's godless scepticism, Reid and his followers sought to re-establish the validity of perception by arguing for the objective nature of God-given reality. Thus they could be read as condemning the uncertainties introduced by the imagination, as Hamilton's exposition of Reid's thought suggests: 'a thing to be known *in itself* must be known as *actually existing* . . . A possible object, an *ens rationis*, is a mere fabrication of the mind itself.'[51]

[50] Cf. Terence Martin, *The Instructed Vision: Scottish Common Sense Philosophy and the Origins of American Fiction* (Bloomington, Ind., 1961), 57–103.

[51] Sir William Hamilton, *The Works of Thomas Reid, DD*, 2 vols. (Edinburgh, 1835), ii. 805, 810; Martin, *Instructed Vision*, 89.

Dugald Stewart subsequently spelt out the dangers to the intellect: frequently the imagination 'produces a youth of enthusiastic hope, while it stores up disappointment and disgust for our future years'.[52] This metaphysical argument could be readily appropriated by moral critics of fiction. Thus Samuel Miller, a guest of the New York Friendly Club during Brown's period of membership, condemned novels for presenting 'unreal and delusive pictures of life'.[53] Above all, it was the highly subjective, internalized mode of Rousseau's *Confessions*, with its lack of a clear-cut ethical dimension, that aroused conservative suspicions.[54] Scepticism concerning the mind's fictions led to a corresponding emphasis on the reading and writing of history as a healthy corrective.[55]

Given the problematic status of novel-writing in post-revolutionary America, Brown's claims for moral seriousness take on a specific defensive quality. In the Preface to *Wieland* he conforms to the current demand for the grounding of experience in external reality by insisting on the factual basis of extraordinary events. He claims 'historical evidence' for the use of ventriloquism, and refers the reader to an 'authentic case' parallel to the younger Wieland's delusion. Only when he has marshalled this verifiable evidence does he defend his use of a subjective mode for instructive purposes: 'it is the business of moral painters to exhibit their subject in its most instructive and memorable forms' (*W* 3).

In appropriating the Godwinian novel in the service of a conservative ideal of a literature of public engagement, Brown makes a singular contribution to the tradition of novelistic commentary on national events generally thought to be inaugurated by Maria Edgeworth in *Castle Rackrent* (1800) and by Scott.[56] When Brown invoked Godwin's fiction as a model of ethical purpose in his letter describing *Sky-Walk*, he also claimed that such intellectual narratives were 'unexampled in America'.[57] In Walstein's School of History' (1799), his major theoretical state-

[52] Dugald Stewart, *Works*, 7 vols. (Cambridge, Mass., 1829), iii. 212; Martin, *Instructed Vision*, 95.

[53] Samuel Miller, *A Brief Retrospect of the Eighteenth Century*, 2 vols. (New York, 1803), ii. 174.

[54] Cf. Henry Mackenzie, *Anecdotes and Egotisms, 1745–1831*, ed. H. W. Thompson (Oxford, 1927), 184.

[55] Martin, *Instructed Vision*, 73–4.

[56] For Scott's debt to Edgeworth, see General Preface, *Waverley Novels*, i, pp. xii–xvi.

[57] Brown, quoted in Pattee, 'Introduction' to *Wieland*, p. xx.

ment on fiction, he reaffirmed the writer's public duty when he attributed to Walstein's pupils the conviction 'that the narration of public events, with a certain licence of invention, was the most efficacious of moral instruments'.[58] This elaborate defence of the role of authorship invites comparison with earlier conservative efforts to establish the writer as a national spokesman in epic poetry. As a schoolboy, Brown planned epic poems on the exploratory voyages of Columbus, Pizarro, and Cortez, obviously desiring to emulate the grand designs of writers such as Timothy Dwight and Joel Barlow, who chose the epic mode to set out their visions of America's origins and progress.[59] In a review of Southey's *Joan of Arc* (1796), written several months after the publication of *Wieland*, Brown claimed that prose literature was an even more important vehicle for national commentary, for it alone could accommodate 'the statements of motive and the enumeration of circumstances' vital to 'beneficial truths'.[60] That this national purpose is already present in *Wieland* is evident from its subtitle. In this 'American Tale' Brown surveys the ills of an entire society, and offers a profoundly disenchanted view of the new promised land.

If Brown exploits Godwinian techniques to review the nation's condition, he also expresses deep dissatisfaction with their original radical tendency. In 'Walstein's School of History', a critical study of the first-person narrative, he formulates his distrust of Godwin's belief in the sanctity of private judgement. The shifting and ambivalent nature of his commentary shows the same mixture of commitment and scepticism towards Godwin's ideas that is characteristic of *Wieland* as a whole.

'Walstein's School of History'

Brown's major theoretical statement on fiction appeared in two parts in the *Monthly Magazine* for July and August 1799, after he had completed *Wieland*, *Ormond*, and the first part of *Arthur Mervyn*. At first glance, Brown might seem to echo Godwin's

[58] Brown, 'Walstein's School of History. From the German of Krants of Gotha', *MM* 1/5 (Aug. 1799), 335–8, and 1/6 (Sept.–Dec. 1799), 407–11, 407.

[59] Dunlap, *Memoirs*, 10; on conservative literary ideals of social commitment, see Elliott, *Revolutionary Writers*, 30–5, 45–54.

[60] Brown, review of Robert Southey, *Joan of Arc*, *MM* 1/3 (June 1799), 227.

theory of imaginative writing as set out in the unpublished 'Of History & Romance'. Like Godwin, Brown argues for the superiority of romance over history and seeks to redefine history in terms of insight into individual character. For Brown, however, trained in the principles of Scottish Enlightenment thought, it is the physician who provides a role for the moral writer to emulate, and scientists such as Buffon, Linnaeus, and Herschel who most successfully unite the insights of 'historian and romancer'.[61] Brown's interest in history owes more to the conservative defence of perceivable reality than to radical attempts to reappropriate the past. Unlike Godwin in the post-revolutionary decade, Brown shows little interest in depicting character in a historically specific context. Only in two fragments of uncertain date, 'Sketches of the History of Carsol' and 'Sketches of the History of the Carrils and the Ormes', does he directly engage with historical movements, and, if one accepts Warner Berthoff's argument for their composition after 1800,[62] this marks a significant shift of focus towards historical writing. But from 1798 to 1800, it is essential to Brown's public and national aims that his works have a recognizable present-day American setting.

Brown sets his discussion of the first-person narrative in a framework which brings to mind Robison's account of the Illuminati's methods of education. According to Weishaupt, the society's founder and university professor at Ingolstadt, each novice studies historical characters under the guidance of an exemplary mentor: 'The knowledge of human character is . . . of all others the most important. Characters in history are proposed to him for observation, and his opinion is required. After this he is directed to look around him, and to notice the conduct of other men' (*PC* 119). This gives a distinctively ambiguous resonance to Brown's account of Walstein, an imaginary high-minded teacher at a Continental university, who gathers around him a group of dedicated pupils.

The works of Walstein and his disciples seem to offer a suspicious blend of Godwin's and Rousseau's autobiographical

[61] George Louis Leclerc, Comte de Buffon, *Histoire naturelle générale et particulière* (1749–67); Carl Linnaeus, *Systema Naturae, Fundamenta Botanica, Genera Plantarum, Critica Botanica* (1735–8); William Herschel' (1738–1822), astronomer; 'Walstein', 336; Brown, 'The Difference between History and Romance', *MM* 2/4 (Apr. 1800), 252.

[62] Warner Berthoff, 'Charles Brockden Brown's Historical Sketches: A Consideration', *American Literature*, 28 (1956), 147–54.

modes. All have the same dangerous internal consistency: 'the same explication of motives, the same indissoluble and well-worn tissue of causes and effects, the same unity and coherence of design, the same power of engrossing the attention'.[63] Brown unfolds a subtle critique of autobiographical narrative which centres on its lack of ethical focus. The first part of the essay deals with the works of Walstein, who is dedicated to promoting human happiness through the representation of exemplary historical figures of great 'intellectual vigour'. His two works are minute explorations of the lives of Cicero and the Marquis of Pombal, ancient and modern statesmen.[64] Though conscious of the 'uncertainty of history', Walstein presents these models as worthy of emulation by all men. In order 'to illuminate the understanding, to charm the curiosity, and sway the passions of the reader', he argues that it is necessary to let the characters speak for themselves. So Walstein undertakes the hazardous task of making Cicero 'narrator of his own transactions', which might, Brown suggests, open the way for errors and incongruities. But, in the event, Walstein achieves an admirable 'imposture' which has an imaginative 'self-consistency' denied by the literal truth. This persuasive defence of a first-person narrative places imaginative consistency above mere factual accuracy, a priority shared by Godwin in his argument for the 'reality of romance'.[65]

Indeed, Brown goes so far as to pronounce Walstein's artful 'exhibition of talents and virtue' as of greater benefit to individual improvement than the actual lives of his subjects. For the fate of Cicero and Pombal, patterns of excellence who attempted to reform through the institutions of government and the law, only shows the 'insufficiency of the instrument chosen by them'. Instead the true benefactor of mankind should work towards a Godwinian 'change of national opinion' by 'assailing errors and vices, argumentatively and through the medium of books'.[66]

In the second part of his essay Brown develops this preference for individual improvement over systematic reform, exploring the potential for benevolent actions in everyday life. As a corrective to

[63] 'Walstein', 335.

[64] Ibid. 336; Sebastião José de Carvalho e Mello, Marquis of Pombal (1699–1782), was chief minister in Portugal from 1756 and an opponent of aristocratic and Jesuit influence.

[65] 'Walstein', 337, 338; Godwin, 'Of History & Romance'.

[66] 'Walstein', 337, 338.

Walstein's exclusive focus on public figures, he describes the activities of one of Walstein's most promising pupils, Engel. This younger author argues for the merits of fictitious models of virtuous conduct in ordinary life, since in the lives of general and statesman 'the temptations to abuse their power are so numerous and so powerful'. Here Brown seems in accord with Godwin's later scepticism about high-minded public aspirations, dramatized in St Leon's disastrous efforts for large-scale improvement. But his conclusion that 'governments and general education cannot be rectified' underlines his distance from Godwin's gradualist theory of political progress. Rejecting all possibility of institutional reform, Brown turns his attention to the limited good that can be achieved by individuals in an ordinary community, where 'every man is encompassed by numerous claims, and is the subject of intricate relations'.[67] The most important of these essentially political relations are matters of property and marriage, and the writer's task is to show the possibilities for benevolent action in support of these bulwarks of social order. Thus Engel plans an exemplary history of the 'intricate relations' of Olivo Ronsica, an entirely fictitious hero.

Brown's sketch of Olivo Ronsica's adventures draws on both the plot of *Caleb Williams* and prevailing notions of the Illuminati's methods of recruitment, anticipating the recurrent blend of the two themes in his subsequent fiction:

> Olivo is a rustic youth, whom domestic equality, personal independence, agricultural occupations, and studious habits, had endowed with a strong mind, pure taste, and unaffected integrity. Domestic revolutions oblige him to leave his father's house in search of subsistence. . . . He bends his way to Weimar. . . . He forms a connection with a man of a great and mixed, but, on the whole, a vicious character.[68]

This scheme of action is developed most directly in *Arthur Mervyn; or, Memoirs of the Year 1793*, a multiple first-person narrative in which the principal spokesman listens to Arthur's story of his energetic pursuit of benevolence, then introduces a debate on its authenticity. Here Brown's critical deployment of Godwin's first-person narrative establishes the technique used with greater sophistication in *Wieland*. Brown undercuts Engel's exemplary plan of action through the gradual revelation of Mervyn's unreliability as 'narrator of his own transactions'.

[67] 'Walstein', 408, 409. [68] Ibid. 410.

The novel's division into two parts creates further complications. *Arthur Mervyn*, First Part, was published in early 1799, but the Second Part did not appear until summer 1800, after the other three major novels.[69] As with previous divisions in *Alcuin* and 'Walstein', this suggests progressive stages in Brown's critique of Godwin, as he departs from one set of relatively sympathetic aims in pursuit of another more critical purpose. In the First Part, the tale is relatively straightforward. Arthur starts out as a mixture of Caleb Williams and Benjamin Franklin, a provincial hero 'willing to be guided by the advice of others, and by the lights which experience should furnish' (*AM* 9). He seems to have been intended as a portrait of natural excellence, initially unspoilt by society, by contrast with the sophisticated villainy of his patron Welbeck.

But in the Second Part Brown questions the sincerity of Mervyn's 'tedious but humble tale' (*AM* 16) by telling his story from a different point of view. This plunges Arthur's faithful listener into doubt: his conviction that 'the face of Mervyn is the index of an honest mind' is undercut by 'the unanimous report of Mervyn's neighbors' (*AM* 229–30, 232).[70] By juxtaposing several contradictory accounts, Brown alerts the reader to the implausibility of Mervyn's earlier innocence and to the unreliability of his Godwinian claims to frankness and impartiality. 'It is not necessary that I should stop every person that I meet in the street to inform him of my sentiments', wrote Godwin in his early discussion of sincerity (*PJ* iii. 305), but this is virtually what Mervyn does in the second half of the book. His enquiring spirit collapses into obsessive righteousness, and his indefatigable pursuit of benevolence breaks down social restraints in a comic manner: he is always entering other people's houses without knocking. Finally Mervyn emerges as a calculating opportunist, while the apparent villain Welbeck is revealed as the helpless victim of early poverty and his own irrational compulsions. Mervyn's confrontation with the wretched, remorse-stricken Welbeck points up his total self-preoccupation: 'Let me gain, from contemplation of thy misery, new motives to sincerity and rectitude!' (*AM* 334) Brown exploits the first-person

[69] The first nine chapters of *Arthur Mervyn* appeared in the *New-York Weekly Magazine*, June–Aug. 1798, then were published with the rest, Feb. 1799; Norman S. Grabo, 'Historical Essay', *AM* 451.

[70] Cf. Godwin's 1793 discussion of sincerity: 'the face, the voice, the gesture, are so many indexes to the mind', *PJ* iii. 294.

narrative to present an image of character and social interaction that completely subverts the optimistic assumptions of Engel's theory. It is this growing scepticism about the ethics of personal testimony that is captured in *Wieland*, which was written between the two parts of *Arthur Mervyn*.

The Transformation

Brown's use of an unreliable narrator to capture and baffle the reader's curiosity is central to his development of the Godwinian novel for conservative purposes. As in *Caleb Williams*, Brown's instructive aim does not involve programmatic statement, but rather acts on the reader through manipulation of point of view. What arrests the reader's attention is the filtering of the entire sequence of events through Clara's consciousness. Long sections of the novel dramatize the passing of a few moments in her mind, and this gives rise to the peculiar sense of proximity that is one of the strengths of Godwin's novels. As John Neal commented of Brown: 'His novels are not so much narratives, as they are dramas—long, continued soliloquies, which you are made to overhear, in your participation.'[71] Brown moves beyond Godwin, however, in emphasizing Clara's limited point of view, which reinforces his thematic interest in subjective delusion at a formal level. In the following passage, in which Clara returns to the room where she heard voices planning her murder, Brown exploits an authentic Gothic atmosphere to convey the confusion between imaginary and real that conservatives described as a consequence of revolutionary freedom:

> Suddenly the remembrance of what had lately passed in this closet occurred. Whether midnight was approaching, or had passed, I knew not. I was, as then, alone, and defenceless. The wind was in that direction in which, aided by the deathlike repose of nature, it brought to me the murmur of the water-fall. This was mingled with that solemn and enchanting sound, which a breeze produces among the leaves of pines. The words of that mysterious dialogue, their fearful import, and the wild excess to which I was transported by my terrors, filled my imagination anew. My steps faultered, and I stood a moment to recover myself.
>
> I prevailed on myself at length to move towards the closet. I touched the

[71] Neal, 'American Writers, No. II', 239.

lock, but my fingers were powerless; I was visited afresh by unconquerable apprehensions. A sort of belief darted into my mind, that some being was concealed within, whose purposes were evil. . . .

My fears had pictured to themselves no precise object. It would be difficult to depict, in words, the ingredients and hues of that phantom which haunted me. A hand invisible and of preternatural strength, lifted by human passions, and selecting my life for its aim, were parts of this terrific image. All places were alike accessible to this foe . . . (*W* 84–5)

Clara's isolated situation is strongly reminiscent of Radcliffe's Gothic plot: the heroine is alone in the dark, seemingly at the mercy of inexplicable fears.[72] What gives this scene its peculiar intensity is its analytical rigour, as Clara charts the collapse of external awareness into a subjective nightmare of fear and uncertainty. This process begins when the immediate data of sense-experience—the 'murmur' of the waterfall and the 'enchanting sound' of the breeze—irresistibly bring to mind 'that mysterious dialogue' of her earlier terrors. With this transformation of immediate sensations into remembered experience, she loses the ability to place herself in relation to the external world: 'My steps faultered'. This physical disorientation marks the loss of a coherent sense of self, which she struggles to regain: 'I stood a moment to recover myself'. She attempts to ballast herself by reaching out to solid objects—'I prevailed on myself . . . to move towards the closet. I touched the lock'—but she fails to connect inner and outer worlds: 'my fingers were powerless'. Instead the external world is completely blotted out by 'unconquerable apprehensions' which expand to fill her entire consciousness.

Scenes full of suspense like this make the reader far more than an observer: instead, he or she becomes a participant in the heightening tension and uncertainty, sharing in the plot's revelations. Like Clara herself, the reader can neither find a rational explanation for mysterious events nor dismiss them as superstitious phenomena. Developing Godwin's exploration of states of mind in which 'reason had no power' (*CW* ii. 141 [1]/154), Brown foregrounds Clara's unreliability as a witness. In a narrative full of unanswered questions, Clara asks: 'What but ambiguities, abruptnesses, and dark transitions, can be expected from the historian who is, at the same time, the sufferer of these disasters?' (*W* 147)

These 'ambiguities, abruptnesses, and dark transitions' centre on

[72] On Radcliffe's plot, see Moers, *Literary Women*, 134–8.

Clara's interaction with her brother Theodore and the mysterious interloper Carwin, as they too fall prey to subjective delusion and give their own limited versions of events, which contradict Clara's account. To point up the dangers of private judgement once it is released from institutional restraints, Brown exploits the theme of religious delusion. Theodore's religious mania, in particular, shows the underlying link between inherited 'enthusiasm' and revolutionary fanaticism.

Given Brown's conviction of the inextricability of public and private realms, his interest in abnormal states of mind deserves notice. In the passage cited above, he taps the resources of conventional Gothic fiction to analyse disturbed mental states, and throughout his novel-writing career he rejected Gothic paraphernalia in favour of naturalized images of terror. In the Preface to *Edgar Huntly; or, Memoirs of a Sleep-Walker*, he dismissed 'Puerile superstition and exploded manners; Gothic castles and chimeras', in favour of more realistic scenes of Indian atrocities,[73] but the real mystery in the novel is created by the hero's periods of somnambulism. As he wrote of *Arthur Mervyn* in February 1799: 'To excite and baffle curiosity, without shocking belief, is the end to be contemplated.'[74] Even the central incident of *Wieland* was based on a real event. According to the *New-York Weekly Magazine* in 1796, one Sunday afternoon in December 1791, a devout farmer living near New York had succumbed to religious mania and murdered his wife and children.[75]

A psychological frame is invoked to explain the disturbing events of *Wieland*. From his earliest writings, Brown made little distinction between moral and physical science, and sought to bring the same method of analysis to bear on both. Especially pertinent in this respect is the way that current psychological theories, based on Common Sense assumptions about the workings of the mind, could be turned to reactionary political ends, highlighting man's irrational potential and thus his need for external controls. Brown's interest in mental processes had been encouraged by the staunch Federalist Elihu Hubbard Smith, who had been taught by Benjamin Rush.

[73] Brown, Preface to *Edgar Huntly, Works*, iv. 3.

[74] Brown to James Brown, 15 Feb. 1799, Dunlap, *Memoirs*, 207.

[75] The parallel case of James Yates was reported in the *New-York Weekly Magazine*, 20 July 1796; Warfel, *American Gothic Novelist*, 104.

Although Rush was one of the original signers of the American Declaration of Independence, by the early 1790s he had defected from his early republicanism, and went so far as to characterize the 'excess of the passion for liberty' among his countrymen as a new 'species of insanity' to which he gave a clinical name, 'anarchia'.[76] Brown's explanation of Wieland's obsession is especially indebted to Rush's seminal essay, 'The Influence of Physical Causes Upon the Moral Faculty' (1786), where he argued that the mental faculties were, like the external senses, subject to physical disease.[77] In particular, the moral sense, imagination, and will, were influenced by involuntary factors such as environment and hereditary defects. Clara echoes this line of thought in her early speculation on Theodore's 'diseased condition': 'The will is the tool of the understanding, which must fashion its conclusions on the notices of sense. If the senses be depraved it is impossible to calculate the evils that may flow from the consequent deductions of the understanding' (*W* 35). This theory made it difficult to distinguish between a responsible and an irresponsible act, as in Wieland's insanity, where his insistence on the 'rectitude of his motives' (*W* 224) obscures his moral responsibility. In addition, Clara's uncle invokes Erasmus Darwin's classification of mental diseases in *Zoonomia* (1794–6) to account for Theodore's delusion (*W* 179). Brown's explanatory note refers to Darwin's definition of 'mania mutabilis', in which the patient substitutes 'imaginations for realities', focusing on a 'mistaken or imaginary idea' while carefully concealing 'the object of his desire or aversion'.[78]

Such attempts at clinical diagnosis only throw into relief Clara's conviction that 'Ideas exist in our minds that can be accounted for by no established laws' (*W* 87). It is this admission that the deeper processes of the mind may be inexplicable that has attracted many twentieth-century critics to Brown's novels.[79] Several scenes in the

[76] For Rush's early involvement with Paine, see Foner, *Tom Paine*, 74, 84, 136–8; *The Letters of Benjamin Rush*, ed. L. H. Butterfield, 2 vols. (Philadelphia, 1951), i. 462–7, 523, quoted in Foner, *Tom Paine*, 138.

[77] Cf. D. Davis, *Homicide*, 72–4.

[78] Erasmus Darwin, *Zoonomia; or, The Laws of Organic Life*, 2 vols. (London, 1794, 1796), ii. 356.

[79] See Fiedler, *Love and Death*, 142–61; Donald A. Ringe, 'Charles Brockden Brown', in *Major Writers of Early American Literature*, ed. Everett Emerson (Madison, Wis., 1972), 273–94; Norman S. Grabo, *The Coincidental Art of Charles Brockden Brown* (Chapel Hill, NC, 1981).

novel cry out for modern psychological interpretation: Clara dreams of being enticed into a pit and killed by her brother, while Wieland's first murderous impulse is to strangle his wife on his sister's bed. But his 'passion more than fraternal' for Clara makes him hesitate to execute judgement on her: 'Any victim but this, and thy will be done!' (*W* 185, 153)

Yet this exploration of family affairs owes more to Brown's discussion of the 'condition of a nation' than to exclusively private concerns, and it serves to highlight the full extent of his internalization of public concerns. Brown is not primarily interested in the isolated psychological occurrence, but in inherited conditioning. Though Clara challenges Carwin, 'Hast thou not made him [Theodore] the butcher of his family; changed him who was the glory of his species into worse than brute?' (*W* 197), the whole shocking tactic of the plot is to show that this is not the case. Instead Brown shows how the republic carries the seeds of its own destruction. The Wielands' rational idyll proves to be unstable from the start: their grandfather's rebellion against traditional expectations, and their father's pursuit of his imaginary God to America, set up the conditions which lead to disaster.

In his analysis of the disintegration of the Wieland family, Brown presents an imaginative reworking of conservative attacks on revolutionary philosophers as destructive of family ties in the name of universal philanthropy. Burke's classic presentation of the French Revolution as a parricidal drama in *Reflections* had already been transformed into narrative by Godwin in *Caleb Williams*, but this theme had a different, more disturbing resonance for American conservatives, recently separated from their parent country. Fears of retribution took on a new urgency in the wake of myths of intellectual conspiracy, fostered in part by Robison's *Proofs of a Conspiracy*. Sharing in this heightened fear of 'enthusiasm', Brown is especially drawn to Robison's account of the leaders of the Illuminati, who sought to mould man's inherent capacity for self-delusion to their own ends: 'What more contemptible than *fanaticism*,' wrote Weishaupt, 'but call it *enthusiasm*; then add the little word *noble*, and you may lead him [man] over the world' (*PC* 223). This pessimistic reading of human potential, the reverse of all that Godwin sought to cultivate in his readers, underlies Brown's critical portraits of high-minded intellectuals in *Wieland*. As he later commented:

Men are liable to error, and though they may intend good, may commit enormous mistakes in the choice of means. While they imagine themselves labouring for the happiness of mankind, loosening the bonds of superstition, breaking the fetters of commerce, out-rooting the prejudice of birth . . . they may, in reality, be merely pulling down the props which uphold human society, and annihilate not merely the chains of false religion but the foundations of morality . . .[80]

Crucial to Theodore's 'transformation' or 'illumination' through excessive self-reliance is the novel's Calvinist framework.[81] Godwin had already exploited theological rhetoric as an instrument of political coercion in *Caleb Williams*, but here Brown effectively combines suspicion of old and new religions to point up the disastrous consequences of revolutionary freedom. The fearsome quality of the elder Wieland's avenging God brings to mind the distrust of institutionalized religious tyranny, represented by the rituals of Roman Catholicism, in the eighteenth-century Gothic novel. But, at the same time, Wieland's attachment to an extremist Continental sect invokes the secret plots of the Illuminati. It is essential to Brown's critique of Godwin that freedom of conscience should entail more dangers than the despotism of established authority. Thus he emphasizes the exclusively personal character of the elder Wieland's faith: 'Social worship . . . found no place in his creed. . . . His own belief of rectitude was the foundation of his happiness' (*W* 11, 12). It is this reliance on inner light, unmediated by ecclesiastical institutions, that leads to Wieland's literal illumination when he burns to death.[82]

A generation later, Theodore's sole reliance on internal sanctions—'moral necessity, and calvinistic inspiration' (*W* 25)—makes him vulnerable to his father's irrational tendency. Theodore's rejection of all guidance but a private sense of rectitude leads him into the initial error of misconstruing Carwin's voices as supernatural commands. Encouraged by these signs of divine approval, he

[80] Brown, late diary entry, n.d.; D. Clark, *Pioneer Voice*, 190; cf. *PJ* i. 104.

[81] The novel's Calvinist setting, but not its political resonance, is discussed in Joel Porte, 'In the Hands of an Angry God: Religious Terror in Gothic Fiction', in G. P. Thompson (ed.), *The Gothic Imagination: Essays in Dark Romanticism* (Pullman, Wash., 1974), 42–64; on links with *Paradise Lost*, see Michael T. Gilmore, 'Calvinism and Gothicism: The Example of Brown's *Wieland*', *Stud. N* 9 (1977), 107–18.

[82] Cf. Scott's suspicion of 'inward light' as a rule of action, discussed above, pp. 87, 98.

becomes the victim of what Tschink called the 'deviations of fanaticism', and longs for 'direct communication' with the invisible world: 'the audible enunciation of thy pleasure . . . some unambiguous token of thy presence' (*W* 167). However, the voices ordering him to kill his wife and children do not come from Carwin, but are purely imaginary. Theodore's defence of his crimes shows a mind that has become logical to the point of automatism; and his account of his murder of his wife in defiance of 'the stubbornness of human passions' (*W* 172) brings to mind Godwin's notorious example of the workings of impartial justice in the first edition of *Political Justice*. Faced with the choice of saving archbishop Fénelon or his chambermaid from a fire, the truly rational thinker would save Fénelon because of his greater benefit to mankind, even if the chambermaid was his own wife or mother: 'What magic is there in the pronoun "my", that should justify us in overturning the decisions of impartial truth?' (*PJ* iii. 146, i. 128)[83] Similarly, Theodore rejects legislative restraints and appeals instead to an absolute concept of divine justice: 'Thou, Omnipotent and Holy! . . . I know not what is crime: what actions are evil in their ultimate and comprehensive tendency or what are good. Thy knowledge, as thy power, is unlimited. I have taken thee for my guide, and cannot err' (*W* 176). In the absence of external controls, Theodore invents his own rule of action modelled on his father's rituals of obedience to an unappeasable persecuting God. But these apparently divinely sanctioned commands prove to be completely warped by his own desires: his incestuous desire for Clara is displaced and enacted when he kills his wife on his sister's bed. Thus the unregulated operation of impartial justice destroys the Wielands' rational idyll and releases into the world a homicidal monster. Theodore's brief reign of terror enacts in miniature the feared disintegration of social order in the wake of the spread of revolutionary thought: 'It seems a prodigy,' wrote Robison. 'Yet it is a matter of experience, that the farther we do advance, in the knowledge of our mental powers, the more are our moral feelings flattened and done away' (*PC* 471).

Brown further dramatizes this anxiety that advances in knowledge have outstripped man's moral development through the activities of Carwin, the casual intruder into the Wielands' intellectual retreat, who provides a catalyst for its anarchic energies. A composite

[83] Cf. Godwin's later defence of this statement, *TP* 37–42.

villain, overloaded with competing significances, Carwin's late entry into the novel may indicate Brown's increased desire to point up his public argument. Carwin's actions show Brown's critique of speculative enquiry at its most direct. Through Carwin's unbridled and amoral curiosity, Brown travesties Caleb's governing compulsion: 'I scrutinized every thing, and pried every where. . . . I cannot justify my conduct, yet my only crime was curiosity' (*W* 205). Carwin's first appearance also suggests Brown's scepticism about Jefferson's ideal of a democratic nation of independent-minded farmers. In answer to Clara's 'airy speculations' about uniting 'progressive knowledge' with 'the practice of agriculture', Carwin knocks at the door dressed as a labourer but quoting poetry, and the 'exquisite art of this rhetorician' proves a major source of his fascination (*W* 51, 74).

Moreover, Carwin's role as a satanic intruder recalls Godwin's praise for men of great ambition and talents, as exemplified by Milton's Satan: 'great talents are great energies, and . . . great energies cannot flow but from a powerful sense of fitness and justice' (*PJ* i. 324). For Brown, by contrast, it is 'great energy employed in vicious purposes' that 'constitutes a very useful spectacle'.[84] Although Carwin is obviously indebted to Falkland's blend of high idealism and perverted values, his mysterious European past establishes him as one of the suspiciously competent '*Men of Talents*' (*PC* 477) who appeared in the aftermath of the Revolution.[85] Pleyel first encountered him in Spain, where he had undergone a '*transformation*' (*W* 67) into a Spaniard and assumed the Roman Catholic faith. Now a penniless wanderer near the Wieland estate, it seems that Carwin can change religion, nationality, and social status at will. In this respect he is an exemplary product of the subversive 'seminary of Cosmo-politism' (*PC* 102) feared by conservatives.

Carwin's 'great energy employed in vicious purposes' is figured most dramatically through his ventriloquism, which he exploits to feed his obsessive curiosity about Clara's personality. In keeping with Godwin's later suspicion of men of talents in *St Leon*, it is the misappropriation of scientific knowledge for personal gratification that Brown emphasizes. Carwin's gift may also owe something to Falkland's 'voice . . . supernaturally tremendous' (*CW* i. 12 [1]/7)

84 Warfel, *American Gothic Novelist*, 95.
85 Cf. Jane Tompkins, *Sensational Designs*, 52.

that deprives Caleb of his freedom, for it becomes an instrument of psychological domination over the entire Wieland household. What focuses Brown's pervasive critique of Godwinian autonomy is Carwin's sheer opportunism. As Carwin confesses to Clara: 'I meditated nothing. My views were bounded to the passing moment' (*W* 201).[86] This amoral expediency reflects a commonplace feature of the revolutionary villain in anti-Jacobin novels such as Isaac d'Israeli's *Vaurien* (1797) and Charles Lucas's *The Infernal Quixote* (1800).[87] The character of Rivers in Wordsworth's play *The Borderers* (1797–8) shows a similar predilection for abstract intellectualizing divorced from moral concerns. In the 'Essay Prefaced to the Early Version', Wordsworth draws attention to Rivers's 'irresistible propensities to embody in practical experiments his worst and most extravagant speculations . . . his perverted reason justifying his perverted instincts'.[88] Similarly, Carwin's irresponsible meddling travesties Godwin's faith in independent enquiry, unfettered by prescription and prejudice.

As in Theodore's apparent rejection of all guidance but his reason, this perversion of the intellect opens up the possibility that if men are released from external constraints, they may base their motives to action on uncontrollable instinct rather than impartial judgement. The fatal interaction of Carwin's unscrupulous scientific meddling and Theodore's over-disciplined intellect subverts Godwin's optimistic philosophy from all sides, unleashing widespread social destruction, and prefiguring the inescapable whirlwind of the monster's rage in *Frankenstein*. As Carwin admits: 'Had I not rashly set in motion a machine, over whose progress I had no controul, and which experience had shewn me was infinite in power?' (*W* 215–16)

The figure of the unscrupulous intellectual, blind to his own compulsions, haunted Brown's subsequent novels. There is some truth in John Neal's comment that 'his principal character is always the same—always Carwin—always an adventurer'.[89] Equally, his plot is always a variant on the master and servant, implicitly parent and child, relationship in *Caleb Williams*. That this bond also reflects his fascination with revolutionary plotters is clear from the

[86] Cf. *PJ* i. 68–9. [87] Kelly, *Fiction of the Romantic Period*, 59–64.

[88] Wordsworth, [On the Character of Rivers], 'Essay Prefaced to the Early Version' [1797–9], *The Borderers*, ed. Robert Osborn (Ithaca, NY, 1982), 67.

[89] Neal, 'American Writers, No. II', 241.

fragmented *Memoirs of Carwin the Biloquist*, begun as a sequel to *Wieland* but never completed.[90] Here Brown exploits the Godwinian plot to present a full-length study of the Illuminati's methods of education. Sharing Caleb's provincial origins, insatiable curiosity, and great ambition, Carwin attains the 'superior power' (*W* 259) he covets when he discovers his secret talent for ventriloquism. Later he meets a fascinating European named Ludloe who proceeds to indoctrinate him in the revolutionary 'system of deceit, pursued merely from the love of truth' (*W* 275). To this end, Ludloe has few scruples about exploiting ventriloquism as an instrument of political coercion: 'No more powerful engine . . . could be conceived, by which the ignorant and credulous might be moulded to our purposes' (*W* 263). Already seen in Carwin's disruption of the Wielands' rational idyll, the full destructive power of this abuse of exceptional talents is spelt out in the stranger's comments on the philosopher's stone in *St Leon*:

> The talent he possessed, was one upon which the fate of nations and of the human species might be said to depend. . . . It might be abused, and applied to the most atrocious designs. It might blind the understanding of the wisest, and corrupt the integrity of the noblest. . . . It might render its possessor the universal plague or the universal tyrant of mankind. (*SL* ii. 32–3)

Under the influence of Ludloe's schemes of 'Utopian felicity', Carwin fantasizes the replacement of corrupt humanity by a 'new race, tutored in truth' (*W* 277, 278). While recalling the destructive 'transformation' of the new American republic in *Wieland*, this project also looks ahead to Frankenstein's scheme to benefit mankind through the creation of a 'new species' (*F* 49). Brown and Mary Shelley come to share a disenchanted view of Godwin's 'probable conjecture' that the final dissolution of legislative restraints will lead to a rational Utopia in which 'every man will seek, with ineffable ardour, the good of all' (*PJ* ii. 529, 528).

On the whole, the disconcerting reversals of *Wieland* hold in check the movement towards revolutionary stereotypes implicit in the concept of Carwin, which is taken further in Brown's relatively static treatment of ideas in *Ormond; or, The Secret Witness*. More central to Brown's purpose in the earlier novel is the fact that

[90] Brown began *Memoirs of Carwin the Biloquist* in Aug. 1798 while *Wieland* was in the press, and published it in instalments in 1803; Alexander Cowie, 'Historical Essay', *W* 335–6.

Carwin's confession of his errors fails to account for Wieland's leap into madness. This utter failure of rational explanation is brought home by Brown's skilful use of narrative point of view, which presents a critical commentary on Godwinian enquiry from the inside. It is this subtle analysis of Clara's 'transformation', as she too is implicated in the family obsession with mysterious voices, that forms Brown's most powerful indictment of the 'erroneous and imperfect discipline' (*W* 5) of the Wielands' upbringing.

Watching her brother's mental disintegration, Clara exclaims: 'What was my security against forces equally terrific and equally irresistable?' (*W* 179) The answer Brown seems to give is that her rational education has in fact deprived her of the 'security' she seeks. Freedom from inherited precedent and tradition removes not only social controls, but stable mental structures of perception and judgement as well. This insight is depicted most graphically in Clara's withdrawal to her solitary house. Its modernity, a timber-built dwelling, simply designed, with no room for the secret passages and dungeons beloved of Radcliffe's novels, only reinforces Clara's lack of stable values, for it is the very emptiness of the Wielands' external world that makes them vulnerable to morbid fantasies.[91] Here Clara broods successively on the mysterious events of her father's death, her brother's obsessional tendencies, and her own legacy of possible madness, but mistakenly holds Carwin responsible for everything.

Clara's deep-seated fascination with her brother is especially significant. The psychological tensions of the novel's climactic scene confirm Brown's departure from a Godwinian exploration of the intrusion of a corrupt system on private life. In a meeting closely modelled on the final exchange between Caleb and Falkland, the insane Theodore comes to claim Clara as another victim. Already Clara has succumbed to a fatal empathy with her brother: 'Was I not likewise transformed from rational and human into a creature of nameless and fearful attributes?' (*W* 179–80) Nevertheless, she prepares to defend herself by killing him if necessary, but at the last moment her spirit of rational self-reliance collapses in a sense of transgression against a Falkland-like brother, 'thus supreme in misery; thus towering in virtue' (*W* 223). Similarly, Caleb comes to identify himself with his persecutor, claiming that it is he, and not Falkland, who is a 'cool, deliberate, unfeeling murderer' (*CW* iii.

[91] Cf. Hazlitt, 'Mind and Motive' [1815], *Works*, xx. 45.

296 [1]/323). Yet Brown does not share in Godwin's indictment of the 'system of nature' (*CW* iii. 285 [1]/320): instead it is the loss of an internal 'consciousness of rectitude' that leads to Theodore's suicide and Clara's mental breakdown (*W* 230).

It is equally crucial to Brown's revisionist purpose that this is not the end of the story. Three years later, writing from Montpellier, Clara produces a final chapter in which she criticizes her earlier 'infatuation and injustice' (*W* 235) in relating this history of disasters. Significantly, Clara's recovery is attributable to external factors, the apocalyptic burning down of her house and the geographical shift, and her new acceptance of human limitations forms the antithesis of Godwin's faith in internal renovation: 'I have not the consolation to reflect that my change was owing to my fortitude or to my capacity for instruction' (*W* 235). In his vision of America as blighted by an inescapable climate of transformation, Brown presents a return to Europe as the only 'method of cure' (*W* 235). Here Clara's mental balance is restored by a sense of established social rituals and traditions: 'My curiosity was revived, and I contemplated, with ardour, the spectacle of living manners and the monuments of past ages' (*W* 237). It is no accident that this 'cure' is recommended by Clara's uncle, who, as physician and friend, has watched over her during her illness. This well-travelled doctor proves the only effective replacement for the father-figures that have proved deluded. Finally the 'deviations of fanaticism' are controlled, if not banished, by medical science.

If Brown follows Godwin in offering a notional alternative to 'things as they are', then, the type of improvement he envisages could not be more removed from Godwin's faith in the individual's development of his or her own rational capacity, enacted through the provisional conclusion to *Caleb Williams*. By contrast, Brown's 'better . . . remedy' (*CW* iii. 286 [1]/320) involves a return to inherited values and sources of external authority and control. In *Wieland* he prophesies that the dissolution of institutional restraints sought by Godwin will only release uncontrollable individual energies and lead to widespread social destruction. For Brown it is this freedom from needful controls, rather than the repressive power of social institutions, which leads to psychic dislocation, and necessitates an equally violent 'cure'.

Although Brown's psychological exploration turns Godwin's rational philosophy on its head, his treatment of topical issues through family drama reaffirms the interdependency of public and private concerns that is the distinctive quality of *Caleb Williams*. Brown's use of competing first-person narratives shows the potential of the Godwinian novel as a form for critical revaluation of Godwin's ideas, strengthening its appeal for the second generation of Romantic writers. Although the shift to subjective concerns in later Gothic fiction is traditionally associated with *Frankenstein*, this intensified focus on mental states is already evident in *Wieland*. Nevertheless, it is the novels of Mary Shelley that show the most arresting development of Godwin's characteristic themes and techniques. In *Frankenstein* and *The Last Man* Mary Shelley gathers up the entire Godwinian tradition and enacts its concerns on a world-scale.

5

Frankenstein: Mary Shelley's Myth-Making

The Godwin School

> Did I request thee, Maker, from my clay
> To mould me man? Did I solicit thee
> From darkness to promote me?—
>
> *Paradise Lost*[1]

The epigraph and subtitle to *Frankenstein; or, The Modern Prometheus* (1818) signal Mary Shelley's challenging expansion of the Godwinian novel to incorporate major Western creation myths. To understand Mary Shelley's commanding position in the Godwin school, however, we must consider not only the early *Frankenstein* but also her ambitious formal experiments in her novels of the 1820s, *Valperga* (1823) and *The Last Man* (1826).[2] Until recently, critics of Mary Shelley's novels have focused on *Frankenstein* alone, and many readings have been conditioned by the autobiographical Introduction published with the revised text of 1831.[3] Although

[1] *PL*. x. 743–5; Mary Shelley read *Paradise Lost* and *Paradise Regained* in 1815 and 1816, *MSJ* i. 62, 89, 96.

[2] Mary Shelley's three later novels, *The Fortunes of Perkin Warbeck: A Romance* (1830), *Lodore* (1835), and *Falkner: A Novel* (1837), show an increased conformity to social and financial pressures and are not studied here.

[3] Mary Shelley, Introduction to *Frankenstein*, Standard Novels, No. 9 (London, 1831), reprinted in *F* 222–9. For a representative selection of modern critical views, see George Levine and U. C. Knoepflmacher (eds.), *The Endurance of Frankenstein: Essays on Mary Shelley's Novel* (Berkeley, Calif., 1979). Psychoanalytical readings include Harold Bloom, '*Frankenstein*, or The New Prometheus', *Partisan Review*, 32 (1965), 611–18, reprinted in *The Ringers in the Tower* (Chicago, 1971), 119–29; Lowry Nelson, Jr., 'Night Thoughts on the Gothic Novel', *Yale Review*, 52 (1963), 236–57; and see below, n. 12. More historical readings include Paulson, *Representations of Revolution*, 239–47; Mary Poovey, ' "My Hideous Progeny": Mary Shelley and the Feminization of Romanticism', *PMLA* 95 (1980), 332–47, reprinted in *The Proper Lady and the Woman Writer: Ideology as Style in the Works of Mary Wollstonecraft, Mary Shelley, and Jane Austen* (Chicago, 1984), 114–42.

there has been some attention to the original aims of the 1818 text,[4] Mary Shelley's role in Godwin's 'new school' has not been explored.

Frankenstein was dedicated to Godwin, and, for several conservative reviewers, its anonymous publication in March 1818 provided an opportunity to attack the entire Godwin circle. 'It is piously dedicated to Mr. Godwin, and is written in the spirit of his school', wrote J. W. Croker in the *Quarterly*:

> Mr. Godwin is the patriarch of a literary family, whose chief skill is in delineating the wanderings of the intellect, and which strangely delights in the most afflicting and humiliating of human miseries. His disciples are a kind of *out-pensioners of Bedlam*, and . . . are occasionally visited with paroxysms of genius and fits of expression, which make sober-minded people wonder and shudder.[5]

This defensive response highlights Mary Shelley's affinity with the Godwinian tradition of fiction, which had been brought to public attention again by the publication of *Mandeville*—dismissed by Croker as 'intolerably tedious and disgusting'—four months earlier.[6] Other reviewers surmised that *Frankenstein* had been written by Godwin or Percy Shelley, and drew parallels with Godwin's earlier novels. The *Edinburgh Magazine* declared that the novel was 'formed on the Godwinian manner', with 'all the faults, but many likewise of the beauties of that model', and compared its 'monstrous conceptions' with the 'wild and irregular theories of the age' also present in *St Leon*.[7] More receptive to the intellectual aims of the Godwinian novel, Scott compared *Frankenstein* and *St Leon* as novels which aimed 'less to produce an effect by the marvels of the narrations, than to open new trains and channels of thought'.[8]

While early reviewers recognized Mary Shelley's major intellectual allegiance, they also simplified it. The immediate association of *Frankenstein* with Godwin and Percy Shelley obscured the extent to which Mary Shelley offered an imaginative critique of Godwin's

[4] Poovey, *Proper Lady*, 112–33; Chris Baldick, *In Frankenstein's Shadow: Myth, Monstrosity, and Nineteenth-Century Writing* (Oxford, 1987), 30–62; Anne K. Mellor, *Mary Shelley: Her Life, her Fiction, her Monsters* (New York and London, 1988), 38–140.

[5] [J. W. Croker], review of *Frankenstein*, *Quarterly Review*, 18 (Jan. 1818), 382.

[6] [Croker], review of *Mandeville*, *Quarterly Review*, 18 (Oct. 1817), 176.

[7] Review of *Frankenstein*, *Edinburgh [Scots] Magazine*, 2nd ser. 2 (Mar. 1818), 253.

[8] Scott, 'Remarks on *Frankenstein*', *Blackwood's*, 2 (1818), 613–20, reprinted in *Scott on Novelists and Fiction*, 261.

concerns. In the 1820s Mary Shelley once again encountered the problem of gaining acceptance of her work in its own right. Although *Valperga*, an uncompromising study of fourteenth-century Italian tyranny, was admired by Godwin and Percy Shelley as an advance on *Frankenstein*, *Blackwood's* found in it 'no inspiration, but that of a certain *school*, which is certainly a very modern, as well as a very mischievous one'.[9] For the more liberal *Examiner* the novel's Godwinian themes only added to its merits, but there was still no attempt to discriminate between the works of Godwin and Mary Shelley: 'Like *Caleb Williams*, written by the father—*Valperga*, the work of the daughter, clings to the memory.'[10] At least one reviewer of *The Last Man* found it true to the 'genius of her family' in its expression of 'visionary theories', but did not read closely enough to appreciate its relentless undercutting of such theories.[11]

Despite this early recognition of Mary Shelley's intellectual commitment, twentieth-century critics have interpreted her relations with the Godwin circle largely in private terms. Mary Shelley's complex position as daughter of Godwin and Wollstonecraft, then wife of Percy Shelley and friend of Byron, has lent itself to readings which posit a psychological frame of reference, excluding both the intellectual stimulus provided by the Godwin school and her independent revaluation of these concerns. More ambitious but equally selective are feminist accounts of *Frankenstein* as a displaced enactment of specifically female experience, which depict Mary Shelley as the beleaguered heroine of her 1831 Introduction, and the tales as a nightmare of male aggression in the sexual, aesthetic, or political sphere.[12]

[9] Review of *Valperga*, *Blackwood's*, 13 (Mar. 1823), 284.

[10] [On *Valperga*], *Examiner*, 826 (30 Nov. 1823), 775.

[11] Review of *The Last Man*, *Monthly Magazine*, 1 (Mar. 1826), 333.

[12] Cf. Elizabeth Nitchie, *Mary Shelley: Author of Frankenstein* (New Brunswick, NJ, 1953), 140. Author-centred readings of *Frankenstein* include Moers, *Literary Women*, 90–110; Marc A. Rubenstein, ' "My Accursed Origin": The Search for the Mother in *Frankenstein*', *SIR* 15 (1976), 136–47; Susan Harris Smith, '*Frankenstein*: Mary Shelley's Psychic Divisiveness', *Women and Literature*, 5/2 (Fall 1977), 42–53; Barbara Johnson, 'My Monster/My Self', *Diacritics*, 12/2 (Summer 1982), 2–10. For more wide-ranging feminist readings, see Sandra M. Gilbert and Susan Gubar, *The Madwoman in the Attic: The Woman Writer and the Nineteenth-Century Literary Imagination* (New Haven, Conn., 1979), 221–47; Mary Jacobus, 'Is there a Woman in this Text?', *New Literary History*, 14 (1982), 117–41; Gayatri Chakravorty Spivak, 'Three Women's Texts and a Critique of Imperialism', *Critical Inquiry*, 12 (1985), 243–61.

It should not be forgotten that this focus on authorial experience begins with Mary Shelley's retrospective comments on her novel of 1818. After 1822 her journal, formerly remarkable for its privacy and self-restraint, highlights her mental reconstruction of her life with Percy Shelley as 'a tale, romantic beyond romance' (*MSJ* ii. 447). This suggests the initial impetus of *The Last Man* as a memorial to her former relationships with Percy Shelley and Byron, and it gives some scope for a reading of the 1831 Introduction to *Frankenstein* as a formal composition in which Mary Shelley, like Lionel Verney, the narrator of *The Last Man*, presents a selective and aestheticized version of the past, 'bringing forward the leading incidents, and disposing light and shade so as to form a picture in whose very darkness there will be harmony' (*LM* 193). As in Godwin's retrospective account of the aims of *Caleb Williams*, Mary Shelley's later emphasis on the overtly literary genesis of *Frankenstein* forms an essential part of its remaking as a Romantic text. In stark opposition to Godwin's view of man's rational potential, she dramatizes herself as the passive, Radcliffean heroine of her own tale, which bodies forth the 'hideous progeny' of private and involuntary experience: 'My imagination, unbidden, possessed and guided me' (*F* 229, 227).

If we remove *Frankenstein* from the biographical constraints of the later Introduction and restore it to the context of its first publication in 1818, the intellectual stimulus provided by the Godwin school offers a more accurate guide to Mary Shelley's aims. The reading lists in her journal from 1814 to 1817 provide ample evidence of her engagement with the literature and polemics on the French Revolution. She was saturated in her parents' writings from an early age, and reread them throughout her life. Her systematic study of *Political Justice*, *Caleb Williams*, and *St Leon* in 1815 was matched only by her continuous reading of Wollstonecraft's *Historical and Moral View of the French Revolution, A Short Residence in Sweden, Norway and Denmark* (1796), and *The Wrongs of Woman* (1798).[13] Her parents' ideas permeate her fiction. In her early years her intellect was trained and directed by Godwin, and despite the loss of personal contact after her elopement with Percy Shelley, Mary Shelley persisted in her father's regimen of daily study, blending literature with works of political,

[13] Mary Shelley read these works in 1814 and 1815, and again in 1816 and 1817, *MSJ* i. 85–93, 94–102.

historical, and scientific theory. Later, in the brief but immensely stimulating period with Percy Shelley and Byron, she developed the international perspective that is a consistent feature of her first three novels. After Percy Shelley's death it was Godwin again who offered criticism and encouragement, to the extent that he rewrote sections of *Valperga* before seeing it through the press.[14] As with Percy's revisions to *Frankenstein*, this has been viewed as an act of appropriation as much as assistance,[15] and it is certainly true that Mary Shelley later mapped her upbringing in terms of a shift from one challenging taskmaster to another: 'I was nursed and fed with a love of glory. To be something great and good was the precept given me by my father. Shelley reiterated it' (*MSJ* ii. 554). But there is little indication that she was intimidated by pressures to excel, as some critics have maintained.[16] Claire Clairmont's pointed remark seems to support this notion of an overbearing emphasis on literary fame: 'In our family . . . if you cannot write an epic poem or novel, that by its originality knocks all other novels on the head, you are a despicable creature, not worth acknowledging.'[17] Yet of all her family, Mary Shelley alone produced such a novel in the post-revolutionary period.

In the words of an early reviewer, the central event of *Frankenstein* forms 'one of those striking conceptions which take hold of the public mind at once and for ever'.[18] More recently, Chris Baldick has shown how the novel's imaginative boldness has established it as a modern myth.[19] But if the novel can be seen as the source for a range of later images and works, it also has a literary and intellectual history. The economical yet profoundly memorable plot derives its major preoccupations from the imaginative concerns of earlier Godwinian writers. The highly charged opposition of creator and creature re-enacts the complex bond of fear and fascination between Falkland and Caleb. In the earlier novel, Caleb is cast as a monster for daring to challenge Falkland's authority, but it is Falkland who becomes an inhuman tyrant. Mary

[14] Godwin to Mary Shelley, 14–18 Feb. 1823, Kegan Paul, *William Godwin*, ii. 277.

[15] Mellor, *Mary Shelley*, 68–9.

[16] Gilbert and Gubar, *Madwoman in the Attic*, 221–47; Poovey, *Proper Lady*, 119–21.

[17] Claire Clairmont, quoted in Mrs Julian Marshall, *The Life and Letters of Mary Wollstonecraft Shelley*, 2 vols. (London, 1889), ii. 248.

[18] Gilfillan, 'Mrs Shelley', 292.

[19] Baldick, *In Frankenstein's Shadow*, 1–9, 30–62.

Shelley builds on Godwin's use of the pursuit to destabilize moral values: in the complex equivocations of *Frankenstein*, the abandoned creature returns to challenge his monstrous father, and the pair act out a drama of enticement and threat that leads to widespread social destruction.

But Mary Shelley's critique of solitary ambition owes more to the sceptical treatments of benevolent ideals in *St Leon* and *Wieland* than to *Caleb Williams*. In *Frankenstein* as in *St Leon*, occult practices lead to moral isolation and the destruction of the family: 'I possessed the secret of eternal life,' recalls St Leon, 'but I looked on myself as a monster that did not deserve to exist' (*SL* iv. 27). As in Brown's treatment of public issues through the 'picture of a single family' (*W* 51), Mary Shelley exploits the first-person narrative as a means of internalizing public issues, moving away from the direct public engagement of the 1790s to explore the psychology of political leaders. In the potent image of the monster strangling Elizabeth on her wedding night, Mary Shelley draws on Brown's pivotal scene of murder on the marital bed, while the formal sophistication of *Frankenstein* develops the narrative complexity of *Wieland*. If Brown conflates Calvinist 'enthusiasm' with the conservative myth of the Illuminati, both of these dangerously self-sufficient outlooks are implicitly present in Frankenstein's troubled history. The earlier novelist's interest in patterns of psychological domination and submission, figured through the scientific motif of ventriloquism, takes on a newly menacing quality in Mary Shelley's preoccupation with automatism and galvanism.[20]

However, Mary Shelley's debt to the Godwinian tradition is not simply a matter of basic similarities in plot and technique: the novel's bold imaginative simplicity also makes available its challenging political and philosophical concerns. The stimulus provided by Godwinian writings in the 1790s does not fully account for the intellectual strenuousness of Mary Shelley's enterprise. To appreciate the sheer range and complexity of *Frankenstein*, we also need to take into account the decline of revolutionary ideals in the literature

[20] On 18th-cent. mechanical men, see Radu Florescu, *In Search of Frankenstein* (London, 1977), 55, 220–3; the experiments of the Bolognese physiologist Luigi Galvani were described in John Aldini, *An Account of the Late Improvements in Galvanism, with a series of Curious and Interesting Experiments performed before the Commissioners of the French National Institute, and repeated lately in the Anatomical Theatres of London* (London, 1803).

of the second decade of the nineteenth century. Mary Shelley's drive towards cultural revaluation reflects the central preoccupations of a disorientated age, and has more in common with the radical international perspectives of Byron and Percy Shelley than has been allowed.

The Decline of Revolutionary Ideals

To some extent *Frankenstein* presents a critique of the optimistic tendencies of Percy Shelley's thought, and Mary Shelley's entry in her journal for 25 February 1822 may be seen as an indication of her critical response to Romantic idealism: 'let me in my fellow creature love that which is & not < imagine > fix my < love > affections on a fair form endued with imaginary attributes' (*MSJ* i. 399).[21] However, Mary Shelley's scepticism is not confined to aesthetic and private concerns: instead she pursues this questioning of subjectivity into all categories of knowledge. If she stressed the value of exploring the cavern of the mind, carrying the 'torch of self-knowledge into its < inmost > dimmest recesses' (*MSJ* i. 400), in her fiction this forms no more than a starting-point for her formidable insight into the range of social, cultural, and political constructs which shape and control individual perception.

This questioning of earlier cultural certainties reflects a wealth of contemporary doubts about progressive theories of man's origins and purpose. Mary Shelley's pessimistic outlook has commonly been attributed to her private experience of bereavement and loss.[22] Even before the drowning of Percy Shelley in July 1822, her journal provides much evidence of depressive swings between periods of intense longing for literary fame and morbid preoccupation with 'lost hopes, and death such as you have seen it' (*MSJ* i. 395).[23] Yet her very next diary entry suggests a wider context for this dwelling on 'the shadowy side', for it points up her uncertainty about meaningful explanations of humanity's purpose. After reading Canto III of Dante's *Inferno*, she declared:

[21] Cf. P. D. Fleck, 'Mary Shelley's Notes to Shelley's Poems and *Frankenstein*', *SIR* 6 (1967), 226–54.

[22] R. Glynn Grylls, *Mary Shelley: A Biography* (Oxford, 1938), 47, 98–100, 110–13.

[23] Cf. Leigh Hunt to Mary Shelley, July 1819, Grylls, *Mary Shelley*, 110 n.

They say that Providence is shewn by the extraction that may ever be made of good from evil—that we draw our virtues from our faults—So I am to thank God for making me weak—I might say thy will be done—but I can never applaud the permitter of self degradation . . . (*MSJ* i. 396)

Although Mary Shelley's erosion of consoling systems of belief found its fullest expression in *The Last Man*, this profound scepticism is already evident in *Frankenstein*, where she reworks the orthodox Christian scheme of man's origins. In both novels Mary Shelley confronts the demise of hierarchical structures of thought. An age of revolutionary progress collapses into undifferentiated chaos: political and social constructs are blotted out by the arresting images of the vengeful monster pursuing his creator, and the invincible plague hunting down the human race.

Underlying this dissolution of meaning is Mary Shelley's pressing awareness of having lived through a period of unnerving revolution in politics and society. While writing *Frankenstein* between June 1816 and May 1817, she was reminded of events of the 1790s by the savage government response to renewed popular unrest, the Luddite disturbances of summer 1816, which ended in the hanging of six leaders, and the Spa Fields riot of December 1816.[24] A year earlier the final dramatic events of Napoleon's career had been played out, culminating in his defeat and the restoration of despotical governments in Europe. It was with some justification that Percy Shelley wrote in the Preface to *The Revolt of Islam*: 'those who now live have survived an age of despair'.[25] In their course of reading, the Shelleys sought an intelligible explanation of how the progressive ideals of the French Revolution had collapsed in despotism at home and abroad.[26] Thus they studied rational explanations of revolutionary excesses in the works of Godwin and Wollstonecraft, alongside sinister conservative myths of intellectual conspiracy in Burke's *Reflections* and Barruel's *Memoirs, Illustrating the History of Jacobinism*.[27] In addition, literary works of the

[24] Thompson, *Making of the English Working Class*, 627–8, 691–700; cf. Mary Shelley to Leigh Hunt, 2 Mar. 1817, *MSL* i. 29.

[25] Shelley, *Poetical Works*, 33.

[26] Gerald McNiece, *Shelley and the Revolutionary Idea* (Cambridge, Mass., 1969), 10–41; cf. Burton R. Pollin, 'Philosophical and Literary Sources of *Frankenstein*', *Comparative Literature*, 17 (1965), 97–108.

[27] See Ch. 3, n. 61; cf. Walter E. Peck, 'Shelley and the Abbé Barruel', *PMLA* 36 (1921), 347–53, and James Rieger, *The Mutiny Within: The Heresies of Percy Bysshe Shelley* (New York, 1967), 63–7.

past were open to historical appropriation, as Godwin had already demonstrated in his treatment of Milton's account of rebellion and creation in *Paradise Lost* (*PJ* i. 323–4).

Something of the human cost of these 'great and extraordinary events' was brought home to Mary and Percy Shelley in their personal experience of devastated Europe,[28] the final result of Napoleon's campaign as he retreated from Moscow in the wake of the Cossack advance. In 1814 their elopement trip took them through land ravaged by Russian troops only five months earlier. Mary Shelley wrote in the *History of a Six Weeks Tour* (1817), 'Nothing could be more entire than the ruin which these barbarians had spread as they advanced',[29] and she later incorporated this description of a war-torn countryside into *Frankenstein* to point up the devastating impact of the monster's crimes (*F* 186). The Shelley's second Continental trip in 1816 took them to Geneva, the birthplace of Rousseau, which prompted Mary Shelley to reflect on the course of 'that revolution, which his writings mainly contributed to mature, and which, notwithstanding the temporary bloodshed and injustice with which it was polluted, has produced enduring benefits to mankind, which all the chicanery of statesmen, nor even the great conspiracy of kings, can entirely render vain'.[30] It is no accident that Frankenstein is also 'by birth a Genevese' (*F* 27), although the novel suggests a more critical attitude to Rousseau than is conveyed here. The Shelleys travelled on to view the 'hollow shew of monarchy' (*MSJ* i. 134) at Versailles, the setting for early scenes in the revolutionary drama as described by Burke (*R* 164–70). This sense of momentous upheaval in all areas of life lay behind Percy Shelley's recommendation of the French Revolution to Byron as 'the master-theme of the epoch in which we live', and as a fit subject for epic treatment.[31] As early as 1812 Percy Shelley himself planned a novel, *Hubert Cauvin*, to be 'illustrative of the causes of the failure of the French Revolution to benefit human-kind'.[32] In August 1814 he began writing *The Assassins*, a political

[28] [Mary Shelley], *History of a Six Weeks Tour through a Part of France, Switzerland, Germany, and Holland, with Letters descriptive of a Sail round the Lake of Geneva, and of the Glaciers of Chamouni* (London, 1817), 18.

[29] Ibid. 19.

[30] Mary Shelley to [?Fanny Imlay], 1 June 1816, *MSL* i. 20.

[31] Shelley to Byron, 8 Sept. 1816, *PBSL* i. 504.

[32] Shelley to Elizabeth Hitchener, 7 Jan. 1812, *PBSL* i. 223.

romance based on Barruel's account of the Illuminati, but this was never completed.[33]

In the event, Mary Shelley alone succeeded in writing a fictional commentary on 'these portentous and monster-breeding times'.[34] Comparison with other literary responses to the decline of revolutionary hopes only serves to highlight the originality of *Frankenstein*. In political works and imaginative writings alike, visions of a secular revelation through the progress of science and reason gave way to premonitions of apocalypse.[35] This trend is commonly associated with the 1820s, which certainly saw an upsurge in images of catastrophe, depopulation, and decay.[36] But, in fact, themes of decline and fall took on a new resonance immediately after Napoleon's final defeat at Waterloo in June 1815.

Underpinning Mary Shelley's vision of universal fragmentation is the widespread decline of faith in revolutionary progress as 'nothing out of nature's certain course' in the first two decades of the nineteenth century.[37] For her potent images of monstrous birth and incurable disease, she returns to the revolutionary polemics of the 1790s. Lee Sterrenburg has argued that the monster imagery of *Frankenstein* reflects the stereotypes of anti-Jacobin propaganda, notably the characterization of Godwin himself as a demonic philosopher, and that the novel as a whole shows Mary Shelley's unequivocal rejection of her radical heritage.[38] However, while Mary Shelley's attitude to Godwin's thought was always deeply divided, her redeployment of revolutionary imagery shows a greater continuity with the Godwinian tradition than Sterrenburg

[33] *MSJ* i. 19; Percy Shelley used the myth of the Illuminati in his early novels, *Zastrozzi* (1810) and *St. Irvyne; or, The Rosicrucian* (1811).

[34] Robert Southey, *Sir Thomas More; or, Colloquies on the Progress and Prospects of Society*, 2 vols. (London, 1829), i. 18.

[35] My account is indebted to Laurence Goldstein, *Ruins and Empire: The Evolution of a Theme in Augustan and Romantic Literature* (Pittsburgh, 1977); Thomas McFarland, *Romanticism and the Forms of Ruin: Wordsworth, Coleridge, and Modalities of Fragmentation* (Princeton, NJ, 1981), 2–55; A. J. Sambrook, 'A Romantic Theme: The Last Man', *Forum for Modern Language Studies*, 2 (1966), 25–33.

[36] See below, pp. 191–3.

[37] Wordsworth, *The Prelude* (1805), ix. 253, *The Prelude, 1799, 1805, 1850*, ed. Jonathan Wordsworth, M. H. Abrams, and Stephen Gill (New York and London, 1979).

[38] Lee Sterrenburg, 'Mary Shelley's Monster: Politics and Psyche in *Frankenstein*', in Levine and Knoepflmacher (eds.), *The Endurance of Frankenstein*, 143–71.

allows. Like Godwin, Mary Shelley reworks images of revolutionary transgression in conservative writings to highlight the social origins of monstrous deeds.

In *Reflections*, as well as exploiting the images of parricidal transgression noted earlier, Burke drew on images of monstrosity and disease to bring home the revolutionaries' perversion of the natural order. Especially influential was his use of the Comte de la Tour du Pin's account of the activities of the Parisian militia, which threatened to create a military democracy, that 'species of political monster, which has always ended by devouring those who have produced it' (*R* 333). At the start of *Letters on a Regicide Peace* (1796), Burke claimed that this prophecy of a cannibalistic 'republic of regicide' had been fulfilled:

> Out of the tomb of the murdered monarchy in France has arisen a vast, tremendous, unformed spectre, in a far more terrific guise than any which ever yet have overpowered the imagination, and subdued the fortitude of man. . . . The poison of other states is the food of the new republic.[39]

Barruel further exploited this notion of devouring offspring when he declared that the French Revolution had proved itself 'a true child of its parent sect [the Illuminati]; its crimes have been its filial duty'.[40]

Godwin and Wollstonecraft, however, turned Burke's early imagery of physical deformity back on itself to subvert his entire notion of hierarchical society based on the 'method of nature' (*R* 120). For Godwin it was paternal tyranny rather than filial rebellion that dislocated man from his true potential and created the monstrous. In *Political Justice* he used images of monstrosity to convey the psychological distortions induced by 'things as they are'. Thus the man who resigns himself to a state of passive obedience is no more than an 'abortion', a 'brute', and the 'most mischievous and pernicious of animals' (*PJ* i. 457, 232).[41] Refuting optimistic thinkers such as Leibniz, he drew attention to the physical deterioration of victims of ignorance and superstition: 'Observe the traces of stupidity, of low cunning . . . of withered hope, and narrow selfishness, where the characters of wisdom, independence and disinterestedness, might have been inscribed' (*PJ* i. 457). But it

[39] Burke, *Letters on the Proposals for Peace with the Regicide Directory of France* [1796], *Works*, v. 256.

[40] Barruel, *Memoirs*, i, p. xvi.

[41] Cf. entry for 28 Aug. 1814, *MSJ* i. 21.

was Wollstonecraft who provided her daughter with the most imaginatively succinct reinterpretation of conservative imagery when she openly declared that monstrous offspring are the products of an oppressive system: 'whilst despotism and superstition exist, the convulsions, which the regeneration of man occasions, will always bring forward the vices they have engendered, to devour their parents'.[42]

This emphasis on the potentially uncontrollable aspects of nature was taken up by later writers. Although Burke described revolutionary theories as a virulent 'plague' of 'epidemical fanaticism', he did not doubt that 'precautions of the most severe quarantine' would lessen the danger (*R* 262, 185).[43] By contrast, writers in the Shelley group emphasized man's inability to control nature, a theme already implicit in *St Leon*, where the harvest in Soleure, the family's Swiss pastoral retreat, is ruined by a storm which also sweeps away Marguerite's belief in the 'immoveable basis' of man's harmonious bond with nature (*SL* i. 40). Moreover, this suspicion of a hostile nature seemed to be confirmed by historical events, as in Napoleon's catastrophic reversal of fortunes at Moscow, which he himself is said to have attributed to malevolent external forces:

> the obstacles that made me fail did not come from men; they all came from the elements. In the south, the sea has been my undoing; in the north, the burning of Moscow and the cold of winter. Thus water, air, and fire, all of Nature, nothing but Nature—these have been the enemies of a universal regeneration which Nature herself demanded! The problems of Providence are insoluble.[44]

This sense of nature's belittlement of man's political ambitions, pervasive in Mary Shelley's novels, gives a historically specific meaning to her use of earlier traditions of cultural fragmentation.

Like other works by Byron and Percy Shelley in this period, *Frankenstein* presents a secular version of eighteenth-century cultural surveys. Throughout the eighteenth century optimistic Enlightenment thought was undercut by a powerful undercurrent which denied all worldly values. In an orthodox Christian

[42] Mary Wollstonecraft, *An Historical and Moral View of the Origin and Progress of the French Revolution, and the Effect it has Produced in Europe*, 1 vol. only, facsimile reprint of 2nd edn. (1795), introd. Janet Todd (New York, 1975), 259.

[43] Cf. Susan Sontag, *Illness as Metaphor* (New York, 1978), 81.

[44] Napoleon Buonaparte, in *Conversations with Las Cases* (1816), quoted in Melvin J. Lasky, *Utopia and Revolution: On the Origins of a Metaphor* (Chicago, 1976), 481.

perspective, the more the Enlightenment built for the future, the more it invited punishment by its emphasis on man's invincibility. As in Michael's prophecy of the Deluge in *Paradise Lost* (xi. 742–54), the world was to be punished by catastrophe so that it could be rebuilt in glory. In Edward Young's *The Last Day* (1713) and *Night Thoughts* (1742–6), seeing nature as a universe of death was a way of achieving spiritual pre-eminence over it.[45] Thus Jean-Baptiste Cousin de Grainville, a priest of the *ancien régime* and a critic of the *philosophes*, could develop the theme of world catastrophe for highly orthodox theological ends. In his novel, *Le Dernier Homme* (1805), translated anonymously as *The Last Man; or, Omegarus and Syderia*, Grainville prophesied a predominantly secular exhaustion of the planet, but also offered a vision of repopulation based on scriptural precedents.[46]

While indebted to these earlier images of catastrophe, the Shelleys' international and ultimately global outlook reflects the influence of more optimistic trends in Enlightenment thought. This bred a series of secular Utopias; Louis-Sebastian Mercier's *L'An 2440* (1770), for instance, offered a sketchy precedent for Godwin's vision of a world regenerated by reason at the end of *Political Justice*.[47] A far more influential analysis of cultural decay was provided by the French rationalist, the Comte de Volney, in *The Ruins; or, A Survey of the Revolutions of Empires* (1791). Structured as a secular apocalypse, the *Ruins* highlights man's capacity to transcend historical alienation through rational debate. As a militantly anti-Christian, optimistic account of revolutionary change, it gained great popularity among radicals in the 1790s.[48] Its Utopian qualities had an even greater imaginative appeal for liberal thinkers of the next generation, faced with the problem of the historical defeat of revolutionary ideals.

Mary Shelley drew extensively on Volney's version of history in both *Frankenstein* and *The Last Man*. The later novel is full of Volney's haunting images of decayed civilizations and depopulated landscapes, while in *Frankenstein*, the *Ruins* is cited as a work of reference in the monster's story of his education. Mary Shelley

45 See Goldstein, *Ruins and Empire*, 73–81.

46 Jean-Baptiste François Xavier Cousin de Grainville, *Le Dernier Homme*, privately published (Paris, 1805), anonymously trans. as *The Last Man; or, Omegarus and Syderia: A Romance in Futurity* (London, 1806).

47 Sambrook, 'Romantic Theme', 25.

48 Thompson, *Making of the English Working Class*, 98–9.

draws on two major aspects of Volney's thought. First, Volney's account of orthodox Christianity as a myth based on projected human wishes and fears, which can then be exploited to uphold paternal despotism, provides the key to her systematic reworking of *Paradise Lost*. In addition, she develops Volney's critique of man's encroachment on nature as the origin of political tyranny: in *Frankenstein* as in *The Last Man*, moral error is equated with the rational achievements of empirical science.[49]

To counterbalance this view of the development of society as a chain of tyrannies, Volney makes an appeal to divinely appointed legislators, whose belief in shared 'eternal and immutable laws' form the basis for his myth of an eternal state (*RE* 84). This essentially optimistic conclusion inspired Percy Shelley's review of post-revolutionary Europe in *The Revolt of Islam*, which posits an alternative to legitimate despotism and an antidote to revolutionary despair in the psychological 'Temple of the Spirit' (xii. 41).[50] However, unlike Percy, Mary Shelley remains profoundly sceptical about Volney's faith in the ultimate triumph of reason.

Contemporary scientific speculations about the world's origins gave further support to Volney's critique of paternal despotism, for they too challenged the orthodox view of creation derived from Genesis. Mary and Percy Shelley's scepticism concerning man-made schemes of order was powerfully reinforced by their shared interest in evolutionary processes. The works of Erasmus Darwin in particular, *The Botanic Garden* (1791), *Zoonomia,* and *The Temple of Nature* (1803), opened up an alternative to Godwin's theory of man's progressive improvement through the unconstrained operation of reason.[51] Though Darwin remained optimistic about man's prospects, he also argued that evolution would continue by its own inherent activity, once begun, and his notes on the struggle for existence and sexual competition prefigure the darker view of natural selection to be developed by Charles Darwin in *The Origin of Species* (1859).

[49] See Patrick J. Callahan, '*Frankenstein*, Bacon and the "Two Truths" ' *Extrapolation,* 14/1 (Dec. 1972), 39–48; Percy Shelley read Bacon's *Novum Organum* in 1815, *MSJ* i. 92.

[50] Cf. Kenneth Neill Cameron, 'A Major Source of *The Revolt of Islam*', *PMLA* 56 (1941), 175–206.

[51] Percy Shelley ordered copies of Darwin's *Zoonomia* and *The Temple of Nature* in Dec. 1812, *PBSL* i. 342, 345; see Brian W. Aldiss, *Billion Year Spree: The History of Science Fiction* (London, 1973), 8–35.

The notion that mankind is merely one more transitory element in the world's evolution was more immediately present in the geological theories of Cuvier and Laplace, discussed at length in the *Edinburgh Review* in 1814.[52] On the basis of their study of geological formations, including fossils which showed evidence of the extinction of species, they argued for the world's origin in successive catastrophes. In highlighting the irregular and arbitrary features of natural phenomena, they refuted the account of the Deluge in Genesis, and confounded Thomas Burnet's geological hypothesis of a controlling divine purpose in his *The Sacred Theory of the Earth* (1681–9).[53] Even Godwin acknowledged the force of convulsion theories, which he invoked in *Political Justice* to refute optimistic accounts of God's controlling purpose. The possibility of the end of the world surfaces at intervals throughout a work often criticized as unrealistically Utopian: 'The human species seems to be but, as it were, of yesterday. Will it continue forever? The globe we inhabit bears strong marks of convulsion ... vicissitude, therefore, rather than unbounded progress, appears to be the characteristic of nature' (*PJ* i. 453). The Shelleys were also familiar with the works of Saussure, the Genevan geologist, though it was Buffon's better-known *Théorie de la terre* that captured Percy Shelley's imagination after his trip to the source of the Arveiron in July 1816.[54] In a letter to Peacock he commented on the inevitability of the earth's degeneration, as shown by the 'slow but irresistible' ravage of the glacier advancing into the valley: 'I will not pursue Buffons sublime but gloomy theory, that this earth which we inhabit will at some future period be changed into a mass of frost.'[55] Buffon's vision of the gradual encroachment of a new ice age gives a specific urgency to Frankenstein's final pursuit of the

[52] Reviews of Georges Cuvier, 'Essay on the Theory of the Earth', trans. from the French by R. Kerr (Edinburgh, 1813), and Pierre Simon, Marquis de Laplace, 'Essay philosophique sur les probabilités' (Paris, 1814), *Edinburgh Review*, 22 (Jan. 1814), 454–75, and 23 (Sept. 1814), 320–40.

[53] On Burnet's theory, see Stephen Jay Gould, *Time's Arrow, Time's Cycle: Myth and Metaphor in the Discovery of Geological Time* (1987; Harmondsworth, 1988), 21–59.

[54] Horace Bénédict de Saussure, *Voyages dans les Alpes*, 4 vols. (1779–96), mentioned by Shelley to Peacock, 22 July–2 Aug. 1816, *PBSL* i. 499; Georges Louis Leclerc, Comte de Buffon, *Théorie de la terre*, in his *Histoire naturelle générale et particulière* (1749–67), vol. i, read by Mary Shelley in June 1817, *MSJ* i. 174–6; cf. *MSJ* i. 112–21.

[55] Shelley to Peacock, 22 July–2 Aug. 1816, *PBSL* i. 498–9.

monster to the North Pole: time is running out from the start of Frankenstein's narrative, told to Walton aboard a ship locked in Arctic ice. 'We are still surrounded by mountains of ice, still in imminent danger of being crushed in their conflict', writes Walton after Frankenstein's tale has ended (*F* 211), and it is only when he resolves to abandon the expedition that the ship is released.

It was Byron rather than Percy Shelley, however, who shared Mary Shelley's apocalyptic tendencies, as he too made extensive use of current scientific theories to support a pessimistic imaginative vision. Byron was so impressed by Cuvier's notion of successive creations that he presented it as an alternative to the Christian scheme in the Preface to *Cain* (1821), and his allusions to Cuvier in *Don Juan* (1819–24) give an apocalyptic tinge to the narrator's sense of worldly transience.[56] Moreover, Cuvier's 'Essay on the Theory of the Earth', translated and reviewed as early as 1814, also stimulated Byron's entirely secular vision of world catastrophe in 'Darkness', which was composed at the same time as the early chapters of *Frankenstein* at Diodati in 1816. A comfortless sketch of planetary decay, this poem gained high praise in early reviews: the *Literary Gazette* welcomed it as 'the finest specimen we have hitherto had of his Lordship's abilities', and made comparisons with Dante.[57] What Byron emphasizes is the end of all possibility of human relationship: 'men forgot their passions in the dread | Of this their desolation . . . no love was left' (ll. 7–8, 41). As in Frankenstein's final pursuit of the monster to the barren polar regions, distinctions of human individuality fall away. Finally nothing remains but the overwhelming presence of the material world, devoid of animation: 'Seasonless, herbless, treeless, manless, lifeless | . . . a chaos of hard clay' (ll. 70–1).

Already in 1816, then, cultural pessimism is a key feature of the radical tradition, and Mary Shelley's development of this global theme suggests her continuity with rather than disruption of the central concerns of Byron and Percy Shelley. But Mary Shelley alone exploits the novel as a myth-making form which is capable of critical scrutiny of political ideals. In *Frankenstein* she expands Godwin's characteristic blend of philosophy and fiction to present

[56] Byron, Preface to *Cain: A Mystery* (1821), *Poetical Works*, 521; *Don Juan* (1819–24), ix. 36–7.

[57] *London Literary Gazette*, quoted in Sambrook, 'Romantic Theme', 29.

an uncompromising critique of optimistic myths of revolutionary change.

The Modern Prometheus

Percy Shelley's apparently innocuous statement in the 1818 Preface to *Frankenstein* highlights the aspects of the novel it seems designed to conceal: he identified the work's 'chief concern' as

> the exhibition of the amiableness of domestic affection, and the excellence of universal virtue. The opinions which naturally spring from the character and situation of the hero are by no means to be conceived as existing always in my own conviction; nor is any inference justly to be drawn from the following pages as prejudicing any philosophical doctrine of whatever kind. (*F* 7)

Certainly *Frankenstein*'s first reviewers were not convinced by this disclaimer. Seizing on the novel's dedication to the author of *Political Justice* and *Caleb Williams*, the revisionary subtitle, and the epigraph from *Paradise Lost*, they were quick to recognize the work's 'incongruity ... with our established and most sacred notions'.[58] For this juxtaposition of allusions alone signals Mary Shelley's provocative fictional aims: she recasts the Godwinian plot as a creation story, reworking both the Greek and Roman myth of Prometheus and the Judaeo-Christian myth as mediated by *Paradise Lost*, and adding a critical commentary on Godwin's rational account of social origins in *Political Justice*.

It is no accident that these accounts may be read in terms of rebellion as well as creation, conveying Mary Shelley's suspicion of Utopian enactments of revolutionary change. Through the use of mythic parallels in a context which undermines their original significance, Mary Shelley establishes a broader cultural and historical setting for her critical assessment of present-day revolutionary events. Indeed, the subtitle and setting of *Frankenstein* explicitly invoke the careers of the revolutionary leaders, Rousseau and Napoleon. Although it is the myth of the 'Modern Prometheus' as Romantic artist that has attracted critical attention in recent years, the novel's first readers would have recognized the topical

[58] Review of *Frankenstein*, *Edinburgh [Scots] Magazine*, 253.

identification of Prometheus with both Rousseau and Napoleon.[59] For the anonymous critic of the *Edinburgh Magazine*, the extravagance of *Frankenstein* reflected the 'stupendous drama' of the Napoleonic Wars, in which 'the events which have actually passed before our eyes have made the atmosphere of miracles that in which we most readily breathe'.[60] Mary Shelley was undoubtedly familiar with Napoleon's reappropriation of classical myth, for she read the *Manuscrit venu de St. Hélène* (1817), a literary hoax which purported to be Napoleon's own review of his victories and defeats.[61] 'A new Prometheus, I am nailed to a rock to be gnawed by a vulture. Yes, I have stolen the fire of Heaven and made a gift of it to France', Napoleon is said to have written while in exile.[62]

Mary Shelley's invocation of Rousseau and Napoleon as modern Prometheans invites further comparison with Byron's analysis of failed revolutionary leaders in Canto III of *Childe Harold*, completed and read to the others at Diodati in 1816. Here the narrator's tour of the battlefields of Europe leads him to view the chaotic aftermath of the French Revolution in terms of the equivocal features of its leaders, imaged through Prometheus's gift of fire to humankind. While he attributes Napoleon's dual role as 'Conquerer and captive of the earth' to a Promethean 'fire | And motion of the soul' which leads 'Beyond the fitting medium of desire' (iii. 37, 42), he describes Rousseau's extreme sensibility, which was commonly held responsible for the French Revolution, in terms of the uncontrollable natural phenomenon of lightning:

> His love was passion's essence:—as a tree
> On fire by lightning, with ethereal flame
> Kindled he was, and blasted. (iii. 78)

Initially fascinated by the power of lightning, Frankenstein similarly comes to experience its full destructive force: 'I am a blasted tree' (*F* 35, 158). With this fatal mixture of creativity and destruction, the

[59] On Prometheus and the Romantic artist, see Bloom, '*Frankenstein*', and Christopher Small, *Ariel Like a Harpy: Shelley, Mary, and Frankenstein* (London, 1972); cf. Edward Duffy, *Rousseau in England: The Context for Shelley's Critique of the Enlightenment* (Berkeley, Calif., 1979), 73–4, 112–13.

[60] *Edinburgh [Scots] Magazine*, 249.

[61] *MSJ* i. 100 and n.; [J. Fréderic Lullin de Châteauvieux], *Manuscrit venu de St Hélène d'une manière inconnue* (1817), claimed to be the autobiography of Napoleon.

[62] Buonaparte, quoted in Lasky, *Utopia and Revolution*, 481.

Promethean activity of Napoleon and Rousseau bears directly on the course of recent history:

> good with ill they also overthrew,
> Leaving but ruins, wherewith to rebuild
> Upon the same foundation, and renew
> Dungeons and thrones, which the same hour refill'd
> As heretofore, because ambition was self-will'd. (iii. 82)

Mindful of these equivocal images of revolutionary activity, Mary Shelley exploits the dual resonance of the original Prometheus legend along with the Christian myth of rebellion and forbidden knowledge used in earlier Godwinian narratives. As both creator of man out of clay, and fire-stealer who defied the gods' tyranny over mankind and was then punished, Prometheus offered a fitting emblem for the losses and gains of revolutionary aspiration in early nineteenth-century writings.[63] While drawn to the Prometheus myth as a subject for poetry, Byron and Percy Shelley rejected Prometheus's ambition and emphasized instead his resistance to oppression and exemplary fortitude. As Byron put it in 'Prometheus' (1815): 'Thy Godlike crime was to be kind, | To render with thy precepts less | The sum of human wretchedness, | And strengthen Mankind with his own mind' (ll. 35–8).[64] But Mary Shelley's use of fiction gives greater scope for the conflation of mythic archetypes: the novel's competing narratives invite us to construe Frankenstein's activity as both rebellion and tyranny. In appropriating creative powers, Frankenstein re-enacts Prometheus's theft of fire and Satan's rebellion, but in the subsequent rejection of his creation he re-enacts the tyranny of Zeus and God.[65] Like Frankenstein himself, the monster is cast as victim and oppressor, and his reading of *Paradise Lost* confuses rather than clarifies the issue:[66]

> Like Adam, I was created apparently united by no link to any other being in existence; but . . . he had come forth from the hands of God a

[63] Judith Shklar, *After Utopia: The Decline of Political Faith* (Princeton, NJ, 1957), 53–7.

[64] Cf. Percy Shelley's internalized treatment of classical myth in *Prometheus Unbound* (1820).

[65] Paul A. Cantor, *Creature and Creator: Myth-Making and English Romanticism* (Cambridge, 1984), 103–9.

[66] See also Leslie Tannenbaum, 'From Filthy Type to Truth: Miltonic Myth in *Frankenstein*', *Keats–Shelley Journal*, 26 (1977), 101–13.

perfect creature, happy and prosperous, guarded by the especial care of his Creator ... but I was wretched, helpless, and alone. Many times I considered Satan as the fitter emblem of my condition ... (*F* 125)

It is a short step from this blurring of the identities that Milton kept separate to a more opportunistic appropriation of roles in which each character keeps collapsing into its opposite. As the monster threatens Frankenstein: 'Slave ... You are my creator, but I am your master' (*F* 165).

Mary Shelley's political allusions add a further layer to this dissolution of stable referents. The monster reads *Paradise Lost* as 'a true history ... of an omnipotent God warring with his creatures' (*F* 125), drawing on Godwin's earlier rereading of Satan's rebellion to highlight paternal tyranny. But this reappropriation of Milton's scheme has a more specific point of reference in Volney's account of cultural decay as the product of paternal despotism, itself 'the offspring of inordinate desire' (*RE* 37). In particular, Frankenstein's obsession with solitary creation brings to mind Volney's account of the Christian scheme of redemption as based on the interaction of 'this God of compassion' and 'his well-beloved son, engendered without a mother' (*RE* 107). For Frankenstein desires a race of offspring, not for their independent qualities, but because they will reflect back an exalted self-image: 'No father could claim the gratitude of his child so completely as I should deserve theirs' (*F* 49). Mary Shelley thus presents an imaginative enactment of Volney's critique of orthodox religion as subjective error writ large, a 'political expedient with which to rule the credulous vulgar', which is open to exploitation by 'bold and energetic spirits, who formed vast projects of ambition' (*RE* 162). This subversive account of Christianity lies behind the novel's reversal of Miltonic orthodoxies.

The novel's multiple first-person narrative carries through this dissolution of moral certainties. As Robert Hume has noted, the Gothic form typically inverts romance structures, as the quest for ideals is parodied in a circular journey to nowhere.[67] Building on Godwin's reworking of allegorical quests for knowledge in *St Leon*, Mary Shelley exploits a form peculiarly suited to the sceptical treatment of ideals. However, the formal complexity of *Frankenstein* makes for a uniquely penetrating critique of ideals. Its threefold

[67] Robert D. Hume, 'Gothic Versus Romantic: A Revaluation of the Gothic Novel', *PMLA* 84 (1969), 282–90.

structure enacts a series of heroic quests which invalidate the possibilities of heroism. Thus Walton's narrative of a literal voyage of discovery is replaced by Frankenstein's account of solitary scientific invention, which encloses the monster's story of his education, at the heart of which is the history of the De Lacey family. At the same time, these narratives are packed with tantalizing glimpses of other life histories: Walton gives a brief account of the career of the ship's master; Frankenstein narrates the story of his mother's early poverty and marriage; and, most important in terms of the novel's reversal of sympathies, Elizabeth gives a complete history of Justine, the Frankensteins' servant, who dies for one of the monster's crimes.

The status of these voyages of discovery is thrown into question by the unreliability of the three principal narrators. As in *Caleb Williams*, the drama of revolutionary struggle takes place in a subjective account which assigns the task of evaluation to the reader. But Mary Shelley foregrounds the issue of unreliability in a highly sceptical manner that has more in common with Hogg's *Confessions of a Justified Sinner* than with *Caleb Williams*. Her juxtaposition of contradictory and cross-referring narratives highlights the confrontation of world-views which is central to her wider aims, and is most evident in the contrasting language in the debates between Frankenstein and his creature. Walton's narrative offers yet another perspective: structured as a series of letters to his sister, it offers the possibility of continuing domestic relationship, by contrast with the wholesale destruction of affective values in Frankenstein's tale.

In this way Mary Shelley exploits the text's different voices to present a survey of cultural values, setting the Frankensteins' family romance against a map of empires. Drawing on Godwin's history of the effects of different political societies on private life,[68] she also commands the geographical range of the works of Byron and Percy Shelley. The centre of the novel's action is the republic of Geneva, the former seat of Calvinism and the birthplace of Rousseau, where the Frankensteins are firmly established as enlightened bourgeois in the era of the French Revolution. Indeed, Frankenstein takes pride in his family's tradition of public service in

[68] *PJ* i. 14, 24 (Bk. 1, ch. 3, 'The Spirit of Political Institutions', ch. 4, 'The Characters of Men Originate in External Circumstances'); cf. the hero's travels in *Fleetwood*, mentioned in *MSJ* i. 11, 19.

support of the republican ideals praised by Rousseau in his early works.[69] It is at Ingolstadt, however, identified by Barruel as the origin of the 'monster Jacobin' engendered by the Illuminati,[70] that Frankenstein completes his revolutionary education and creates the monster. In the ensuing pursuit, the novel's claustrophobic psychological intensity is offset by geographical expansion. Frankenstein's journey to Scotland to create the monster's mate involves a cultural education. Accompanied by his childhood friend, Clerval, he travels from the inhuman isolation of the Alps to the cultivated valleys of the Rhine. Once in England, he is briefly inspired by 'the divine ideas of liberty and self-sacrifice' (*F* 158) associated with the leaders of the Civil War, and he passes through the country of the Lake poets on his journey north. The monster's own travels bear out his claim that he has the power to desolate the world, for he murders Clerval off the coast of Ireland, and entices Frankenstein to the polar regions. In addition, his story offers insight into the workings of different political systems, ranging from the simplified patriarchal idyll in the De Laceys' cottage in Germany, a refuge from revolutionary Paris, to Turkish despotism, in Safie's tale of paternal oppression.

Other doubled characters besides Frankenstein and his creature highlight the wider cultural and political significance of these geographical shifts. At one level Mary Shelley's critique of solitary ambition offers a brief retrospect on the poetry of her Romantic contemporaries.[71] Through Clerval, the image of Frankenstein's 'former self' (*F* 155), she voices dissatisfaction with the notion of speculative detachment from humanity associated with Wordsworth's *The Excursion*.[72] Echoing the doubts of Percy Shelley in 'Mont Blanc' (1816), she undercuts the Lake poets' belief in the redemptive possibilities of a benign natural environment. Frankenstein is repeatedly drawn to the 'terrifically desolate' Alps, which he compares with the landscape of the English lakes (*F* 92, 159). His elevated intuition that the mountains are 'the habitations of another race of beings' (*F* 90) suggests his desire to find a benevolent controlling power in nature. But this aspiration is parodied and drained of meaning when his invocation of the

[69] Cf. Rousseau's address to the citizens of Geneva: 'you have no masters other than wise laws instituted by yourselves and administered by upright magistrates of your own choosing', *Discourse*, 57, 61.

[70] Barruel, *Memoirs*, iii. 444.

[71] Butler, *Romantics, Rebels, and Reactionaries*, 140–2.

[72] Cf. entry for 14 Sept. 1814, *MSJ* i. 25.

'Wandering spirits' of Mont Blanc heralds not the consoling presence he desires but the reappearance of 'the wretch whom I had created' (*F* 93). Clerval's preference for the peopled valleys of the Rhine offers a further commentary on Frankenstein's rejection of humanity, which directly echoes *Childe Harold* (iii. 46):

> Look at . . . that group of labourers coming from among their vines; and now that village half-hid in the recess of the mountain. Oh, surely, the spirit that inhabits and guards this place has a soul more in harmony with man, than those who pile the glacier, or retire to the inaccessible peaks of the mountains of our own country. (*F* 153)

This opposition between solitary desire and human community culminates in the final reckless pursuit to the icy northern regions, the antithesis of the emotional warmth signalled by Elizabeth's Italian origins. Through this polarization of values, Mary Shelley presents a parodic, simplified version of Percy Shelley's earlier quest-narrative, *Alastor; or, The Spirit of Solitude* (1816), for she construes the poet-figure's excessively sensitive personal sensibility, what Percy terms his 'generous error', as straightforwardly solipsistic.[73]

Mary Shelley's allusions to Coleridge again point up the dangers of solipsism and suggest that, like Percy Shelley, she makes little distinction between the aesthetics of Wordsworth and Coleridge. Here the issue is complicated by her alterations to the 1831 text, which have encouraged the exclusive focus on Romantic introspection that forms a major strand in modern criticism of *Frankenstein*.[74] In the 1818 text, Walton alludes in passing to the killing of the albatross in *The Rime of the Ancient Mariner* (1797, 1817), and his account of his early career as a poet is surely meant to point up the subjective origins of his illicit quest for knowledge: 'for one year [I] lived in a Paradise of my own creation' (*F* 15, 11). In this perspective Frankenstein's allusion to *The Ancient Mariner* appears more critical than apologetic, for it highlights his erroneous rejection of the monster, which breeds the guilt-ridden fantasy that ' "a frightful fiend | Doth close behind him tread" ' (*F* 54). But in

[73] On the allegorical complexities of *Alastor*, see Timothy Clark, *Embodying Revolution: The Figure of the Poet in Shelley* (Oxford, 1989), 96–142; Shelley, Preface to *Alastor; or, The Spirit of Solitude* (1816), *Poetical Works*, 15.

[74] See above, n. 59; L. J. Swingle, 'Frankenstein's Monster and its Romantic Relatives: Problems of Knowledge in English Romanticism', *Texas Studies in Literature and Language*, 15 (1973), 51–65.

the later text Mary Shelley's adaptation of the references to Coleridge defuses this critical dimension and invites us to view Frankenstein as the victim of unfathomable psychological impulse. For Walton now glosses his allusion to Coleridge's poem: 'I have often attributed my attachment to, my passionate enthusiasm for, the dangerous mysteries of ocean, to that production of the most imaginative of modern poets. There is something at work in my soul, which I do not understand' (*F* 231). This statement prepares for the reception of Frankenstein as another Ancient Mariner whose 'varied intonations' and 'soul-subduing music' captivate his audience (*F* 232). Like the Wedding Guest, Walton is compelled to hear out the tale of this alienated being, and is finally left 'forlorn',[75] inviting the reader to overlook the critical scrutiny of Frankenstein's story which the 1818 text demands.

As already seen, the full range of references in the 1818 *Frankenstein* tell a different story, indicating Mary Shelley's concern not with psychological idiosyncrasy for its own sake, but with the relationship between private states of mind and the construction of political society. But even this political frame of reference is by no means clear-cut. The text's layered perspectives invite competing interpretations: Frankenstein's narrative seems to offer a conservative warning of the dangers of revolutionary idealism; but, from the monster's point of view, the story is one of social oppression and abandonment by a tyrannical God. To explore this bipartisan quality further, we need first to look at Frankenstein's account of his creation of the monster.

Here Mary Shelley's use of the conservative myth of intellectual conspiracy might suggest an unequivocal Burkean reading of revolutionary transgression, since it is at the University of Ingolstadt, where Weishaupt had founded the Illuminati in 1775, that Frankenstein is inspired to create the monster. But the fact that Mary Shelley also draws on Volney's critique of the dominant values of paternalistic society suggests a more radical undercurrent to her analysis. In his early apprenticeship to the sixteenth-century occultists and alchemists Cornelius Agrippa and Paracelsus, Frankenstein's state of mind recalls Volney's account of paternal oppression, which fosters the subjective delusions of religious faith:

[75] Coleridge, *The Rime of the Ancient Mariner* (1797, 1817), l. 623, *The Complete Poetical Works of Samuel Taylor Coleridge*, ed. E. H. Coleridge, 2 vols. (Oxford, 1912).

'Smitten with his imaginary world, man despised the world of nature: for chimerical hopes he neglected the reality' (*RE* 162). At Ingolstadt, similarly, Frankenstein resents having 'to exchange chimeras of boundless grandeur for realities of little worth' (*F* 41) when Krempe, his early, unsympathetic tutor, criticizes his outmoded studies. By contrast, the teachings of Waldman inspire him to fulfil his earlier dreams of 'new and almost unlimited powers' (*F* 42). Crucially, Waldman praises the masters of empirical science in the precise terms that Volney condemns: 'They penetrate into the recesses of nature . . . they can command the thunders of heaven, mimic the earthquake' (*F* 42). Here Mary Shelley directly invokes Volney's prophecy of man's downfall as a presumptuous 'mortal creator': 'Thou hast measured the extent of the heavens, and counted the stars, thou hast . . . conquered the fury of the sea and the tempest, and subjected all the elements to thy will! But oh! how many errors are linked with these sublime energies!' (*RE* 23) However, Waldman's dismissal of questions of the moral use of such powers also echoes conservative warnings about unregulated intellectual activity: 'The labours of men of genius, however erroneously directed, scarcely ever fail in ultimately turning to the solid advantage of mankind' (*F* 43). Frankenstein's corresponding lack of ethical restraints underscores Mary Shelley's anxiety that, as Southey later observed, 'the moral culture of the species' may not have kept 'pace with the increase of its material powers'.[76]

Frankenstein himself broaches this concern when he warns Walton against man's egotistical desire to become 'greater than his nature will allow' (*F* 48). Extending Godwin's critique of Alexander's imperialistic ambitions, admired by Falkland as 'the generation of love and virtue' (*CW* ii. 16 [1]/111), Mary Shelley diagnoses this isolating obsession as the origin of political tyranny and conquest:[77] 'If no man allowed any pursuit whatsoever to interfere with the tranquillity of his domestic affections, Greece had not been enslaved; Caesar would have spared his country; America would have been discovered more gradually; and the empires of Mexico and Peru had not been destroyed' (*F* 51). It is this scheme of opposing political values that lies behind the diverse cultural preferences of Frankenstein and Clerval, as signalled by the juxtaposition of Clerval's reading of Persian, Arabic, and Hebrew

[76] Southey, *Sir Thomas More*, i. 206; cf. *PC* 471.

[77] Cf. *VRW* 155.

literature with Frankenstein's enthusiasm for 'the manly and heroical poetry of Greece and Rome' (*F* 64). Heroic aspiration is presented most ambiguously in Frankenstein's address to the sailors who wish to abandon Walton's expedition. Reversing his earlier advice to Walton—'Learn from . . . my example' (*F* 48)—Frankenstein echoes the speech of Dante's Ulysses to his fellow-explorers, for which he is consigned to the fiery ditch reserved for evil counsellors.[78] Frankenstein's adoption of heroic formulas at this point subtly emphasizes his loss of self-awareness: 'Did you not call this a glorious expedition? and wherefore was it glorious? . . . because danger and death surrounded, and these dangers you were to brave and overcome. For this was it a glorious, for this was it an honourable undertaking' (*F* 212). It is no accident that Dante also presents Ulysses' fatal voyage of discovery in opposition to familial relationships,[79] thus endorsing the multiple levels of Mary Shelley's political analysis.

Within this framework of heroic allusion, Mary Shelley presents an internalized treatment of the errors of paternal despotism by pursuing the social and psychological consequences of Frankenstein's egotism. She portrays Frankenstein's desire to benefit the species through discovering the origins of life as a self-aggrandizing pursuit. In planning a 'new species' who 'would bless [him] as its creator and source' (*F* 49), Frankenstein evades domestic obligations to his family and the social restraint of a reciprocal relationship with his childhood love, Elizabeth. Totally obsessed, he fails to notice seasonal changes just as he neglects his family: 'I wished, as it were, to procrastinate all that related to my feelings of affection until the great object, which swallowed up every habit of my nature, should be completed' (*F* 50). In highlighting the dangers of 'enthusiasm' specifically in terms of its destructive effects on the natural order as represented by the family, Mary Shelley seems to be offering a Burkean critique of revolutionary aspiration, and a subversive rejoinder to Godwin's early rational views.[80]

However, the complexity of Mary Shelley's response to Godwin's thought should be emphasized. By 1798 Godwin had revised his

[78] Cf. Dante: 'Call to mind from whence ye sprang: | Ye were not formed to live the life of brutes, | But virtue to pursue and knowledge high'; *The Divine Comedy*, trans. Henry Francis Cary as *The Vision; or, Hell, Purgatory, and Paradise*, 3 vols. (London, 1814; 2nd edn., corr. with additional notes, 1819), *Hell*, xxvi. 115–17.

[79] Cf. ibid. 93–7.

[80] Cf. Sterrenburg, 'Mary Shelley's Monster'; Mellor, *Mary Shelley*, 86–7.

account of moral action to take account of the private affections, and he had already dramatized the tension between egotistical aspiration and domestic affections in *St Leon*, a concern clearly evident in *Frankenstein*. But while Mary Shelley endorsed Godwin's later position on the domestic affections, she also expressed dissatisfaction with his tentative speculations about a future rational Utopia at the end of *Political Justice*: 'The men . . . will probably cease to propagate. The whole will be a people of men, and not of children' (*PJ* ii. 528). In a grim foreshadowing of her vision of world depopulation in *The Last Man*, Mary Shelley travesties these Utopian expectations on a grand scale. Frankenstein aspires to create a 'new species', but ends up fearing a 'race of devils', and his fantasy of benefiting mankind is replaced by the apocalyptic dread of inflicting a 'curse upon everlasting generations' and wiping out 'the whole human race' (*F* 49, 163). Frankenstein's ultimate crime against the family is his act of creation without a woman. He fantasizes that his offspring will reflect back an exalted image of his own masculinity, but his dream after bringing the monster to life only confirms his transgression of the natural order:

> I thought I saw Elizabeth, in the bloom of health, walking in the streets of Ingolstadt. Delighted and surprised, I embraced her; but as I imprinted the first kiss on her lips, they became livid with the hue of death; her features appeared to change, and I thought that I held the corpse of my dead mother in my arms. (*F* 53)

Here Mary Shelley offers psychological rather than historical insights into Frankenstein's motives to action: the unexpected return of repressed subconscious impulses suggests a move away from Godwinian social analysis towards a more conventional psychological explanation.

While this imagery of familial transgression suggests Mary Shelley's Burkean sympathies, elsewhere in the narrative she remains deeply sceptical about the integrity of the patriarchal family, the basis of Burke's hierarchical order. All the families in the novel are internally divided long before the monster wreaks havoc.[81] Walton's family consists of one married sister; the De Laceys have lost their mother and take in another motherless girl,

[81] Kate Ellis, 'Monsters in the Garden: Mary Shelley and the Bourgeois Family', in Levine and Knoepflmacher (eds.), *The Endurance of Frankenstein*, 123–42; William Patrick Day, *In the Circles of Fear and Desire: A Study of Gothic Fantasy* (Chicago, 1985), 139–43.

Safie; the Frankenstein family is made up of a series of adoptions and substitutions. Victor Frankenstein's mother, Caroline Beaufort, his betrothed, Elizabeth, and the servant Justine, are themselves the survivors of broken families. Artificially constructed, the Frankenstein family is bonded together on implicitly incestuous lines: Caroline is Baron Frankenstein's former ward and Elizabeth is brought up as Frankenstein's sister, a relationship emphasized in an 1831 addition, where Frankenstein's mother offers him the homeless Elizabeth as a 'gift' (*F* 235). In the 1831 text Mary Shelley also expanded her account of Frankenstein's idyllic upbringing, highlighting his parents' 'deep consciousness of what they owed towards the being to which they had given life' (*F* 234) by contrast with his own parental negligence. Yet this abundance of parental care equally nurtures Frankenstein's egotism. Even in the first edition, the family remains a closeted and inward-looking sphere, which gives Frankenstein an 'invincible repugnance to new countenances' (*F* 40). Once on the road to Ingolstadt, however, he is critical of a youth spent 'cooped up in one place' (*F* 40), and his creation of the monster dramatizes his rejection of affective bonds. It is the monster's own story, however, that presents the most thoroughgoing critique of a society based on paternalistic domestic ties.

The Monster's Story

Given its tortuous prehistory, the very form of the monster invites competing interpretations. Identified, on the one hand, with Burke's spectre of revolutionary excesses, the monster subverts the Burkean metaphor of organic growth and continuity: constructed out of arbitrary bits and pieces, fragmented relics of the past, it defeats the very idea of a coherent tradition. As an incomplete 'new man', it also suggests the disastrous consequences of a sudden break with past traditions.

Crucial to this problem of definition is the novel's shifting points of view. Mary Shelley's use of the first-person narrative throws earlier polemical oppositions into doubt, and becomes more radically subversive of all forms of order. By giving the monster a voice, she internalizes its significance, showing how a state of tyranny creates and perpetuates divided selves. But, at the same time, the monster's power to erode stable values anticipates that of the plague in *The Last Man*, which challenges and finds wanting all political systems.

Mary Shelley's equivocation in defining the monstrous, and what it means to be fully human, approaches the heart of her intellectual purpose. Nowhere is this problem of definition more acute than in Frankenstein's curiously imprecise account of his first meeting with his creature:

> He held up the curtain of the bed; and his eyes, if eyes they may be called, were fixed on me. His jaws opened, and he muttered some inarticulate sounds, while a grin wrinkled his cheeks. He might have spoken, but I did not hear; one hand was stretched out, seemingly to detain me, but I escaped, and rushed down stairs. (*F* 53)

The rest of the novel pivots on Frankenstein's failure to respond when the creature presents the outrageous demand of his own existence. Instead Frankenstein retreats into a fantasy world, and continually presents the monster in terms of dualistic reversal: 'my own vampire, my own spirit let loose from the grave, and forced to destroy all that was dear to me' (*F* 72). Rather than generously acknowledging his creature, he greets him with frenzied expressions of 'rage and horror . . . anger and hatred . . . furious detestation and contempt' (*F* 94). Denying the monster the humanizing experience of parental love, Frankenstein further refuses to create him a mate with whom he can live on equal terms. His failure to admit his creature's independence presents the antithesis of Godwin's eminently rational account of parental obligations: 'thou standest before me vested in the prerogatives of sentiment and reason; a living being, to be regarded with attention and deference. . . . I rejoice in the restraint to which your independent character subjects me, and it will be my pride to cultivate that independence in your mind' (*SL* ii. 28). Frankenstein's negligence leaves the creature no option but to repeat his own tyrannical actions. As Percy Shelley put it in his review of *Frankenstein* for the *Examiner*: 'Treat a person ill and he will become wicked . . . divide him, a social being, from society, and you impose upon him the irresistible obligations—malevolence and selfishness.'[82]

The monster's physical deformity is powerfully suggestive of the

[82] Shelley, 'On *Frankenstein*' [1818, first published in the *Athenaeum*, 10 Nov. 1832], *Works*, vi. 264.

psychological distortions induced by the pressures of hierarchical society. In this respect Mary Shelley's treatment of parental tyranny prefigures Percy Shelley's exploration of incest as a metaphor for paternal religion in *The Cenci* (1819), the play that he wanted her to write.[83] Mary Shelley admired this study of 'sad reality', as opposed to the 'beautiful idealisms of moral excellence' in *Prometheus Unbound* (1820), as the finest of her husband's works.[84] Like Frankenstein, Count Cenci has 'cast nature off' (III. i. 286), and he regards his offspring, his daughter Beatrice, as an extension of himself—'This particle of my divided being' (IV. i. 117)—rather than as a separate individual. This denial of Beatrice's independent existence leads to the wholesale erosion of social bonds in the play. Cenci's incestuous union with his daughter figures his reactionary wish to perpetuate a corrupt system, and he envisages the offspring of their union as a further monstrous birth:

> A hideous likeness of herself, that as
> From a distorting mirror, she may see
> Her image mixed with what she most abhors. (IV. i. 146–8)

Similarly, the monster, bereft of parental care, comes to see himself as a 'filthy type' of his maker, 'more horrid from its very resemblance' (*F* 126).

Mary Shelley exploits images of incompletion to define a failure in relationship. Although Frankenstein literally endows the monster with life, the creature's half-finished appearance reflects his withholding of love. The creature's inability to find relationship leads him to define himself as 'a monster, a blot upon the earth, from which all men fled, and whom all men disowned' (*F* 116). Throughout the novel understated images of restoration to life highlight Frankenstein's travesty of biblical and Miltonic creation myths. In the opening sequence Walton's efforts to restore the half-frozen Frankenstein to 'animation' by rubbing him with brandy forms only one aspect of his care; it is his sympathy that makes Frankenstein exclaim: 'you have benevolently restored me to life' (*F* 20, 21). The blind De Lacey's exemplary response to the monster,

[83] According to Mary Shelley, Percy Shelley was inspired by the story of the Cenci family while in Rome in 1819, and 'urged the subject to me as one fitted for a tragedy . . . but I entreated him to write it instead', Note on *The Cenci* (1839), *Poetical Works*, 335.

[84] Shelley, Dedication to Leigh Hunt, *The Cenci* (1819); Preface to *Prometheus Unbound* (1820); *Poetical Works*, 275, 207.

the antithesis of his creator's negligence, is at once an indication of his own humanity and a means of glimpsing the monster's true potential: 'Excellent man! . . . You raise me from the dust by this kindness' (*F* 130).[85] But the monster's history finally repeats his creator's internal dislocation: 'My heart was fashioned to be susceptible of love and sympathy; and . . . wrenched by misery to vice and hatred' (*F* 217). Resigning himself to the state of barbarism that Godwin and Volney saw as the present character of political society, he dismisses himself, in Godwin's phrase, as 'an abortion' (*F* 219).

Mary Shelley explores the wider psychological and political implications of this monstrous imposition by allowing the monster to tell his own story, which makes a direct appeal to the reader's sympathies. By contrast with Frankenstein's melodramatic outbursts, the monster's eloquence reflects a blend of Miltonic authority and Godwinian persuasion, further validating his marginalized point of view. Like Caleb Williams, he seeks an alternative to the processes of 'human laws, bloody as they may be' by appealing to the reader as judge: 'Let your compassion be moved, and do not disdain me. Listen to my tale: when you have heard that, abandon or commiserate me, as you shall judge that I deserve' (*F* 96). As he tells Frankenstein: 'On you it rests, whether I . . . lead a harmless life, or become the scourge of your fellow-creatures.' By the end of his tale, however, the reader is surely implicated in his sense of universal injustice: 'Am I to be thought the only criminal, when all human kind sinned against me?' (*F* 219)

The monster's story offers an alternative to Frankenstein's bourgeois upbringing, and goes on to challenge the entire set of relations of which his creator is part. Even in his first responses to the external world, modelled on Rousseau's theory of natural man,[86] he appears the antithesis of Frankenstein, who desires to penetrate the secrets of nature and establish his own pre-eminence. But the monster outgrows Rousseau's notion of happiness arising from the satisfaction of physical passions. Instead his developing moral and intellectual awareness reflects Godwin's theories of education determined by external circumstances, as set out in *The Enquirer* and developed further in *Mandeville*. More like the

[85] Cf. Adam to Eve: 'needs must the power | That made us . . . | Be infinitely good . . . | That raised us from the dust', *PL* iv. 412–16.

[86] Rousseau, *Discourse*, 81–105.

orphaned Mandeville than Godwin's early rational enquirer, the monster has an overwhelming sense of his lack of natural ties: 'No father had watched my infant days, no mother had blessed me with smiles and caresses' (*F* 117). In this perspective, it is deprivation of familial bonds rather than the family environment itself that creates the monstrous. If Mary Shelley offers a glimpse of what lies outside social models based on the 'method of nature' (*R* 120), ultimately this can only be rendered in negative terms, and this underscores her scepticism about all social constructs.

The monster's education drives home this negative vision. His lack of biological origins is offset by a complete cultural development, but this only reflects back on Frankenstein's quest: 'Increase of knowledge only discovered to me more clearly what a wretched outcast I was' (*F* 127). The monster's programme of reading breeds a profound sense of alienation from the dominant forms of patriarchal society, presenting the vices of advanced society as if for the first time. Appropriately, his disenchantment begins with a reading of Volney's *Ruins*, which gives him an appalling degree of insight into the governments and religions of different nations:

> Was man, indeed, at once so powerful, so virtuous, and magnificent, yet so vicious and base? . . . For a long time I could not conceive how one man could go forth to murder his fellow, or even why there were laws and governments . . . the strange system of human society was explained to me. I heard of the division of property, of immense wealth and squalid poverty; of rank, descent, and noble blood. (*F* 115)

His subsequent reading-matter encapsulates the major stages of Western civilization: Plutarch's *Parallel Lives* offers a view of classical republican heroism; *Paradise Lost* expounds orthodox Christianity; and Goethe's *The Sorrows of Young Werther* introduces eighteenth-century subjectivity. But the monster is unable to place himself in relation to any of these cultural movements. His indecision about whether he is Adam or Satan is clarified by his reading of Frankenstein's laboratory journal. Here the monster learns of his literally fragmented origins and Frankenstein's early hostility, now echoed in his curse of his creator as a tyrannical God (*F* 126).

Significantly, the monster's marginalized position is shared by other figures excluded from the sources of social power. Anticipating Mary Shelley's critique of imperialism in *The Last Man*, the monster identifies with colonized groups when he resigns his claim to a place in advanced society and plans to retreat to the wilds of South America with his mate (*F* 142–3). More central in *Frankenstein* is the victimization of women, a theme taken up in *Valperga*. Those women who are, like the monster, victims of Frankenstein's withholding of love, approach the monster's vision of universal persecution, anticipating their deaths at his hands.

Especially instructive is the fate of Justine, the Frankensteins' servant. Even before she is wrongfully convicted of murdering Frankenstein's younger brother William, her history of alienation enacts in miniature the division between Frankenstein and his creature. She recalls that when she returned to her own family after being brought up in the Frankenstein household, her mother 'accused her of having caused the deaths of her brothers and sister' (*F* 61). Another false accusation in the public sphere leads to her execution for the monster's crime. Pressurized by her Roman Catholic confessor, she collapses in moral confusion and admits to the murder, telling Elizabeth, 'I almost began to think that I was the monster that he said I was' (*F* 82).[87] The verdict of the court makes a mockery of 'the justice of our judges' in which Baron Frankenstein has so much faith (*F* 76). In this way the monster drives home the arbitrary nature of the justice meted out to himself, for it is through his planting of William's locket on Justine while she is asleep that he marks her out for false accusation: 'thanks to the lessons of Felix, and the sanguinary laws of man, I have learned how to work mischief' (*F* 140).

Elizabeth too comes to share the special quality of the monster's insight, prefiguring her deathly confrontation with him on her wedding night. Like Justine, after William's death she blames herself for a crime she has not committed: 'I have murdered my darling infant!' (*F* 67) Yet her speech in Justine's defence at the trial implicates her in the shortcomings of Genevan justice: it heightens opinion in favour of her own goodness and against Justine's apparent crime (*F* 80). After Justine's execution, she resigns all faith in man-made schemes of justice:

> Now misery has come home, and men appear to me as monsters thirsting for each other's blood . . . Alas! Victor, when falsehood can look so like the truth, who can assure themselves of certain happiness? I feel as if I were

[87] Cf. Wollstonecraft on the error of 'blind obedience', *VRW* 107.

walking on the edge of a precipice, towards which thousands are crowding, and endeavouring to plunge me into the abyss. (*F* 88)

As in *Caleb Williams*, the occasion of the legal trial focuses larger epistemological issues. Elizabeth's recognition that truth and falsehood cannot be distinguished moves beyond a critique of institutional justice to suggest that the entire system of political society upheld by the Frankensteins may devolve into a chaos of arbitrary perceptions. An isolated outburst, this apocalyptic premonition underscores the radical scepticism at the heart of Mary Shelley's political analysis. In the final, mutually obsessed pursuit among the dwindling ice-floes of the polar regions, men and monsters are indistinguishable, anticipating the erosion of all forms of order in *The Last Man*.

Given this escalating disruption of meaning, it is tempting to argue that Mary Shelley offers a stable point of reference through Walton's intervention at the start of the novel. It is certainly true that the outer frame provided by Walton's voyage of discovery relegates Frankenstein's story to the status of historical accident, and, to some extent, Walton's ostensibly exemplary domestic sympathies provide a critical gloss on Frankenstein's monstrous egotism. Like Frankenstein, Walton dreams of 'the inestimable benefit which I shall confer on all mankind to the last generation' (*F* 10), but this does not prevent him from writing letters home. Whereas Frankenstein laments his morality, Walton recognizes the insufficiency of the individual, and laments his lack of a friend (*F* 13).

However, Walton's position is full of contradictions. He writes that he longs for a companion, yet he has put himself in the situation where he seems least likely to meet one. When he does meet with Frankenstein, he claims to 'love him as a brother' (*F* 22), but as the full extent of Frankenstein's delusion becomes evident, this response appears idealizing and uncritical. Their final exchange remains deeply ambivalent. Although Walton abandons his dreams of 'utility and glory' (*F* 213) in compliance with the will of the sailors, his return to society is presented in largely negative terms: 'Thus are my hopes blasted by cowardice and indecision. I come back ignorant and disappointed' (*F* 213). Frankenstein is even more unwilling to relinquish his ambitions: though he admits the delusive quality of his 'fit of enthusiastic madness' in creating the monster, he finds little to blame in his past conduct (*F* 214). Instead he remains fascinated by the pursuit of knowledge and seeks to encourage Walton's hopes, just as he imposes a legacy of vengeance on the monster. Thus his presentation of his experience as a cautionary tale collapses in contradictions: 'Seek happiness in tranquillity, and avoid ambition. . . . Yet why do I say this? I have myself been blasted in these hopes, yet another may succeed' (*F* 215).

More unsettling still is the dramatic appearance of the monster in Frankenstein's cabin. In bringing the unmanageable product of solitary ambition to the surface of the narrative, Mary Shelley issues an unanswerable challenge to the shaky pattern of consolation offered by Frankenstein's self-centred review of his conduct and Walton's largely uncritical endorsement of his values. For this unaccommodated creature alone has the self-reflective capacity to make a gesture beyond the novel's collapse of relationship when he ceases to react to his creator as a dehumanized tyrant and recognizes his finer qualities: 'Oh Frankenstein! generous and self-devoted being!' (*F* 217) Such an unexpected glimpse of the monster's affective potential reminds us of his early benevolent actions, described by the De Laceys in the words '*good spirit, wonderful*' (*F* 110). The monster's review of his past conduct presents a notional image of man's capacity for benevolence: 'Once I falsely hoped to meet with beings, who, pardoning my outward form, would love me for the excellent qualities which I was capable of bringing forth' (*F* 219). In addition, this image is concretely shown through Walton's momentary willingness to 'pardon' the monster's 'outward form' and hear his tale. As in *Caleb Williams*, however, this exemplary awareness is unaffordable within the constraints of 'things as they are', and the monster's extravagant plans for self-immolation complete the novel's breakdown of meaning.

At one level, Walton's listening to the monster's speech, with its cluster of images of thwarted potential, points, albeit precariously, towards a change in the structure of human relationships, and invites comparison with the provisional ending to *Caleb Williams*. Indeed, the structural complexity of *Frankenstein* supports this view, for its multiple first-person narrative seeks to place the reader as true arbiter of political justice in Godwin's manner. But Mary Shelley lacks Godwin's optimistic faith in man's capacity for rational judgement. While she accounts for the monster's deformity in terms of social oppression, her treatment of Frankenstein as an exemplar of egotistical ambition suggests a less historical approach, moving towards the conventional psychological focus of her later revisions. Yet this loss of Godwin's early confident ability to discriminate between humanity and the monstrous empowers the imaginative reach of *Frankenstein*, reaffirming and extending the mythic patterns of the Godwinian novel. Mary Shelley's compensating drive towards large-scale revaluation of systematic forms of belief becomes central in her next two novels.

6

Mary Shelley's Novels of the 1820s: History and Prophecy

Valperga: 'A Book of Promise'

Shortly before her return to England in August 1823, Mary Shelley wrote to Leigh Hunt deprecating *Valperga* as 'merely a book of promise, another landing place in the staircase I am climbing'.[1] Yet this image also suggests the novel's importance as a transitional work. At first sight it has little in common with either *Frankenstein* or *The Last Man*. The product of several years' reading and research, *Valperga* is a slow-moving, episodic narrative which displays a wealth of historical detail. It centres on the unscrupulous ambitions of Castruccio Castracani degli Antelminelli, later Prince of Lucca, a power-hungry aristocrat who played a leading role in the fourteenth-century feuds among the states of northern Italy. Mary Shelley wrote to Maria Gisborne in June 1821 that it was 'a child of mighty slow growth': she first thought about the subject at Marlow in 1817, researched it throughout 1818 and 1819, and began writing in a rare period of serenity in October 1820.[2]

Though largely unread today,[3] *Valperga* was admired by Godwin and Percy Shelley as a significant advance on *Frankenstein*. Godwin may have criticized its length, but he also praised it as a work of 'more genius' than *Frankenstein*, possibly because it resembled his own latest experiment in historical fiction, *Mandeville*.[4] Mary Shelley's study of Castruccio's character as it is moulded by the feud between the Guelphs and the Ghibellines owes much to Godwin's treatment of the effects of hereditary 'party

[1] Mary Shelley to Leigh Hunt, 3(5) Aug. [1823], *MSL* i. 361.

[2] Mary Shelley to Maria Gisborne, 30 June 1821, *MSL* i. 203; cf. *MSJ* ii. 505 and n.; for Mary Shelley's reading 1818–20, see *MSJ* i. 265–8, 345–7.

[3] Cf. Frederick L. Jones, 'Introduction' to *The Letters of Mary Wollstonecraft Shelley*, 3 vols. (Norman, Okla., 1944), i, p. xxx.

[4] Godwin to Mary Shelley, 15 Nov. 1822, Marshall, *Life*, ii. 52; cf. Godwin to Mary Shelley, 14–18 Feb. 1823, Kegan Paul, *William Godwin*, ii. 277.

spirit' on the individual (*V* i. 12).[5] But while following her father's extension of the Godwinian novel into the realm of history, Mary Shelley departs from his subjective narrative mode in favour of a more capacious form that will embody her developing preoccupation with the anatomy of political, social, and cultural certainties. Drawing on Scott instead, she adopts an impersonal third-person narrative voice to present the main story of Castruccio's rise to power. Although *Valperga* was generally recognized as another product of the 'mischievous' Godwin school,[6] its externalized point of view conciliated those reviewers who had been alienated by *Frankenstein*. The *British Magazine* praised *Valperga* as an attempt to 'restore the old style' of *Don Quixote* and *Tom Jones*, and compared its epic qualities favourably with *Waverley*.[7] In a letter to the publisher Charles Ollier, Percy Shelley too described *Valperga* as superior to the *Tales of My Landlord*, especially in 'the beauty and the sublimity' of the character of the prophetess Beatrice.[8]

These comparisons with Scott alert us to Mary Shelley's enrichment of the Godwinian narrative in response to other models of intellectual fiction in the early 1820s. In turning to Scott as a model, she recognized that the issues of political rule implicit in *Frankenstein* could only be discussed adequately through a more inclusive analysis of society. Her journal contains ample evidence of her thorough engagement with Scott's novels, which she read as they were published, some of them more than once.[9] Scott's use of history to present the past as a coherent whole has already been discussed in relation to Godwin's historical writings of the previous decade.[10] But Scott's pursuit of this vision of ordered social evolution equally needs to be seen in relation to social criticism of the early 1820s, in which the polarized debate of the 1790s was revived.

[5] Mary Shelley read *Mandeville* in Dec. 1817, Apr. 1818, and Mar. 1819, *MSJ* i. 185, 206, 251; and reread *Fleetwood* and *Caleb Williams* in June 1820, *MSJ* i. 323.

[6] Review of *Valperga*, *Blackwood's*, 13 (Mar. 1823), 284.

[7] Review of *Valperga*, *British Magazine; or, Miscellany of Polite Literature* (1823), 33–41.

[8] Shelley to Charles Ollier, 25 Sept. 1821, *PBSL* ii. 353; Ollier did not publish *Valperga*.

[9] Mary Shelley read *Waverley* in 1815, 1817, and 1821, *MSJ* i. 90, 166, 388; *Tales of My Landlord: The Black Dwarf/Old Mortality* in 1817 and 1820, *MSJ* i. 99, 162–3, 346; *Rob Roy* (1817) in 1818 and 1821, *MSJ* i. 192, 388; *The Bride of Lammermoor* in 1820, *MSJ* i. 320; and *Ivanhoe* (1819) in 1820 and 1821, *MSJ* i. 323, 387.

[10] See above, pp. 85–8.

On the one hand, with the Holy Alliance representing the interests of the restored monarchies in Europe, conservative nostalgia for a Burkean model of a naturally evolving organic society became more deeply entrenched.[11] For instance, in the *Lay Sermons* (1816–17) Coleridge drew on Burke's central image of a 'great primaeval contract of eternal society' (*R* 195) to convey his own vision of the 'happy organization of a well-governed society', which he was to develop further in *On the Constitution of the Church and State*.[12] By contrast, the republication of Paine's writings in 1818 and 1819 announced new efforts to retrieve a liberal view of the past.[13] Especially relevant to *Valperga* is the work of the Swiss historian J. C. L. de Sismondi: in the *History of the Italian Republics* (1809–26), written as a protest against Napoleon's campaign to gain control of Italy, he sought to present fourteenth-century republican Florence as a living inspiration for liberal thinkers.[14] Godwin too made a major contribution to this revival of a republican past: in 1820 he was already planning his massive *History of the Commonwealth of England*, though only the first volume was published before Mary Shelley completed her own revaluation of political ideals in *The Last Man*.[15]

Thus, while the historical scope of *Valperga* owes much to Scott's more naturalistic, documentary art, its central imaginative threads reflect the selective and theoretical concerns of earlier Godwinian novels. Mary Shelley had learned from *St Leon* and *Mandeville* that a historically distanced setting gave unusual scope for a displaced treatment of contemporary social pressures on the individual. Her choice of subject indicates her lasting fascination with revolutionary

[11] My account is indebted to Elie Halévy, *The Liberal Awakening, 1815–1830* (1923), trans. from the French by E. I. Watkin (London, 1926, 1961), 128–32.

[12] Coleridge, *The Statesman's Manual; or, The Bible the Best Guide to Political Skill and Foresight, A Lay Sermon, Addressed to the Higher Classes of Society* (1816), *Lay Sermons*, ed. R. J. White (Princeton, NJ, 1972), 21; read by Mary Shelley in Jan. 1817, *MSJ* i. 153.

[13] Paine, *Theological Works*, 7 parts (London, 1818); *Political and Miscellaneous Works, with Life by Richard Carlile*, 2 vols. (London, 1819); Mary Shelley reread Paine's *Age of Reason*, *Common Sense*, and *Rights of Man* in Mar. 1820, *MSJ* i. 311–12, 346.

[14] Jean-Charles-Leonard Simonde de Sismondi, *History of the Italian Republics, Being a View of the Origin, Progress, and Fall of Italian Freedom*, i–viii (Paris, 1809), reviewed in *Quarterly Review*, 7 (June 1812), 257–74, studied by Mary Shelley in 1819 and 1820, *MSJ* i. 247, 268.

[15] Godwin, *History of the Commonwealth*, vol. i, appeared in June 1824; Mary Shelley to Marianne Hunt, 13(18) June 1824, *MSL* i. 146.

leaders. Percy Shelley was not alone in viewing the novel's despotical hero as 'a little Napoleon' who displayed 'all the passions and the errors of his antitype', although his letter to Ollier, describing Mary Shelley's treatment of Italian manners as 'a living and a moving picture of an age almost forgotten', suggests an attempt to play down the novel's topicality.[16] While Castruccio's 'ambition for power, conquest and renown' (*V* i. 161) brings to mind Napoleon's career, it gains a more specific disturbing power in the shadow of the Austrian army's invasion of Naples to restore despotical government in 1821.[17] It is no accident that Castruccio's mercenary exploits include a period of service in the Imperial army, subduing the rebel states of Italy. Certainly it was the contemporary resonance of Mary Shelley's treatment of military aggrandizement that divided critics along party lines. *Blackwood's* was especially critical of what it called 'this perpetual drumming at poor Buonaparte' and accused Mary Shelley of merely 'flinging over the grey surtout and cocked hat of the great captain of France, the blazoned mantle of a fierce *Condottiere* of Lucca'.[18] Conversely, the *Examiner* found much to praise in Mary Shelley's treatment of imperialistic ambition.[19]

An obvious descendant of St Leon and Frankenstein, Castruccio is depicted as the product of the hereditary desire for fame and military glory. Bereft of parental guidance at an early age, he falls in with a group of Italian nobles who share the 'never resting desire, to aggrandize first themselves, and secondly their native town' (*V* i. 65) against which Frankenstein warns Walton. By contrast, the rural lifestyle of Guinigi, the friend of Castruccio's father, offers an exemplary harmony with nature: 'To my eyes . . . the sight of the bounties of nature, and of the harmless peasants who cultivate the earth, is far more delightful than an army of knights hasting in brilliant array to deluge the fields with blood' (*V* i. 47). Drawing on Virgil's contrast of the arts of peaceful cultivation with the devastation of military conquest in the *Georgics*, Mary Shelley engages directly with the political issues implicit in her earlier critique of Frankenstein's desire to impose his will on the natural world.[20] But Castruccio rejects Guinigi's outlook in favour of the pursuit of glory, and educates himself through a series of dubious

[16] See above, n. 8.
[17] Halévy, *Liberal Awakening*, 135.
[18] See above, n. 6.
[19] *Examiner*, 826 (30 Nov. 1823), 775.
[20] *MSJ* i. 247; cf. Mary Shelley to Maria Gisborne, 22 Jan. 1819, *MSL* i. 85.

adventures in the English court of Edward I and the Italian wars in the Netherlands. He returns to his native land as a master of Italian statecraft with a 'mine of undiscovered evil in his character' (*V* i. 244).[21] Now Prince of Lucca, he sets out to conquer the surrounding states. The final stage in his evolution into a military dictator involves his capture of the fortress Valperga, the repository of republican values and the ancestral home of his childhood love, Euthanasia. Here the interpenetration of public and private tyranny is symbolized by Castruccio's entry into Valperga through the secret door he formerly used as Euthanasia's lover (*V* ii. 230). After this pivotal act of treachery, Castruccio's relentless 'craving that seemed to desire the empire of the world' (*V* iii. 171) is depicted increasingly from the outside. The book concludes not with a conventional character assessment but with a public epitaph, pointing up the dehumanizing effects of military ambition.

Although the character of Guinigi offers a notional alternative to tyrannical domination, Mary Shelley undercuts the history of Castruccio more persuasively by introducing different narrative voices. In a strategy which recalls the narrative complexity of *Frankenstein*, she opens up her apparently uncompromising historical account into a more dialogic form reminiscent of earlier Godwinian novels. But, more markedly than in *Frankenstein*, the novel's alternative points of view are voiced by women. To some extent the lives of the two major female characters recall the limited spheres of the women in *Frankenstein*, for they too are defined by their relationship to the central male figure, which eventually destroys them. Euthanasia, Castruccio's childhood love, is betrayed by his political dealings, while he seduces, then abandons, the prophetess Beatrice. In the later novel, however, Mary Shelley develops the role of women to convey a generalized view of despotism in which public and private aspects of masculinist power are inextricably mixed. These strong-minded female characters have an independence rarely glimpsed in *Frankenstein*, or, indeed, in many novels in the period. Both are introduced in terms which establish their claims to social power: Euthanasia, 'independent and powerful . . . was as a queen in Valperga', while Beatrice has a different kind of authority as 'this divine girl, this *Ancilla Dei*' (*V* i.

[21] Mary Shelley read Niccolò Machiavelli, *Life of Castruccio Castracani of Lucca* (1532) in 1820, *MSJ* i. 313.

169, ii. 21). In telling their own stories, they call into question the entire basis of Castruccio's rise to power.

Nothing could be more remote from Castruccio's debasement of human relationships for political ends than the affective values displayed in Euthanasia's account of her early life: 'What is the world, except that which we feel? Love, and hope, and delight, or sorrow and tears; these are our lives, our realities, to which we give the names of power, possession, misfortune, and death' (*V* i. 193). The rest of Euthanasia's narrative establishes her as a figure of unconstrained political optimism. Brought up in republican Florence, she inherits her father's political ideals, which reflect Godwin's gradualist theory of political progress. Believing that the present is 'only a point of rest' in an endless movement towards virtue and independence, she despises the party spirit which enthralls Castruccio: 'we are blind with regard to futurity,' he insists, 'let us work for ourselves alone' (*V* i. 29, 127–8). In addition, her extensive reading of Dante leads her to link the wisdom of self-knowledge with political liberty. Drawing on Godwin's praise of writers such as Shakespeare and Milton as examples of unfettered human potential, Mary Shelley invokes Dante as another 'pledge of a glorious race, which tells us that, in clinging to the freedom which gave birth to his genius, we may awake the fallen hopes of the world' (*V* i. 197–8).[22]

But at the same time Euthanasia's position as a casualty of Castruccio's ambition undercuts this optimistic drive, pointing up Mary Shelley's underlying preoccupation with the decline of political ideals and the erosion of relationship. For Euthanasia's early solitude prefigures the cosmic homelessness of Lionel Verney, the last man. With the death of her entire family from fever, she is left a 'solitary scion of the stock', and she spends her early life in Rome 'amidst a dead race, and an extinguished empire' (*V* i. 207, 206). In this way she is more a spirit of 'ancient times' than a 'modern Italian' (*V* i. 203), and her marginal status as an embodiment of classical republican ideals in a modern age makes her vulnerable to Castruccio's Machiavellian schemes for power. When Valperga falls to Castruccio, Euthanasia's fortitude collapses in irrational guilt and fear. She is finally implicated in the corruptions of modern statecraft when she joins a conspiracy to

[22] Cf. *TP* 81, read by Mary Shelley in June 1817; she read Dante's *Divine Comedy* in 1818 and 1819, *MSJ* i. 173, 247–8, 303.

overthrow Castruccio. Yet the narrator never admits to her death: the ship that carries her into exile in Sicily fails to reach its destination, but no wreck is found.[23] Like Frankenstein's monster, Euthanasia presents an unanswerable challenge to the dominant values of political society, then disappears into darkness.

More overtly provocative is Beatrice's commentary on Castruccio's rule, which highlights Mary Shelley's continuing dissatisfaction with the bond between political despotism and institutionalized Christianity, newly evident in the name of the Holy Alliance. Godwin thought Beatrice the 'jewel of the book', while Percy Shelley praised Beatrice's character as 'perfectly original'.[24] But in fact this powerful creation forms a recognizable blend of Dante's Beatrice, Percy's Beatrice Cenci, and Frankenstein's creature. Mary Shelley also identified her character with Guido's portrait of Beatrice Cenci (*V* ii. 17–18), which Percy had described at length in the Preface to *The Cenci*. More important here is Percy's use of paternal incest as a metaphor for the tyranny of orthodox religion in *The Cenci*, a theme which Mary Shelley had also tackled in *Mathilda* [1819], a short work first published in 1959 and generally read as autobiographical.[25] However, the topic of paternal incest should also be read in the context of Mary Shelley's scepticism concerning religious orthodoxies: for Mathilda as for Frankenstein's creature, 'the holy name of father was become a curse to me'.[26]

In Beatrice's history Mary Shelley uniquely extends this identification between the monster's sense of a malevolent creator and the oppression of women. It is no accident that the orphaned Beatrice is assumed to be the child of the religious fanatic Wilhelmina, who believed herself 'the Holy Ghost incarnate upon earth for the salvation of the female sex' (*V* ii. 26). For this account of Beatrice's origins attempts to restore the balance to the scheme of Christian redemption, already shown to be inadequate to a full account of humanity in *Frankenstein*. As noted in the previous chapter, Volney's reference to the 'well-beloved son, engendered without a mother' (*RE* 107) highlights the exclusive quality of paternal religion criticized by Mary Shelley. By contrast, Beatrice's role as another divine child 'sent upon earth for the instruction and

[23] Cf. Mary Shelley to Maria Gisborne, 3(6) May 1823, *MSL* i. 336.

[24] Godwin to Mary Shelley, 14–18 Feb. 1823, *MSL* i. 323 n.; *PBSL* ii. 353.

[25] Nitchie, 'Introduction' to *Mathilda* [1819], ed. Elizabeth Nitchie (Chapel Hill, NC, 1959), pp. xi–xiv; for a more ambitious reading, see Mellor, *Mary Shelley*, 191–200.

[26] *Mathilda*, 72.

example of suffering humanity' is inspired by 'her mother's soul' (*V* ii. 21, 42). More in keeping with Volney's sense of religion as fraud is the episode in which Beatrice's claims to divine powers are tested by the officers of the Inquisition. Sentenced to trial by ordeal, she walks across burning coals without injury, and this convinces her that she is indeed a prophetess (*V* i. 61). It is only many years later that this ostensible '*Judgment of God*' is revealed as a trick, perpetrated by the hostile father-figures of the Inquisition (*V* iii. 72). Beatrice's special insight into the world as a theatre of suffering is the product of a series of such brutalizing deceptions.

Mary Shelley highlights the wider implications of this displaced critique of religious orthodoxies through Beatrice's 'Anathema' in which she openly denounces the God of orthodox Christianity. Mary Shelley obviously expected to antagonize reviewers who had already criticized *Frankenstein* for its impiety: 'Did the End of Beatrice surprise you,' she wrote to Maria Gisborne in May 1823. 'I am surprised that none of these Literary Gazettes are shocked.'[27] Announcing the 'eternal and victorious influence of evil' brought about by Castruccio's reign, Beatrice directly accuses a malevolent Creator who promotes domestic strife, war, disease, and tyranny:

> Oh! Surely God's hand is the chastening hand of a father, that thus torments his children! His children? his eternal enemies. . . . Did not the power you worship create the passions of man; his desires which outleap possibility, and bring ruin upon his head? . . . And then we are told the fault is ours; good and evil are sown in our hearts, and ours is the tillage, ours the harvest; and can this justify an omnipotent deity that he permits one particle of pain to subsist in his world? (*V* iii. 45–7)

Here Mary Shelley's use of imagery of diseased nature in connection with paternal tyranny prefigures her dramatization of the plague's advance in *The Last Man*. Like the heroine of Percy Shelley's *The Cenci*, who experiences her father's incestuous violence in terms of tainted air which 'eats into [her] sinews' (III. i. 21), Beatrice discovers the 'influence' of Castruccio's tyranny as the very atmosphere of life: it 'circulates like air about us, clinging to our flesh like a poisonous garment' (*V* iii. 44). In *The Last Man* the air is literally contaminated as it forms the agency for the spread of disease, and this image retains its disturbing association with a

27 See above, n. 23; cf. Mary Shelley to Leigh Hunt, 18[19] Aug. 1823, *MSL* i. 374.

Malevolent Creator who has abused his offspring. Beatrice's despairing vision of universal persecution forms only a prelude to her decline into madness and death.

In these women's narratives Mary Shelley exploits devices of historical distancing to give unusually direct expression to the decay of meaning at the heart of her fictional enterprise. By contrast, the structural complexity of *Frankenstein* works to relegate the story of demonic reversal to a fable, and it is in subjective nightmare alone that Victor envisages the race of men, not in their fullest Promethean potential, but turning into corpses. But in Beatrice's narrative this parodic Gothic vision forms the dominant character of experience, undercutting theological and political frames of reference alike. This erosion of systematic forms of belief becomes central in *The Last Man*, where Mary Shelley introduces a succession of consoling explanations only to drain them of significance. Such an extreme vision of cultural dissolution requires a radical extension and remoulding of Godwinian techniques.

The Last Man

> Let no man seek
> Henceforth to be foretold what shall befall
> Him or his children. *Milton*[28]

Mary Shelley's movement away from enabling dialogue in *The Last Man* is implicit even in the epigraph, which replaces Adam's interrogative statement at the start of *Frankenstein* with a dire prediction. After *Valperga* Mary Shelley returns to a theme which she described as 'more wild & imaginative & I think more in my way',[29] but her earlier experimentation with the multiple first-person narrative gives way to a single confessional form, anticipating the conservative stance of the 1831 *Frankenstein*. Set in the future, *The Last Man* is structured as a retrospective analysis of world collapse in which Lionel Verney, the last man, tells of the wiping out of humanity by an incurable plague. The novel's three volumes enact the phases of disintegration set in motion by Frankenstein's quest on a cosmic scale.

[28] *PL* xi. 770–2; cf. epigraph to *Frankenstein*, *PL* x. 743–5; Mary Shelley reread *Paradise Lost* and *Paradise Regained* in 1819 and 1820, *MSJ* i. 303, 346.

[29] Mary Shelley to Leigh Hunt, 2[5] Oct. 1823, *MSL* i. 393.

Verney starts life with every confidence in his ability to control his environment. Exiled from society because of his father's wrongs, he is brought up in Cumberland with his sister Perdita, whose name evokes the pastoral seclusion of *The Winter's Tale*. But Verney's early life owes more to Wordsworth's and Rousseau's images of natural man than to Shakespeare: absorbed in lawless passions, Verney scarcely registers England's transformation from monarchy to republic in the year 2073. However, he begins to develop moral awareness when he meets Adrian, second Earl of Windsor, son of the dethroned monarch and an exemplary figure of sympathy and love. Verney's relationship with Adrian creates a new Eden of affective harmony, which is further heightened when he marries Adrian's sister Idris. Meanwhile Lord Raymond, an exemplar of egotistical ambition, is distracted from his craving for political power into marriage with Perdita. Along with Adrian, the two couples establish an idyllic community at Windsor. Several years pass, now memorialized by Verney as a vision of lost human potential. Raymond becomes Lord Protector of England, but his extravagant plans for public benevolence are forgotten when he starts visiting in secret the exiled Greek Evadne, whose ambition mirrors his own. When Perdita discovers that he has been deceiving her, he resigns the Lord Protectorship and sets off to lead the campaign to free Greece from Turkish oppression.

This collapse of domestic relationship proves to be only the first stage in the decline of advanced political society. In volume two the scene shifts to Greece. Determined to liberate Constantinople from the Turks, Raymond achieves a hollow victory. When he makes a triumphal entry into the besieged city he finds its inhabitants dead of the plague, and his quest for glory ends with his own death and the release of the disease into Europe. Having followed Raymond to Greece with Perdita, Verney forces her to return to England, but she commits suicide on the way home. Reports of outbreaks of plague in Asia and America quickly establish the disease as a threat to the entire human race. Further portents of natural disorder, freak storms and black suns, herald the steady advance of the plague across Europe. Its arrival in England leads to the rapid breakdown of social order. Verney resolves to lead his family and friends in search of some 'uncontaminated seclusion' (*LM* 176) elsewhere in Europe.

A heightened tone of prophetic utterance opens volume three, in which Verney recounts this final exodus and its dramatic collapse into a Gothic pursuit between the 'failing remnant' (*LM* 308) of the species and the plague. At this point Verney himself contracts the plague, and is the only person to do so and recover. As the survivors travel through Paris and Versailles, scenes of former revolutionary activity, internal strife is stirred up by the few remaining men of talents, religious leaders, even as the numbers decline. By the time that the party has crossed the Alps to reach the *mer de glace*, only Verney, Adrian, and two of Verney's children remain. Significantly, at this scene of Frankenstein's meeting with his creature, the plague departs. The survivors drift south into Italy, where they are dwarfed by the ruins of Rome and Venice, and witness the overwhelming profusion of the natural world which threatens to displace the edifices of man-made civilization. They set sail for Greece only to be shipwrecked in a violent storm. Verney alone crawls ashore into an empty world. His subsequent narrative confirms that the monster's experience of cosmic victimization has become that of all mankind. Alienated, despairing, and unbearably lonely, Verney ends his tale by setting out on a futile but compulsive quest for companionship.

This brief account should already indicate Mary Shelley's arresting development of the concerns of *Frankenstein*, fulfilling the monster's prophecy that Frankenstein's failure to honour his obligations will release 'an evil . . . so great, that not only you and your family, but thousands of others, shall be swallowed up in the whirlwinds of its rage' (*F* 96). In addition, this apocalyptic theme requires a more capacious narrative form than is found in earlier Godwinian novels. Muriel Spark has drawn attention to Mary Shelley's originality in following *Frankenstein*, 'the first of a new and hybrid fictional species', with 'an entirely new genre, compounded . . . of the domestic romance, the Gothic extravaganza and the sociological novel'.[30] To do justice to Mary Shelley's synthesis of different forms, however, we also need to recognize the general currency of 'hybrid' fictional modes in the 1820s, a period of remarkable formal innovation in the novel.

While studying Scott's novels throughout 1821 and 1822, Mary Shelley also read Thomas Hope's *Anastasius; or, Memoirs of a*

[30] Muriel Spark, *Child of Light: A Reassessment of Mary Wollstonecraft Shelley* (Hadleigh, 1951), 128, 2; cf. her *Mary Shelley* (London, 1988), 153, 188.

Greek (1819).[31] Set against the conflict between Turkey and Greece in the 1770s, this witty confessional narrative includes a survey of Christian, Greek, and Islamic customs, and its account of an outbreak of plague at Constantinople may have provided a direct stimulus to Mary Shelley's novel. Novelistic interest in cultures remote from the Christian religion is also evident in Tom Moore's *The Epicurean* (1827), in which the philosopher of the title travels to Egypt in pursuit of the elixir of immortality, but ends up as a convert to Christianity. By contrast with these displaced treatments of contemporary issues, the novels of fashionable life that influenced Edward Lytton Bulwer's Godwinian experiments in the late 1820s also deserve notice. Theodore Hook's *Sayings and Doings* (1824–8) and Benjamin Disraeli's *Vivian Grey* (1826–7) offered little more than satirical commentaries on aristocratic manners, but it was the flexibility of this 'silver fork' mode that attracted the Tory MP Robert Plumer Ward to novel-writing.[32] Introducing his first work, *Tremaine; or, The Man of Refinement* (1825), as a 'treatise on moral philosophy, not a novel', Ward sought to promote orthodox religious belief through contemporary political satire, and opened the way for Bulwer's masterly blend of first-person narrative, fashionable novel, and political analysis in *Pelham; or, The Adventures of a Gentleman* (1828).[33] In the same period Peacock departed from his earlier conversational mode to produce more generalized, historical treatments of contemporary political issues in *Maid Marian* (1822) and in *The Misfortunes of Elphin* (1829).[34]

This development of other modes of intellectual fiction, especially in the area of political and cultural analysis, provides the background to Mary Shelley's innovative contribution to the Godwinian tradition in *The Last Man*. Indeed, the range of models available for fictional treatments of contemporary issues may suggest that the concept of a distinctively Godwinian form is no longer valid. For example, Lee Sterrenburg has pointed out that in formal terms *The Last Man* combines confession and anatomy, and thus anticipates nineteenth-century assessments of cultural

[31] Entries for Sept. 1821, Feb. 1822, *MSJ* i. 379–80, 397–8.

[32] See Hazlitt, 'The Dandy School' [1827], *Works*, xx. 143–9; Ellen Moers, *The Dandy: Brummell to Beerbohm* (London, 1960), 52–64.

[33] Robert Plumer Ward, *Tremaine; or, The Man of Refinement*, 3 vols. (London, 1825), i, p. xii; *Pelham* is discussed in Moers, *The Dandy*, 68–82.

[34] *Maid Marian* and *The Misfortunes of Elphin* are discussed in Marilyn Butler, *Peacock Displayed: A Satirist in his Context* (London, 1979), 14–82.

fragmentation such as Carlyle's *Sartor Resartus* (1833–4).[35] But while Sterrenburg's essay gives welcome attention to Mary Shelley's strong sense of contemporary politics, on closer analysis her work cannot be so readily assimilated into this later tradition.

Above all, Mary Shelley lacks any stable system of values from which to conduct an authoritative cultural analysis. Instead her emphasis on man's inability to find a meaningful role maintains the uncompromising secular stance of cultural surveys of the French revolutionary period, notably *Political Justice*, *St Leon*, Godwin's own fictional anatomy of ideals, and Volney's *Ruins*. For it is Mary Shelley's saturation in Godwin and Volney, and her familiarity with the ideas of Plato's *Republic*,[36] to which Godwin and Volney are also indebted, that gives *The Last Man* its remarkable philosophical unity. In particular, the extravagant scale of her parade of political ideals owes much to Volney's apocalyptic vision of the dissolution of an essentially tyrannical cultural order.

Again, Mary Shelley alone has the imaginative discipline to embody these concerns in narrative form. Building on her highly allusive and indirect treatment of public themes in *Frankenstein*, she expands the analytical scope of the Godwinian novel to incorporate a comprehensive survey of intellectual outlooks. In an adventurous strategy, she recasts the retrospective structure of earlier Godwinian narratives as a projection into the future, creating her own dystopian mode. This formal innovation provides crucial support for her dismantling of political systems, for it erodes the dialogic and provisional quality of earlier works such as *Caleb Williams*, rejecting the faith in private judgement it embodies. The narrator of *The Last Man* is faced with the impossibility of controlling history, society, or nature, and this dwarfing of the individual is central to the plot's oppressive imaginative power. While even Frankenstein, in the 1818 text, is presented with moral choices, and his confrontation with the monster initially takes the form of rational debate, here the plague is presented as an invincible force with which man has no community.

This starkly uncompromising narrative form has posed problems for critics ever since the novel's first publication. To some extent,

[35] Lee Sterrenburg, '*The Last Man*: Anatomy of Failed Revolutions', *Nineteenth Century Fiction*, 33 (1978), 342, to which my study is indebted.

[36] Percy Shelley read Plato's *Republic* to Mary in Nov. 1818 and Oct. 1819, *MSJ* i. 235, 300.

the failure of nineteenth-century critics to engage with Mary Shelley's intellectual purpose is a direct consequence of the novel's radically disenchanted view of society. While Mary Shelley's imaginative boldness gives *The Last Man*, in Grylls's words, 'a terror beyond that of *Frankenstein*',[37] her drive to emotional and intellectual extremes was scarcely in keeping with later nineteenth-century confidence in man's material and colonial advances. Even the novel's first reviewers refused to acknowledge its topicality. The *Monthly Review* described the work as 'the product of a diseased imagination', while the *Monthly Magazine* took the opportunity to condemn *Frankenstein* as well on the grounds of the subjectivity Mary Shelley persistently criticized: 'the whole course of her ambition has been to pourtray monsters which could have existed only in her own conceptions, and to involve them in scenes and events which are wholly unparalleled by any thing that the world has yet witnessed'.[38] The *Panoramic Miscellany* similarly avoided discussion of the novel's content except to criticize the choice of a promising subject 'incompetently treated'.[39]

Mary Shelley's fictionalized portrayal of Percy Shelley and Byron in the two leading male characters, Adrian and Raymond, provoked further critical hostility. One reviewer went so far as to ask why Mary Shelley did not write a novel about being '*the last Woman*', since then 'she would have known better how to paint her distress at having nobody left to talk to'.[40] For twentieth-century critics, the notion that 'Lionel Verney was the symbol of Mary's lonely widowhood', while obviously having some force, has continued to inhibit recognition of the novel's impersonal intellectual themes.[41]

As in the case of *Frankenstein*, Mary Shelley herself encouraged a

[37] R. Glynn Grylls, 'Mary Shelley's Novels', letter in *Times Literary Supplement* (11 Apr. 1935), 244, quoted in W. H. Lyles, *Mary Shelley: An Annotated Bibliography* (New York, 1975), 136.

[38] Review of *The Last Man*, *Monthly Review*, quoted in Poovey, *Proper Lady*, 158; review of *The Last Man*, *Monthly Magazine*, 1 (Mar. 1826), 334.

[39] Review of *The Last Man*, *Panoramic Miscellany*, 1 (Mar. 1826), 380.

[40] Review of *The Last Man*, *London Literary Gazette*, 474 (18 Feb. 1826), 103, quoted in Lyles, *Mary Shelley*, 175.

[41] Nitchie, *Mary Shelley*, 16; cf. Edmund Gosse, 'Shelley's Widow', *Silhouettes* (London, 1925), 231–8; Ernest J. Lovell, Jr., 'Byron and Mary Shelley', *Keats–Shelley Journal*, 2 (1953), 35–49; studies which move beyond a biographical framework are Robert Lance Snyder, 'Apocalypse and Indeterminacy in Mary Shelley's *The Last Man*', *SIR* 17 (1978), 435–52; Sterrenburg, '*The Last Man*'; cf. Poovey, *Proper Lady*, 146–58; Mellor, *Mary Shelley*, 141–69.

defensive biographical myth. *The Last Man* formed her major literary project after her return to an inhospitable and repressive England in August 1823. Beset by financial worries and the legacy of scandal surrounding Percy Shelley and her parents, she remained intellectually and emotionally isolated for several years.[42] In her bleakest periods of depression, her journal seems to corroborate biographical readings of her work. As she wrote on 14 May 1824: 'The last man! Yes I may well describe that solitary being's feelings, feeling myself as the last relic of a beloved race, my companions, extinct before me' (*MSJ* ii. 476–7).[43] Her deliberate fictionalization of aspects of Byron's and Percy Shelley's thought must raise the question of how far she is simply reworking previous material in order to retain a hold on the past. Certainly she invited interpretations of *The Last Man* as a memorial to 'the Elect'. As she wrote to John Bowring of her relationship with Percy Shelley: 'Romance is tame compared with all that we experienced together. . . . I have endeavoured, but how inadequately to give some idea of him in my last published book.'[44]

Yet any reading of *The Last Man* as authorial therapy must be set against Mary Shelley's intellectual mastery of depressing circumstances. Grylls has persuasively argued that 'Shelley's death, which she took to be the end of her development, was really the beginning of it'.[45] In December 1822 Mary Shelley wrote to Jane Williams, 'I am more & more convinced that blank as my future life must be, it is only in books and literary occupation that I shall ever find alleviation.'[46] As she became increasingly determined to control and direct her literary powers, Godwin offered a new source of encouragement and support: 'Your talents are truly extraordinary,' he wrote to Mary in February 1823. ' "Frankenstein" is universally known, and . . . is everywhere respected . . . you have cultivated your mind in a manner most admirably adapted to make you a great and successful author.'[47] Mary Shelley's extensive period of

[42] Poovey, *Proper Lady*, 147–8.

[43] On the next day Mary Shelley attributed this depression to her foreboding of Byron's death, reported in the English newspapers on 14 June 1824, *MSJ* ii. 477 and n.

[44] Mary Shelley to John Bowring, 25 Feb. [1826], *MSL* i. 512.

[45] Grylls, *Mary Shelley*, p. xv.

[46] Mary Shelley to Jane Williams, 5 Dec. 1822, *MSL* i. 296.

[47] Godwin to Mary Shelley, 14 Feb. 1823, Kegan Paul, *William Godwin*, ii. 282.

research for *The Last Man* shows no falling-off from the breadth of intellectual preoccupations in *Frankenstein* and *Valperga*.[48]

Especially revealing of Mary Shelley's conscious artistic purpose is her comment in a letter to John Howard Payne on 'the necessity of making the scene < general > universal to all mankind and of combining this with a particular interest which must constitute the novel'.[49] Four years later, in a review of Godwin's *Cloudesley*, she openly rejected 'the merely copying from our own hearts' as a fit basis for works of art.[50] Nowhere is this sense of impersonal artistic creativity more evident than in the Preface to *The Last Man*. Mary Shelley begins with an account of her visit to the Cumaean Sibyl with Percy Shelley in 1818, but her development of the cave image owes more to the Platonic allegory of the Cave of Making than to autobiographical points of reference.[51] Though she is led to the cave by her companion, she alone can construct the truth hidden in the Sibyl's leaves. Crucially this task is imaged through a reversal of Plato's account of intellectual growth. According to Plato, the true philosopher must learn to distinguish between deceptive shadows of justice and truth in the firelit cave and intelligible forms in the light of the sun.[52] For Mary Shelley, however, the deeper into the cavern of mental fictions she penetrates, the closer she comes to the 'truths contained in these poetic rhapsodies' (*LM* 4). In addition, the Sibyl's mysterious 'written characters', cryptic in appearance and inscribed in different languages, evoke Mary Shelley's inclusive vision of past, present, and future cultural traditions: 'ancient Chaldee, and Egyptian hieroglyphics, old as the Pyramids . . . some were in modern dialects, English and Italian . . . they seemed to contain prophecies, detailed relations of events but lately passed; names, now well known, but of modern date' (*LM* 3). Mary Shelley depicts the writer's role as one of transforming these 'scattered and unconnected' fragments into an intelligible language.

Viewed in this perspective, Mary Shelley's allusions to the work of Byron and Percy Shelley move beyond personal reminiscence to

[48] Cf. Mary Shelley to [?Charles Ollier], [?June 1824–Aug. 1825], to John Cam Hobhouse, 19 Feb. [1825], and to John Howard Payne, 27 Sept. [1825], *MSL* i. 431, 466, 502.

[49] Mary Shelley to Payne, 28 Jan. [7 Feb.] 1826, *MSL* i. 510.

[50] [Mary Shelley], review of *Cloudesley*, *Blackwood's*, 27 (May 1830), 712.

[51] The Shelleys visited the Bay of Naples on 8 Dec. 1818, *MSJ* i. 242; on issues of female creativity, see Gilbert and Gubar, *Madwoman in the Attic*, 95–104.

[52] Plato, *The Republic*, trans. A. D. Lindsay, ed. Renford Bambrough, Everyman's Library (London, 1976, 1984), Bk. 6: 514–18, pp. 207–12.

support her analysis of various beliefs by which individuals seek to order their experience. Indeed, Mary Shelley's rigorous focus on mental attitudes calls into question any criticism based on identification with individual characters. Ironically, it was the apparent rationalist Godwin who drew attention to her analytical mode of characterization in his memorable criticism of her manuscript tragedy, submitted to him in 1824: 'Your personages are mere abstractions, the lines and points of a Mathematical Diagram, and not men and women. If A crosses B, and C falls upon D, who can weep for that?'[53] This comment may seem to indicate a weakness in Mary Shelley's depiction of emotionally compelling characters, but it is read more profitably as a pointer to the distinctive quality of her art. Her intention is rarely to make us weep, but rather to make us think. Even in *Frankenstein*, she is chiefly concerned to explore intellectual passions, and her treatment of character in *The Last Man* confirms this shift away from the psychological subtleties of earlier Godwinian novels. It is this interest in the type, rather than the individual, that underlies her rather schematic opposition of characters in the service of her revaluation of political ideals.[54] Even minor characters such as Adrian's mother, the Countess of Windsor, are depicted in symbolic class terms: when she dies the survivors bid farewell to 'the last tie binding us to the ancient state of things' (*LM* 303).

Recognition of Mary Shelley's assimilation of the literary and political debates of the 1790s should not lead us to overlook the sheer topicality of *The Last Man*. The 'last man' theme had already provided Byron and Mary Shelley with a potent source of images for their secular fantasies of cultural decay in 'Darkness' and *Frankenstein*.[55] But this emphasis on world catastrophe gained further momentum in the early 1820s. Cuvier's theory of the world's evolution through successive natural disasters seemed to be confirmed by a series of outbreaks of epidemic disease, which offered concrete evidence of man's inability to control nature.

Other artists also responded to these unsettling times with a heightened emphasis on the millennial recurrence of world-collapse. Beginning in 1817 and working throughout the 1820s, the

[53] Godwin to Mary Shelley, 27 Feb. 1824, Kegan Paul, *William Godwin*, ii. 289.

[54] Cf. Northrop Frye's definition of 'Menippean satire' as exemplified by Peacock's novels, *Anatomy of Criticism* (Princeton, NJ, 1957), 309.

[55] See above, pp. 150–4.

painter John Martin produced a series of epic compositions which depicted Old Testament catastrophes such as the collapse of Nineveh and Babylon, and the Deluge.[56] According to his biographer William Feaver, Martin's epic paintings 'underlined the cyclical, virtually millennial, recurrence of catastrophe in world history' at a time when 'representations of storms, eruptions and earthquake swept like tidal waves through . . . periodicals, broadsheets, panoramas, and paintings'.[57] What appealed to Mary Shelley in this popular trend was its sense of human littleness, dwarfed by towering natural forces, a theme already evident in Scott's depiction of civil conflict.[58] When Raymond makes his apparently triumphal entry into Constantinople, for instance, Verney remains at a distance, watching through a telescope. By placing Verney as a helpless onlooker, Mary Shelley underlines the futility and triviality of Raymond's final heroic gesture. From such a distance, Verney can no longer distinguish Raymond from 'the pigmy forms of the crowd', and the entire human drama is wiped out when the city collapses in 'terrific thunders' (*LM* 144).

In late 1826 Martin produced the first of three paintings of the last man's vision of a dying universe, in which he claimed to be inspired by Thomas Campbell's influential poem, 'The Last Man'.[59] But Campbell's poem was first published in the *New Monthly Magazine* for September 1823, along with an author's note which would have reminded Mary Shelley of Byron's earlier secular prophecy of world decay. 'Many years ago', wrote Campbell, 'I had the idea of this last Man in my head and I distinctly remember speaking on the subject to Lord B[yron]. I recognized, when I read his poem "Darkness", some traits of the picture I meant to draw.'[60] However, Campbell's own poem belongs with more orthodox treatments of world catastrophe, since

[56] William Feaver, *The Art of John Martin* (Oxford, 1975), 39–45, 92–7, 99–103; on Martin's paintings and Godwin's novels, see Gilfillan, 'William Godwin', 21.

[57] Feaver, *John Martin*, 70.

[58] Cf. Scott's description of the moorlands before the battle of Drumclog in *Old Mortality*, *Waverley Novels*, x. 108–10 (ch. 7).

[59] Martin produced paintings on the 'last man' theme in 1826, 1832, and 1849; Feaver, *John Martin*, 95, 184, 223.

[60] Thomas Campbell, author's note to 'The Last Man' [Sept. 1823], l. 19, which concludes: 'I am entirely disposed to acquit Lord Byron of having intentionally taken the thoughts', *Complete Poetical Works*, ed. J. Logie Robertson (Oxford, 1907), 234.

the last man's vision of universal decay provides a test of Christian faith, and his message to the narrator is one of unequivocal trust in God's purposes:

> 'Go, tell the night that hides thy face
> Thou saw'st the last of Adam's race
>   On earth's sepulchral clod
> The darkening universe defy
> To quench his immortality
>   Or shake his trust in God!' (ll. 75–80)

It is precisely this uncritical faith in a benign God that Mary Shelley undercuts when she exploits current fears of epidemical disease for her own secular literary purpose. In 1817 a cholera epidemic in Bengal posed a serious threat to Europe for the first time. As William McNeill has pointed out, what was most disturbing about cholera was its capacity to bypass quarantine stages, which made it seem ineradicable.[61] Though previously confined to Bengal, in 1817 movements of English trade and troops carried it to other areas. By 1818 cholera had spread overland to the northern frontiers of India; by 1821 it had been carried by sea to Indonesia, China, and Japan, and had also crept to the Persian Gulf. This outbreak had scarcely run its course when a second wave began in 1826. Fears of the disease reaching England were widespread, and the demonstrable link between infection, trade, and troop movements was not lost on critics of the present state of society. Thus, in his *Colloquies on the . . . Prospects of Society* (1829), Southey invoked pestilence as a punishment for society's absorption in purely materialistic progress: 'Visitations of this kind are in the order of nature and of Providence . . . and looking to the moral government of the world, was there ever a time when the sins of this kingdom called out more cryingly for chastisement?'[62]

Mary Shelley similarly exploits plague imagery to criticize contemporary moral and political values. As early as May 1817, she read Defoe's *Journal of the Plague Year* (1722) and John Wilson's poem, *The City of the Plague* (1816), but she found a more illuminating use of plague imagery for conservative social commentary in Brown's *Arthur Mervyn*, which is set in post-revolutionary Philadelphia at the time of a yellow-fever epidemic.[63]

[61] William H. McNeill, *Plagues and Peoples* (1976; Harmondsworth, 1979), 341–2.

[62] Southey, *Sir Thomas More*, i. 51.

[63] *MSJ* i. 171, 177.

In this 'theatre of pestilence' (*AM* 144), disease throws into sharp relief the moral degeneration of post-revolutionary society, as grasping self-interest leads to the decay of 'the strongest ties that bind human beings together' (*AM* 133).

On 8 June 1824, Mary Shelley wrote of the resurgence of creative powers that she planned to channel into *The Last Man*: 'I will celebrate thee, O England, and cast a glory on thy name!' (*MSJ* ii. 479) In the event, however, her commentary on national values is profoundly critical. If she adopts the disease metaphor as a familiar analogy for political disorder, she gives special emphasis to the incurable nature of England's sickness. The republican setting of her tale brings to mind the form of government praised by Godwin in the *History of the Commonwealth*, but she also follows Brown in linking republicanism with commerce. Repeated references to the 'busy spirit of money-making . . . peculiar to our country' (*LM* 181) point up the destructive effects of the love of gain on an entire civilization. Thus fear of the plague leads to the 'snapping of dear affinities' within the family and the disintegration of whole communities into a world of outcasts 'wandering separate from each other' (*LM* 191, 194). As in recent events in Bengal, trading routes guide the plague into the heart of Europe: Verney points out that merchants have carried the disease from the East to Athens, fulfilling the ominous speculation of William Dunlap, Brown's early biographer: 'no one will say that on the return of those blessings which foreign commerce is supposed to bestow on nations, we, in the midst of security, shall not be again visited by a disease which constantly exists in some of the countries to which our merchants and sailors resort for profit'.[64] Crucially, the plague is associated not only with trade but with tyranny, a theme already implicit in *Valperga*, where Castruccio's father is an early victim of 'malignant fever, brought by some trading vessels from the Levant', and the death of Euthanasia's republican family from disease exposes her to the brutalities of Castruccio's regime (*V* i. 37, 207). Verney further highlights this link when he comments that the 'extensive commercial relations' of the Turks 'gave every European nation an interest' in the success of their aggrandizing project in Greece (*LM* 115). As the fatal outcome of Raymond's campaign reaffirms, the forces that promote England's encroachment on

[64] Dunlap, *Memoirs*, 101.

other nations in conquest and in commerce also lead to the retribution of the plague.

Finally, though, Verney's narrative diverges from 'the masterly delineations of the author of Arthur Mervyn' (*LM* 187), for Mary Shelley endows the image of the plague with multiple and competing significances. At one level, in keeping with earlier critiques of advanced society, she locates the source of the plague in man's rapacious desire for power, which infects aristocratic and republican values alike. In this respect the republican politician Ryland comes closest to the true meaning of the plague when he criticizes Adrian's optimistic notion that man's energy of mind will save him from destruction: 'Be assured that earth is not, nor ever can be heaven, while the seeds of hell are natives of her soil' (*LM* 159). That man's energy of mind is more likely to lead to universal catastrophe is only too evident from Raymond's disastrous exploits. Verney himself supports this conservative interpretation of the plague as an image of man's incurably diseased consciousness, when he surmises that in the Alps 'we should find health, if in truth health were not herself diseased' (*LM* 287). Yet at another, more profoundly disquieting level, mankind is seen to be simply at the mercy of malevolent external forces: 'Nature, our mother, and our friend, had turned on us a brow of menace' (*LM* 168). As another 'invincible monster . . . more cruel than tempest, less tame than fire' (*LM* 160), pestilence threatens the entire future of the human species. In this sense it carries a truly Gothic burden of significance, forcing characters to move out of the realm of choice into that of destiny. Yet Verney's efforts to find a coherent explanation for the plague need to be seen in the context of his ambivalent role as prophet of universal catastrophe.

The Fall of Empires

Like Frankenstein's monster, the figure of Verney invites competing critical interpretations. On the one hand he has been identified with other larger-than-life figures of Romantic alienation, such as the Ancient Mariner, the Solitary of *The Excursion*, and the hero of Maturin's *Melmoth the Wanderer* (1820).[65] More recently, his

[65] Hugh J. Luke, Jr., 'Introduction' to Mary W. Shelley, *The Last Man* (Lincoln, Nebr., 1965), p. xvii.

limited perspective as the 'last man' has given scope for readings of the novel in terms of modern gender theories.[66] However, this most isolated of first-person narrators is best viewed in the more historically specific context of the Godwinian tradition. Mary Shelley draws directly on earlier critical portraits of solitary seekers after knowledge in *St Leon*, *Childe Harold*, and, to a lesser extent, *Alastor*. In adopting the subjective narrative voice of earlier Godwinian novels, she foregrounds Verney's unreliability as the sole witness of the dissolution of all creeds. She is especially indebted to Godwin's sceptical use of the myth of the Wandering Jew in *St Leon*. Reborn through the secret powers of alchemy, St Leon exults: 'For me the laws of nature are suspended . . . I am destined to be triumphant over fate and time' (*SL* ii. 108). But this unprecedented detachment from historical processes only leads to a crushing awareness of his lack of significance, anticipating the radical displacement of Frankenstein's creature. Mary Shelley similarly underlines Verney's special status through a series of archetypal rebirths. Most important, he is the only character to survive being infected by the plague, after which he gains a superhuman vitality: 'My body . . . was exuberant with health . . . methought I could emulate the speed of the racehorse . . . hear the operations of nature in her mute abodes' (*LM* 250). He comments that the period of violent storms which precedes the exodus from England requires the resistance of 'more than human energy' (*LM* 271), and this is what he eventually possesses. When only four people are left on earth, Verney alone—'an excellent swimmer' (*LM* 322)—survives the shipwreck that claims the lives of the other three.

While Verney presents an extreme version of Godwin's isolated, questing figure, his peculiarly androgynous nature marks a significant departure from earlier novels. Mary Shelley seeks to synthesize within a single personality the value-systems represented by different characters in *St Leon* and *Frankenstein*. In his quasi-Wordsworthian boyhood, Verney exhibits all the traits of a masculinist desire to impose himself on nature: in his daily 'acts of tyranny' he appears 'as uncouth a savage as the wolf-bred founder of old Rome' (*LM* 12, 9). However, Adrian's tutelage in the domestic affections brings about the first of his many rebirths. As

[66] Gilbert and Gubar, *Madwoman in the Attic*, 146–7; Rosemary Jackson, *Fantasy: The Literature of Subversion* (London, 1981), 103.

Verney's previous spirit of confrontation is replaced by love and sympathy, he finds himself 'as much changed as if [he] had transmigrated into another form . . . all was softened and humanized' (*LM* 21–2). He remains an exemplary figure of domestic values for the rest of the novel. Unlike St Leon, he successfully combines a sweeping cultural overview with familial obligations: when he attends a performance of *Macbeth*, he identifies not only with Ross's lament for the decline of his country, but also with Macduff's grief and anger at the destruction of his family (*LM* 204).

Verney's unreliability as prophet of universal catastrophe equally needs to be seen in relation to Volney's *Ruins*, which is structured as an optimistic reading of political upheaval. At the start of his quest for the meaning of the fall of empires, Volney's traveller seems to prefigure Verney's role: 'Who knows but that hereafter some traveller like myself . . . will sit down solitary amid silent ruins, and weep a people inurned, and their greatness changed into an empty name?' (*RE* 8) Like Adam in Book XI of *Paradise Lost*, the traveller speculates that a 'mysterious God' has pronounced a 'secret malediction against the earth', sanctioning the decay of civilization. But the limitations of this despairing view are made apparent when the Genius of the place intervenes and asks: 'Is it the arm of God that has introduced the sword into the city . . . or is it the arm of man? . . . Is it his pride that creates murderous wars, or is it the pride of kings and their ministers?' (*RE* 9) Through a review of the growth of civilization, the Genius educates the traveller into an awareness that notions of divine irresponsibility and blind fatality are the product of human fears and wishes rather than external deity (*RE* 171–2). Thus man must recognize his own responsibility for the tyranny and violence which dominates patriarchal society, a lesson which Verney fails to learn.

The recognition that all schemes of order may be structured on terms of violent confrontation underlies Mary Shelley's critical assessment of political ideals. Like the dreamer in Percy Shelley's *The Triumph of Life* (1822), Verney witnesses an essentially Gothic decay of meaning as successive creeds are parodied and drained of significance by the relentless advance of the plague.[67] Developing the pattern of Utopian expectation and demonic reversal established

[67] Cf. Shelley, *The Triumph of Life* (1822), ll. 208–93.

in *Frankenstein*, Mary Shelley offers a profoundly disenchanted commentary on the age of revolution, which ends in a total rejection of the progressive ideals of her own generation. Furthermore, this generalized treatment of intellectual issues conveys a richer sense of contemporary political debate than is present in *Frankenstein.*

At the outset, the novel's parade of biblical resonances alerts us to Mary Shelley's sceptical redeployment of myth in the manner of *Frankenstein.* Taken together, the epigraphs to *Frankenstein* and *The Last Man* introduce Milton's planned justification of the ways of God to men only to exclude the possibility of intelligible explanation. In Mary Shelley's decontextualized reading, Adam's challenge to an apparently irresponsible Creator—'Did I solicit thee | From darkness to promote me?' (*PL* x. 744–5)—gives way not to consoling insight but to uncomprehending despair at the prospect of the end of the race. The retrospective structure of Verney's narrative reinforces this deterministic outlook, as he succumbs to the belief in blind fatality that Volney's traveller warns against. As he recalls how his youthful optimism has given way to disappointment, he abandons any belief in human potential for improvement: 'What is there in our nature that is for ever urging us on towards pain and misery?' (*LM* 23) Catastrophic external events corroborate his suspicion of a malevolent force ruling the universe, and he resigns himself to the role of passive commentator on the world's decay: 'since what is, must be, I will sit amidst the ruins and smile' (*LM* 290).

Verney's invocation of biblical parallels reinforces this lack of intelligible explanation, pointing up the entirely secular quality of Mary Shelley's eschatology.[68] As in *Frankenstein*, the novel's theological frame of reference highlights the erosion of stable moral referents. Images of the inevitable encroachment of 'the earth's desolator . . . even as an arch-fiend' (*LM* 177) into the paradise of England depict the plague as man's final fall. As when the monster has set fire to the De Laceys' cottage, man is left 'solitary, like to our first parents' with 'the whole . . . earth before him' (*LM* 234), but this proves to be the end rather than the beginning of earthly existence. Verney attempts to explain the survivors' exile from England by analogy with biblical episodes associated with the

[68] Mary Shelley read 'The Bible as far as the Psalms' in 1819, and 'The Bible until the end of Ezekhiel' in 1820, *MSJ* i. 304, 345.

apocalyptic political hopes of the Civil War period.[69] While, like Adam and Eve, they seek to recover an Edenic state of innocence in some 'fertile spot' where they may 'replant the uprooted tree of humanity' (*LM* 237), their quest also recalls the Israelites' flight from plague-stricken Egypt in search of the Promised Land. Yet the hidden promise of these allusions proves illusory: the prospects of the dying race cannot be identified with Adam's and Eve's exile into an imperfect world, and they are no longer a chosen people with a right to a land of their own. In Exodus the plague falls on the Egyptians alone, but here it has no power of moral discrimination. When the fifty survivors reach the Alps, they mistakenly greet 'the divine magnificence of this terrestrial exhibition' (*LM* 305) as a sign of their salvation; but they are speedily dwarfed by this landscape, which engenders a sense of human equality before death.

Moreover, attempts by the survivors themselves to invoke a controlling divine purpose are depicted as the product of self-interested fanaticism. Verney regards the story of the Deluge as a mere 'imposture' (*LM* 296) which divides the people by fostering the illusion of an elect who will be saved from calamity. It is thus an indication of Verney's desperation in the face of inexplicable events that he too wishfully compares the boat carrying the last four members of the race to Noah's ark (*LM* 320), but the futility of this gesture is apparent when the storm destroys all but himself. In his final solitude, he shares Adam's despair—

> How didst thou grieve then, Adam, to behold
> The end of all thy offspring, end so sad,
> Depopulation—

but he lacks the compensating hope provided by God's 'Covenant new' (*PL* xi. 754–6, 867). Though he is further tempted to compare himself with 'that monarch of the waste—Robinson Crusoe' (*LM* 326), he has little of Crusoe's spiritual conviction that Providence 'order'd every Thing for the best'.[70]

Verney's loss of Crusoe's energetic capacity to master the external world equally reflects Volney's vision of the dissolution of an essentially tyrannical cultural order. To some extent *The Last*

[69] On the patterns of 'nonconformist story', see Keeble, *Literary Culture of Nonconformity*, 263–82.

[70] Daniel Defoe, *Robinson Crusoe* (1719), ed. J. Donald Crowley (Oxford, 1972), 108; read by Mary Shelley 27 Apr.–11 May 1820, *MSJ* i. 315–18.

Man invites comparison with Mary Shelley's earlier novels in its treatment of opposed world-views based on Volney's *Ruins*. This theme is most evident in her rather schematic juxtaposition of Raymond and Adrian. Raymond's attitude to the external world forms a repetition of Frankenstein's desire for self-aggrandizement: 'He looked on the structure of society as but a part of the machinery which supported the web on which his life was traced. The earth was spread out as a highway for him; the heavens built up as a canopy for him' (*LM* 31). As in the earlier novel, this masculinist desire to appropriate the world for one's own ends forms the beginnings of tyrannical imposition; but here Mary Shelley also pursues the errors of egotistical ambition in the public sphere by dramatizing Raymond's quest for military dominance in Europe. But she also posits an alternative to this excessive desire for power in Adrian's generous and merging temperament. Like the monster before he is 'wrenched by misery to vice and hatred' (*F* 217), Adrian views the universe as a natural dwelling place rather than a scheme to be exploited: 'Adrian felt that he made a part of a great whole. He owned affinity not only with mankind, but all nature was akin to him . . . while he the focus only of this mighty mirror, felt his life mingle with the universe of existence' (*LM* 31). While at one level this opposition of value-systems invites a reading in terms of gender values, it has a more specific historical meaning in Volney's account of civilized and primitive man (*RE* 21–2, 25–7).

For Mary Shelley introduces this polarization of values only to negate it, drawing on Volney's depiction of all human fabrications as a model of oppression. In this perspective, as Hannah Arendt has commented in her discussion of Plato, 'an element of violence is inevitably inherent in all activities of making, fabricating, and producing, that is, all activities in which men directly confront nature'.[71] Verney's later realization that the entire species is about to perish carries the full force of Volney's apocalyptic intimation that civilization built on attempts to tyrannize over nature must be erased so that it may be rebuilt on entirely different terms:

> Will the earth still keep her place among the planets; will she still journey with unmarked regularity round the sun . . . will beasts pasture, birds fly,

[71] Hannah Arendt, *Between Past and Future: Six Exercises in Political Thought* (London, 1961), 111–12.

and fishes swim, when man, the lord, possessor, perceiver, and recorder of all these things, has passed away, as though he had never been? (*LM* 300–1)

Mary Shelley's wholesale rejection of political systems turns on the fact that Raymond's determination to shape the world to his own ends forms the dominant feature of civilization in *The Last Man*. In re-enacting Frankenstein's story of egotistical desire and demonic reversal in the sphere of world history, Mary Shelley makes a decisive break with Godwinian analysis of the social origins of oppression. Instead she presents Raymond as the model of a tyrant whose imposition of authority on others is rooted in his inability to control his own passions.[72] Despite Raymond's success as a parliamentary orator, his desire for fame as 'benefactor of his country' confirms the egotistical origin of his 'thousand beneficial schemes' (*LM* 76). As Lord Protector, he plans to build canals and bridges, and to abolish poverty and disease in the manner of St Leon.[73] But England proves an inadequate sphere for his self-aggrandizing ambition, which leads him to plan a string of foreign conquests. Invoking the examples of Alexander, Caesar, Cromwell, and Napoleon, he aims 'to unite with the Greeks, take Constantinople, and subdue all Asia. I intend to be a warrior, a conqueror; Napoleon's name shall vail to mine' (*LM* 39–40). As with Frankenstein's abandonment of domestic ties, Raymond's failure in the realm of personal relationships invites us to construe his quest for fame as flight rather than pursuit.[74] Mary Shelley presents Raymond's deception of Perdita as yet another form of subjective folly. Possessed by an 'intense feeling of the reality of fiction' (*LM* 89), he is drawn into a secret liaison with Evadne, but what really attracts him is her 'restless energy of character' (*LM* 81), which offers a satisfying duplication of his own ambition. But his breach of domestic trust has unforeseen consequences: it triggers the world-wide collapse of relationship in the wake of the plague, as predicted by Perdita: 'Nature grows old, and shakes in her decaying limbs,—creation has become bankrupt' (*LM* 97).

Yet the collapse of Raymond's quest to liberate Constantinople

[72] For Shelley's treatment of this theme, see P. M. S. Dawson, *The Unacknowledged Legislator: Shelley and Politics* (Oxford, 1980), 109–33.

[73] Cf. *SL* ii. 105–6.

[74] Cf. *F* 51, and Peacock's covert censure of Byronic introspection, *Nightmare Abbey* (1818), *Works*, iii. 103.

from Turkish oppression suggests that it is civilization rather than nature that proves bankrupt. The portentous scene of Raymond's entry into Constantinople encapsulates the novel's shift from political analysis to phenomena that defeat analysis.[75] Notably it is the dying Evadne, the mirror image of Raymond, who prophesies Raymond's defeat and the end of all relationship: 'This is the end of love! . . . Fire, and war, and plague, unite for thy destruction!' (*LM* 131) On the eve of the assault, Raymond succumbs to the same irrational dread and renounces his Promethean dream of human potential: 'each man I meet appears a corse, which will soon be deserted of its animating spark' (*LM* 135). These portents of psychological disintegration culminate in Verney's dream of Timon's last feast:

> I came with keen appetite, the covers were removed, the hot water sent up its unsatisfying steams, while I fled before the anger of the host, who assumed the form of Raymond. . . . my friend's shape, altered by a thousand distortions, expanded into a gigantic phantom, bearing on its brow the sign of pestilence. (*LM* 146)

Here Mary Shelley recasts Frankenstein's dream of Elizabeth 'livid with the hue of death' (*F* 53) and turning into his mother's corpse, to present the plague as a massive force of retribution for man's dreams of conquest and power. Furthermore, behind both images of demonic reversal lies the 'vast, tremendous, unformed spectre' released by revolutionary transgression in Burke's writings on the French Revolution.[76] The parallel is made explicit when Raymond's men shrink back from the gates of Constantinople: 'as if they expected some Mighty Phantom to stalk in offended majesty from the opening' (*LM* 144).

Yet the exact quality of Raymond's heroic aspiration suggests a more thoroughgoing revaluation of ideals than is at first apparent. At one level, Mary Shelley forcefully develops her earlier critique of tyrannical imposition, the wider relevance of which is glimpsed when Frankenstein refuses to allow the monster to retreat to South America with his mate.[77] Raymond's campaign is not overtly

[75] Sterrenburg, '*The Last Man*', 339.

[76] Burke, *Works*, v. 256.

[77] Cf. George Canning's redeployment of this image: 'To turn [the Negro] loose in . . . the maturity of his physical passions, but in the infancy of his uninstructed reason, would be to raise up a creature resembling the splendid fiction of a recent romance; the hero of which constructs a human form . . . but . . . finds too late that he has only created a more than mortal power of doing mischief'; 'Amelioration of

imperialistic, however, but is directed towards the liberation of Constantinople from Turkish tyranny, and its restoration to the Greeks. Here Mary Shelley unmistakably links the release of the plague with liberal hopes for freedom and equality, anticipating the conservative stance of the 1831 *Frankenstein*. Thus she subverts the hopes of her friends and fellow-writers who supported the Greek struggle for independence in the early 1820s. By contrast with the increasingly hopeless state of affairs in England, the Shelley group found in Greece a land where freedom might still be realized. Mary Shelley herself followed the course of the Greek war with enthusiasm, and she was deeply disturbed by government repression at home: 'no longer England but Castlereagh land or New Land Castlereagh', she wrote in March 1820.[78] Percy Shelley's deep sense of personal involvement in the Greek struggle is conveyed most eloquently and controversially in *Hellas* (1822). In a statement withdrawn from the Preface on the poem's first publication, Percy identified the Greek spirit as evidence of a 'new race . . . nursed in the abhorrence of the opinions which are its chains', which will continue 'to produce fresh generations to accomplish that destiny which tyrants foresee and dread'.[79]

In *The Last Man* Mary Shelley rebuts this optimistic faith in a new civilization rising from the ashes of Greece, and dwells instead on the extinction of the race. Although Verney resembles Ahasuerus, the mythical seer of *Hellas*, in experiencing 'A life of unconsumèd thought which pierces | The Present, and the Past, and the To-come' (ll. 147–8), he is no longer a prophet of glorious struggles, as in the poem's epigraph.[80] If Evadne's appearance on the battlefield outside Constantinople brings to mind the dying soldier in *Hellas*, who 'arose out of the chaos of the slain' (l. 405) to prophesy Greek victory, Evadne's prediction is one of universal calamity. Mary Shelley thus rejects the poem's precarious optimism, seen at its most problematic in the final Chorus which offers the mental choices of regeneration or defeat:

the Condition of the Slave Population in the West Indies (House of Lords)', *Hansard's Parliamentary Debates*, NS 10 (16 Mar. 1824), col. 1103, quoted in Lyles, *Mary Shelley*, 122.

[78] Mary Shelley to Marianne Hunt, 24 Feb. [error for 24 Mar.] 1820, *MSL* i. 137.

[79] Shelley, Preface to *Hellas* [1822], first published in 1892, *Poetical Works*, 448.

[80] The epigraph reads: 'I am a prophet of glorious struggles'; Sophocles, *Oedipus at Colonus*, 1080.

The world's great age begins anew,
 The golden years return,
The earth doth like a snake renew
 Her winter weeds outworn:
. . . . . .
Cease! drain not to its dregs the urn
 Of bitter prophecy!
The world is weary of the past,
 Oh, might it die or rest at last! (ll. 1060–1101)

If this reworking of Percy Shelley's imagery suggests that Mary Shelley is most directly concerned with a revaluation of her husband's optimistic thought, her focus on the demise rather than the regeneration of the species also forms an indictment of Godwin's view of gradual social improvement. Yet, as already seen in *Frankenstein*, her attitude to Godwin's thought is by no means clear-cut. Though she was suspicious of Godwin's early confidence in man's rational potential, she shared his distrust of solitary ambition and his extreme dissatisfaction with the existing system. Thus at one level her vision of social disintegration dramatizes Godwin's prophecy of the inevitable decay of hierarchical institutions: 'Every scheme for embodying imperfection must be injurious. That which is to-day a considerable melioration, will at some future period, if preserved unaltered, appear a defect and disease in the body politic' (*PJ* i. 246). Ultimately, however, Mary Shelley's pessimistic drive erodes Godwin's positive ideals as well. Her vision of material decay and depopulation offers a grotesque parody of his projected rational future state, in which 'Generation will not succeed generation. . . . There will be no war, no crimes, no administration of justice, as it is called, and no government. Beside this, there will be neither disease, anguish, melancholy, nor resentment' (*PJ* ii. 528). Were it not for its prostration through 'disease, anguish, melancholy, [and] resentment', the situation of the last of the race encamped at Versailles might seem to approximate to Godwin's ideal: 'Our habitations were palaces . . . there was no need of labour, no inquisitiveness, no restless desire to get on' (*LM* 279).

Mary Shelley's reassessment of Godwin's faith in individual mental capacities and its Shelleyan development centres on her treatment of Adrian as a figure of disinterested benevolence in apparent contrast to Raymond's egotism. When Raymond abandons his public duties for personal reasons and the republican Ryland flees from office in terror as the plague advances, Adrian alone is willing to take on the Protectorship of England. An androgynous figure throughout, he enacts his alternative system of affective values on a large scale, touring the hospitals to bring 'patience, and sympathy, and such aid as art affords, to the bed of disease' (*LM* 179). But the retrospective structure of the narrative underlines the futility of individual efforts to resist the plague. Adrian's early conviction that the 'will of man is omnipotent, blunting the arrows of death, soothing the bed of disease' is immediately called into question by Verney's description of Adrian's voice as a Shelleyan 'dying flame' flickering on the 'embers of an accepted sacrifice' (*LM* 54). It is further eroded by the spectacle of the plague tightening its grip on the entire population, though Adrian himself remains untouched by disease. The character of the astronomer Merrival, a descendant of the obsessed scientists in *St Leon*, *Wieland*, and *Frankenstein*, presents a more straightforward critique of the gradualist optimism shared by Godwin and Percy Shelley. Ignoring the imminent threat to the survival of the species, Merrival is absorbed in calculations for its long-term benefit (*LM* 159). But when his family is wiped out by the plague, he is driven insane by the loss of the domestic bonds he neglected during their lifetime (*LM* 220).

This paring away of progressive notions of social improvement equally underlies the novel's travesty of Burkean values. In dramatizing an uncontrollable disorder in the natural realm, Mary Shelley develops the critique of Burke's defence of hierarchical government as the 'method of nature' (*R* 120) which is begun in *Frankenstein*. However, the topicality of her later analysis should not be overlooked. Wishing to make the novel's political scenes as authentic as possible, in February 1825 she wrote to the Benthamite John Cam Hobhouse asking if he could arrange for her to attend a House of Commons debate, and her deployment of Burkean language, used extensively by Canning in his speeches, suggests her familiarity with political rhetoric of the day.[81] In the first volume, Verney idealizes Windsor Forest as the heart of England, full of

[81] Mary Shelley to John Cam Hobhouse, 19 Feb. [1825], *MSL* i. 466; cf. Halévy, *Liberal Awakening*, 175; *The Speeches and Public Addresses of the Right Hon. George Canning, during the election in Liverpool, 1816*, a pamphlet record, appeared in 1816.

'majestic oaks' which have 'grown, flourished and decayed during the progress of centuries' (*LM* 28) in a truly Burkean manner. But, outside this rural retreat, England is in a state of political chaos, with parliament fragmented into hostile factions of aristocrats, democrats, and republicans. This internal division gives Raymond the opportunity to triumph by sheer force of personality. In his bid to restore the monarchy, Raymond invokes Burke's notions of 'ancient right and inheritance' in opposition to 'the commercial spirit of republicanism' (*LM* 42, 43), and thus wins the day for the royalist party.

Given this picture of irreconcilable class interests, England has a 'dismembered frame' (*LM* 39) long before the plague wreaks further havoc. Nevertheless, Verney remains confident in the ultimate stability of the social order. He even goes so far as to quote Burke's *Reflections* in support of this belief:

> Strange system! riddle of the Sphynx, most awe-striking! that thus man remains, while we the individuals pass away. Such is . . . 'the mode of existence decreed to a permanent body composed of transitory parts; wherein, by the disposition of a stupendous wisdom . . . the whole . . . in a condition of unchangeable constancy, moves on through the varied tenour of perpetual decay, fall, renovation and progression'. (*LM* 165)[82]

But the opening lines of the next chapter subvert this intuitive belief in natural continuity: 'Some disorder had surely crept into the course of the elements, destroying their benignant influence' (*LM* 166). Subsequent events show 'the decay and fall without the progression'.[83] To dramatize the illusory nature of Burke's notion of perpetual renewal, Mary Shelley draws on current scientific speculations on the arbitrariness of natural phenomena.[84] National stability is literally undermined by violent storms and tidal waves which seem 'about to wrench the deep-rooted island from its centre' (*LM* 167). When the survivors attempt to leave England for the last time, a further episode of freak weather conditions extends this sense of disorientation into the cosmic sphere: 'as if no longer were we ruled by ancient laws, but were turned adrift in an unknown region of space' (*LM* 270).

The exodus from England points up Verney's resignation of the final consoling fiction of man's role as 'lord, possessor, perceiver,

[82] Cf. *R* 120.

[83] Sterrenburg, '*The Last Man*', 332.

[84] See above, pp. 152–4.

and recorder' (*LM* 301) of the external world. In the novel's last volume Mary Shelley dwells on the startling contraction of man's Promethean ambitions for knowledge and power: 'life—life—the continuation of our animal mechanism—was the Alpha and Omega of the desires, the prayers, the prostrate ambition of human race' (*LM* 212). Such a drastic paring down of the quest for ideals exposes the full resonance of the novel's predetermined Gothic structure, which has a special significance for Mary Shelley's development of the Godwinian narrative model.

The Loss of Debate

It is Verney's unique fate to experience the novel's loss of meaning to the full when he undergoes his final rebirth into 'the dead world' (*LM* 325) where he is the only human survivor. In its closing pages the narrative comes to rest on Verney's unimaginable predicament as sole survivor of the inexplicable event which 'closed the history of the human race' (*LM* 311). Public and external themes are displaced by the pressures of individual grief and loneliness. The artistic problems involved in this shift from intellectual issues to subjective concerns may be approached through Lukács' account of the novelistic form produced by 'the Romanticism of disillusionment', in which engagement with external social values is replaced by psychological analysis. Lukács describes such a narrative shift from outer to inner worlds as a 'decisive value-judgement on reality' which reflects a fragmentation of meaning in the social and political realm.[85] Denied stable values in the external world, the individual seeks meaning solely within the self. But this situation may also lead to emotional excess: 'the soul's loneliness, its lack of any support or tie, is intensified until it becomes immeasurable, and, at the same time, the cause of this condition of the soul in a specific world situation is mercilessly revealed'.[86] Such an 'overall dominance of mood' may further invite the pessimistic revelation of the 'ultimate nullity' of all human values.[87]

It is certainly true to say that Verney's quest for stable values is

[85] Georg Lukács, *The Theory of the Novel* (1920), trans. from the German by Anna Bostock (London, 1971), 114; cf. Lukács's retrospective comment, Preface (1962), 17.

[86] Lukács, *Theory of the Novel*, 118.

[87] Ibid. 119.

doomed to failure. Mary Shelley subverts not only the controlling ideology of paternalistic social models but also the radical ideals of the Godwinian tradition. Through the massive Gothic image of the plague, she dismantles all systematic forms of thought, forcing an entire reassessment of assumptions about the knowable world.

Yet this extreme disenchantment needs to be set against the 'overall dominance of mood' in the novel's closing pages, which suggests a move towards subjective experience. Mary Shelley attempts to counteract the novel's drive towards cultural negation by presenting images of her personal experience of loss, and salvaging a role for Verney as Shelleyan artist among the kings of thought in Rome.[88] In an effort to derive aesthetic consolation from the defeat of political and personal hopes, Verney draws attention to the task of writing 'this journal of death' (*LM* 192). Relegated to the passive witness of successive catastrophes, he regains some measure of control over the past by reconstructing events which 'arranged themselves in pictures before me' (*LM* 126). Above all, he finds that writing keeps the notion of community alive, and he casts himself as literal author of the species: 'I became as it were the father of all mankind' (*LM* 113). However, the illusory nature of this consolation is never in doubt: 'I was alone in the Forum; alone in Rome; alone in the world' (*LM* 337).

Mary Shelley's invocation of a Shelleyan poet-figure collapses into another powerfully projected image of the isolated, questing individual which recurs in earlier Godwinian novels. In keeping with *St Leon* and *Frankenstein*, Mary Shelley emphasizes the dehumanizing effects of the loss of sympathy and love. After the shipwreck, it is only a matter of days before Verney fails to recognize himself in a mirror: 'What wild-looking, unkempt, half-naked savage was that before me?' (*LM* 331) This self-alienation confirms his affinity with that earlier 'unfashioned creature' in *Frankenstein* (*F* 232). After a year of utter solitude, Verney's recognition of his disinherited status is marked by a shift into the present tense: 'My person, with its human powers and features, seem to me a monstrous excrescence of nature' (*LM* 340).

The novel's final emphasis on personal isolation is best viewed in relation to Mary Shelley's treatment of Raymond as an exemplar of egotistical ambition, for this too points up the centrality of

88 Cf. Mary Shelley to Maria Gisborne, [*c.*27 Aug. 1822], *MSL* i. 254; see also *MSJ* ii. 467.

individual psychology rather than the historical and social conditions foregrounded in *Caleb Williams*. If there is a sense in which a known personality, that of Byron, becomes the mainspring of the plot, Mary Shelley's focus on individual error also prefigures her revisions to *Frankenstein* for the 1831 edition. Here she recasts her 1818 tale to highlight the 'incurable ill' (*F* 254) of Frankenstein's egotistical desire. This new emphasis on unfathomable psychological depths lies behind Frankenstein's account of his creature as a 'living monument of presumption and rash ignorance' (*F* 245). Like Verney, Frankenstein now presents himself as the victim of forces beyond his control. For instance, he interprets Waldman's lecture on modern chemistry as 'the words of fate, enounced to destroy me. . . . I felt as if my soul were grappling with a palpable enemy' (*F* 241). In this struggle he appears entirely at the mercy of conflicting irrational impulses: 'My internal being was in a state of insurrection and turmoil; I felt that order would thence arise, but I had no power to produce it' (*F* 241). Even the monster, formerly presented as a product of external circumstances, now acknowledges a 'fiend within [him]' and recasts his former 'deeds' as 'sins' (*F* 251, 219, 259).

While Mary Shelley extends the generalized intellectual range of the Godwinian novel, then, there is also a less analytical undercurrent in *The Last Man* which suggests a retreat from social analysis towards essentially private concerns, rather than the interpenetration of public and private realms of experience in Godwin's own novels. This shift towards subjective experience is reinforced by the form of *The Last Man*, which marks a loss in terms of the intellectual debate that is central to the instructive aims of other Godwinian novels under discussion. It is essential to the hard-won optimism of *Caleb Williams* that its artistic strategies stimulate the reader into active participation, challenging the individual to exercise his or her private judgement and to fulfil the duty of impartial enquiry. In this way, despite its prevailing bleakness, Godwin's pioneering intellectual novel indicates the possibilities for mental growth and wider social change. Although Brown registers an extreme distrust of Godwin's individualism in *Wieland*, his use of competing first-person narratives reaffirms a belief in the discriminating powers of the educated reader, and thus maintains the open-ended quality essential to its dialogic precedent. If Brown envisages the catastrophic consequences of unfettered individualism, he also posits an alternative sphere of values through the final geographical shift to Europe.

However, Mary Shelley presents an image of the total disintegration of Godwin's imagined community of enquiring readers. In *The Last Man* there is no 'uncontaminated seclusion' (*LM* 176) to offer an alternative to a catastrophe that wrecks the entire known world. Verney's terminally isolated predicament erodes the very terms of rational debate. Abandoning the structural complexity of *Frankenstein*, Mary Shelley enacts her loss of faith in individual improvement at the level of narrative form. Given the overwhelming grief and powerlessness of her first-person narrator, the reader too is forced into the role of passive witness to man's defeat by forces beyond his rational control.

Yet this single point of view may be seen as entirely proper to the novel's apocalyptic theme, and in this sense Mary Shelley's disenchanted creation myth moves towards the separate genre of science fiction. Despite or because of her profound intellectual uncertainty, Mary Shelley achieved an unparalleled extension of the imaginative scope of the Godwinian novel. Through the unforgettable images at the heart of *Frankenstein* and *The Last Man*, the symbolic concerns of the Godwinian tradition are both revitalized and deflected, and thus made available to mainstream nineteenth-century fiction writers.

Afterword: Rereading the Godwinian Novel

THE form in which the Godwinian novel was received in the nineteenth century was established by the republication of several works in Henry Colburn and Richard Bentley's Standard Novels, a monthly series of one-volume reprints which was launched in 1831 at the price of 6*s*. per volume. *Caleb Williams* was no. 2 in the series, *St Leon* was no. 5, *Frankenstein*, published in one volume with the first part of Schiller's *The Ghost-Seer*, was no. 9, and *Fleetwood*, published the following year, was no. 22.[1] *Edgar Huntly*, which was published with the second part of *The Ghost-Seer* in 1831, was the only one of Brown's novels to appear in the Standard Novels series, *Wieland* and *Ormond* having already been republished by Colburn in 1822.[2] The Standard Novels series presented itself as an attempt to register the permanent fame of certain novels written since the age of Fielding and Smollett, and it marked the first sustained effort by a publisher to exploit the cheaper market for fiction.[3] The major Godwinian novels remained in print and widely available for the next thirty years at least. While this republication ensured their classic status, however, it introduced a different set of concerns from those discussed in this book. The four novels by Godwin and Mary Shelley appeared with Prefaces which presented them in aesthetic and private terms, marginalizing the authors' specific political and philosophical concerns at the time of their first publication.

To some extent this biographical framework appears a response to marketing demands in an age of 'personality'. As Godwin observed in the 1831 Advertisement to *St Leon*: 'The present race of readers are understood to be desirous to learn something of the peculiarities, the "life, character, and behaviour" of an author'

1 Sadleir, *XIX Century Fiction*, ii. 93, 100.

2 Ibid. 100; Reid, 'Brockden Brown in England', 188; *Wieland* and *Ormond* later appeared along with *Caleb Williams* in the Novel Newspaper series (1839–42), Sadleir, *XIX Century Fiction*, ii. 143–4.

3 Sadleir, *XIX Century Fiction*, ii. 94; cf. Altick, *English Common Reader*, 274–5.

before they pronounce judgement on his work.[4] Moreover, in the Standard Novels series, it was a matter of conscious policy to secure revised texts and new Prefaces in which the author's mature judgement was passed on his earlier work.[5] This strategy may be attributed in part to the phenomenal success of the Author's Edition of the Waverley Novels, the first complete edition of Scott's works, which began to appear in 1829.[6] Scott introduced the series with a General Preface giving an account of his early life and literary development, and thus established an influential precedent for autobiographical authorial statements.

Although Godwin gave away little about himself in the 1831 Advertisement to *St Leon*, he and Mary Shelley conformed to Bentley's demand for biographical information in other Godwinian reprints. *Caleb Williams* was prefaced by a lengthy memoir of Godwin's life, written by Mary Shelley, while *Frankenstein* and *Fleetwood* appeared with detailed accounts of authorial literary development in a manner which owes much to Scott. 'I must refer to a very early period of my life, were I to point out my first achievements as a tale-teller', began Scott,[7] a statement virtually echoed by Mary Shelley in the 1831 Introduction to *Frankenstein*: 'It is not singular that, as the daughter of two persons of distinguished literary celebrity, I should very early in life have thought of writing' (*F* 222). This leads into the biographical account of her early life with Godwin and Percy Shelley that has proved so influential in modern criticism.

However, the re-presentation of the Godwinian novel involves more than a response to Bentley's marketing strategy. At issue is the whole question of its original political content and purpose. The later Prefaces show a shift to the subjective and private concerns already seen in Mary Shelley's revisions to the text of the 1831 *Frankenstein*. This dampening-down of earlier radical aims is equally evident in redescriptions of *Caleb Williams*, in which it is difficult to separate Mary Shelley's contribution from Godwin's. In her memoir of Godwin, issued with the 1831 *Caleb Williams*, Mary Shelley emphasized the moderation of Godwin's early political

[4] Godwin, Advertisement to *St Leon*, Standard Novels, No. 5 (London, 1831), p. vi.

[5] Sadleir, *XIX Century Fiction*, ii. 95.

[6] Sir Walter Scott, *Waverley Novels*, New Edition, with the Author's Notes, 48 vols. (Edinburgh, 1829–33), was published by Robert Cadell in monthly volumes at 5*s*. each; Sadleir, *XIX Century Fiction*, ii. 91.

[7] Scott, General Preface, *Waverley Novels*, i, p. ii.

views and glossed over the subversive qualities of his best-known novel: 'All that might have offended, as hard and republican in his larger work [*Political Justice*], was obliterated by the splendour and noble beauty of the character of Falkland.'[8] Meanwhile, in a series of new accounts of *Caleb Williams*, Godwin interpreted Caleb's actions in a range from 'the immeasurable and ever-wakeful curiosity of a raw youth' to the sexual guilt implicit in Perrault's tale of Bluebeard: 'Caleb Williams was the wife, who in spite of warning, persisted in his attempts to discover the forbidden secret' (*CW* 340).[9] Godwin's emphasis on 'the private and internal operations of the mind' (*CW* 339), shorn of his progressive political philosophy, paves the way for modern analyses of the novel in terms of innate psychological drives. What was a systematic analysis of institutional oppression in the 1790s becomes capable of an entirely different reading, which emphasizes man's uncontrollable impulses and thus supports Burke's argument for governmental restraints (*R* 151). The hidden political agenda of this recasting of the Godwinian plot is made explicit in Mary Shelley's new account of Frankenstein's creation of the monster. Her overtly theological vocabulary draws attention to his unequivocal transgression against accepted moral, social, and political boundaries: 'Frightful must it be; for supremely frightful would be the effect of any human endeavour to mock the stupendous mechanism of the Creator of the world' (*F* 228).

Along with this Burkean emphasis on innate moral error comes a new account of artistic creativity that highlights internal origins rather than the stimulus of public debate, and owes more to German idealist thought than to Godwinian rationalism.[10] In contrast to Scott's posture of ostentatious amateurism, both writers emphasize their preconceived intellectual aims.[11] But they describe their starting-point as a scene that embodies an original intuition. Creation is no longer derived from observation and experience, but

[8] [Mary Shelley], 'Memoirs of William Godwin', in *Caleb Williams*, Standard Novels, No. 2 (London, 1831), p. vi.

[9] Godwin, Advertisement to *St Leon*, p. v; see also Advertisement to *Cloudesley: A Tale*, 3 vols. (London, 1830), i, p. iv; cf. Bruno Bettelheim, *The Uses of Enchantment: The Importance and Meaning of Fairy Tales* (1976; Harmondsworth, 1978), 299–303.

[10] Shelley to Horace Smith, 14 Sept. 1821, contains a request for 'the French translation of Kant', *PBSL* ii. 350; cf. *MSJ* i. 37.

[11] Cf. Scott: 'about the year 1805, I threw together about one third part of the first volume of Waverley', *Waverley Novels*, i, p. xi.

from a pre-existing philosophic kernel in a process which brings to mind Carlyle's summary of the Kantian system in his influential essay, 'On the State of German Literature' (1827): 'The Kantist, in direct contradiction to Locke and all his followers . . . commences from within, and proceeds outwards. . . . The ultimate aim of all Philosophy must be to interpret appearances,—from the given symbol to ascertain the thing.'[12] This intuitive logic is most evident in Mary Shelley's account of aesthetic creation: 'Invention, it must be humbly admitted, does not consist in creating out of void, but out of chaos; the materials must, in the first place, be afforded: it can give form to dark, shapeless substances, but cannot bring into being the substance itself' (*F* 226). Locating the origin of her story in the dream-experience recounted in the fifth chapter of the novel, she depicts the artist's role as one of 'making only a transcript' of this symbolic incident (*F* 228). Published a year later, Godwin's account of writing *Caleb Williams* shares the same emphasis on a prior intuition which is then shaped by the artist into intelligible form:

> I formed a conception of a book of fictitious adventure that should in some way be distinguished by a very powerful interest. Pursuing this idea, I invented first the third volume of my tale, then the second, and last of all the first. I bent myself to the conception of a series of adventures of flight and pursuit . . . (*CW* 336–7)

It was this unity of purpose that later appealed to Dickens, who discussed the construction of *Caleb Williams* in a letter to Edgar Allan Poe, highlighting the novel's ostensible starting-point in 'the hunting-down of Caleb, and the Catastrophe'.[13] In this way *Caleb Williams* becomes a thrilling suspense narrative prefiguring nineteenth-century detective fiction.

A more immediately significant figure in the reinterpretation of the Godwinian novel was Edward Lytton Bulwer, a major spokesman for an idealist theory of fiction in the nineteenth

[12] Thomas Carlyle, 'On the State of German Literature' [1827], *The Collected Works of Thomas Carlyle*, Centenary Edition, 30 vols. (London, 1896–9), xxvi. 79; on its popularity, see Rosemary Ashton, *The German Idea: Four English Writers and the Reception of German Thought, 1800–1860* (Cambridge, 1980), 67.

[13] Dickens to Edgar Allan Poe, 6 Mar. 1842, *The Letters of Charles Dickens*, Pilgrim Edition, ed. Madeline House *et al.* (Oxford, 1965–), iii. 107; cf. Poe, 'The Philosophy of Composition' [1846], *The Complete Works of Edgar Allan Poe*, ed. James A. Harrison, 17 vols. (New York, 1902, 1965), xvi. 193–208.

century.[14] A full-scale discussion of Bulwer's theory of the novel lies outside the scope of this study, but what deserves mention here is Bulwer's reappropriation of the Godwinian novel in response to the injunctions of German Romantic aesthetics. Following Carlyle, whom he met for the first time in 1832, Bulwer turned to German philosophical idealism as an alternative to negative aspects of the utilitarian creed.[15] Despite his early association with Bentham and his followers,[16] by 1833 Bulwer's uneasiness about the prevailing demand for the useful led him to criticize the entire materialistic frame of mind which had developed from Locke, Adam Smith, Helvétius, and Bentham. As he wrote in *England and the English* (1833): 'No new, idealizing school has sprung up amongst us, to confute and combat with the successors of Locke; to counterbalance the attraction towards schools, dealing only with the unelevating practices of the world—the science of money-making, and the passionate warfare with social abuses.'[17] In search of a native idealizing tradition, he turned to the leading poets of the day, especially Wordsworth and Shelley, in whose work 'the Imaginative Literature has arrogated the due place of the Philosophical'.[18]

In the realm of narrative fiction, however, Bulwer turned to Godwin, and made selective use of Godwinian themes in *Pelham* and his early 'Newgate' novels, *Paul Clifford* (1830) and *Eugene Aram* (1832).[19] Although *Paul Clifford* includes an analysis of oppressive social conditions in the manner of the 1794 *Caleb Williams*, Bulwer's primary allegiance to the fictional model of the *Bildungsroman*, as exemplified by Goethe's *Wilhelm Meister*

[14] See Michael Lloyd, 'Bulwer-Lytton and the Idealising Principle', *English Miscellany*, 7 (1956), 25–39; Richard Stang, *The Theory of the Novel in England, 1850–1870* (London, 1959), 12–14; Edwin M. Eigner, *The Metaphysical Novel in England and America: Dickens, Bulwer, Hawthorne, Melville* (Berkeley, Calif., 1978), 2–38.

[15] On Bulwer's contact with Carlyle, see Susanne Howe, *Wilhelm Meister and his English Kinsmen: Apprentices to Life* (New York, 1930), 147–50; my account is indebted to Roy Park, *Hazlitt and the Spirit of the Age: Abstraction and Critical Theory* (Oxford, 1971), 43–76.

[16] See V. A. Lytton, 2nd Earl of Lytton, *The Life of Edward Bulwer, First Lord Lytton, by his Grandson*, 2 vols. (London, 1913), i. 390–413.

[17] Edward Lytton Bulwer, *England and the English* (1833), ed. Standish Meacham (Chicago, 1970), 321.

[18] Ibid. 285.

[19] See Louis Cazamian, *The Social Novel in England, 1830–1850* (1903), trans. from the French by Martin Fido (London, 1973), 1–50; Keith Hollingsworth, *The Newgate Novel, 1830–1847: Bulwer, Ainsworth, Dickens and Thackeray* (Detroit, 1963), 65–98.

(1785–96), is evident from his earliest writings.[20] In his review of Godwin's *Cloudesley* for the *New Monthly Magazine* in 1830, he lays claim to Godwin not as a radical political philosopher but as an idealizing intellectual who could combat the dominant empirical epistemology of the utilitarians. Carefully dissociating himself from Godwin's political radicalism, he paid tribute to Godwin as a pioneer of a fictional tradition which transcended its revolutionary context to link the thought of past and future ages:

> there yet seems to be, when I look on Godwin's earlier works, something dimly prophetic in their profound and immoveable calmness, unruffled as they are by party, or personality, or reference to fleeting interests. . . . I regard him as one of those seers, foretold to the latter days, who, though erroneous in their own predictions, were to herald and indicate the Avatar of a glorious and holy Truth.[21]

Significantly, Bulwer was not the first to view Godwin as a figure who could link eighteenth-century rationalism with German idealism. As early as 1804, Henry Crabb Robinson wrote home from Germany: 'in spight of my change of opinions I still am attached to Godwin indeed . . . it is very easy to connect him with or rather to draw him over to the German school'.[22] No doubt responding to the publication of the 1831 *Frankenstein* in the same volume as Schiller's *The Ghost-Seer*, Gilfillan later spoke of Godwin's 'German cast of mind—the same painful and plodding diligence, added to high imaginative qualities', and compared Mary Shelley's 'original creation' in *Frankenstein* with the works of German fiction-writers.[23]

Bulwer's characterization of Godwin as a figure of transcendent genius sets the scene for his reinterpretation of his fiction in terms of its timeless symbolic appeal, a process aided by Godwin's retrospective account of writing *Caleb Williams*. Responding to Godwin's later emphasis on internal processes, Bulwer persistently sought to relocate the Godwinian novel in an anti-mimetic tradition

[20] Howe, *Wilhelm Meister*, 132–9; Carlyle's translation of *Wilhelm Meister's Lehrjahre* (1785–96) was published in 1824.

[21] [Bulwer], 'The Lounger', *New Monthly Magazine*, 28 (1830), 366; cf. [Mary Shelley], review of *Cloudesley*, *Blackwood's*, 27 (May 1830), 711–16.

[22] Letter of 30 Jan. 1804, *Crabb Robinson in Germany, 1800–1805: Extracts from his Correspondence*, ed. Edith J. Morley (Oxford, 1929), 135; cf. letters of 15 Sept. 1802, 21 Apr. 1805, 113, 166.

[23] Gilfillan, 'Mrs Shelley', 284, 295.

based on the aesthetics of the German post-Kantian philosophers.[24] In his Preface to the 1835 edition of *The Disowned* (1828), his early experiment on the apprenticeship theme of *Wilhelm Meister*, he set out his theory of the 'metaphysical' novel, which is largely based on Schiller's theory of epic and dramatic poetry.[25] But he also made use of Godwin's theoretical distinction between drama and the novel, based on the primary interest in philosophy that fiction ought to express. In the Preface to *Cloudesley* Godwin contrasted the implausible unity found in dramatic forms—'sketches half made up, and human passions and characters distorted, to fit a plot'—with the more capacious mode of 'fictitious history', where the writer could intervene with his own comments, explaining the 'inmost thoughts that pass in the bosom of the upright man and the perverse'.[26] This argument for a disruptive philosophical commentary had an obvious appeal for Bulwer, who sought above all to distinguish his concept of metaphysical fiction from the 'multiform representation of real life' in the works of his contemporaries.[27] As a capacious, self-consciously intellectual form which supported a 'typical and pervading moral' rather than a straightforward didactic purpose, Bulwer argued, the metaphysical novel was best exemplified by *Wilhelm Meister*.[28] Although Bulwer described this form as still to be developed in the English-speaking world, he saw the beginnings of such a tradition in the 'dark tales of Godwin and the far inferior compositions of Brown'.[29]

Thus Bulwer realigns Godwin's 'new and startling' blend of philosophy and fiction with a fictional mode based on an entirely different system of thought, which is best exemplified in Friedrich Schlegel's presentation of *Wilhelm Meister* as embodying his ideal

[24] On Bulwer's theory, but not Godwin's place in it, see Stang, *Theory of the Novel*, 153.

[25] Eigner, *Metaphysical Novel*, 57.

[26] Godwin, Preface to *Cloudesley*, i, pp. vii–viii.

[27] Bulwer, 'On the Different Kinds of Prose Fiction, with Some Apology for the Fiction of the Author', *The Disowned*, 2 vols. (3rd edn., London, 1835), i, p. vii.

[28] [Bulwer], 'On Moral Fictions. Miss Martineau's *Illustrations of Political Economy*', *New Monthly Magazine*, 37 (1833), Part 1, 146; cf. Godwin's essay, 'Of Choice in Reading' (*E* 129–46); *The Enquirer* was reissued in 1823.

[29] Bulwer, 'On the Different Kinds of Prose Fiction', p. xi; see also his comparison of Godwin and Goethe in 'On Art in Fiction' (1838), reprinted in Edwin M. Eigner and George G. Worth (eds.), *Victorian Criticism of the Novel* (Cambridge, 1985), 31; and *A Word to the Public; containing Hints towards a Critical Essay upon the Artistic Principles and Ethical Designs of Fiction* (London, 1847), 22.

of 'progressive universal poetry'.[30] In his theory at least, Bulwer finds the lasting significance of the Godwinian novel in a philosophical outlook far removed from Godwin's gradualist theory of political progress.

To pursue this emphasis on internal concerns would be to lose the distinctive social and political alignment of *Caleb Williams* and *Frankenstein* at the time of their first publication. More important to this study is Bulwer's preservation of Godwin's external concerns in *Paul Clifford*, his tale of an abandoned child forced into crime by the pressure of social circumstances, and their subsequent development in other socially engaged novelists such as Dickens and Gaskell. The continuing need to press into service the symbolic representation of social concerns in the Godwinian narrative underlines the formal achievement of the Godwin school. In their myth-making narratives, the Godwinian writers offer ways of articulating historical pressures that remain outside the dominant forms of nineteenth-century representation. The formal experimentation of Mary Shelley and Bulwer in the 1820s already suggests the need for a richer and more diverse treatment of contemporary society than is found in Godwin's novels of the 1790s, anticipating the more capacious, though widely diverging, modes of Dickens and George Eliot. In *Valperga* especially, Mary Shelley registers the limitations of Godwin's first-person narrative in exploring the full complexities of class society. Her focus on a triangle of figures whose thoughts and actions are determined by larger political movements from which they cannot withdraw prefigures the more comprehensive analytical mode of George Eliot's *Romola* (1863), set in fifteenth-century Florence, which shares a strikingly similar preoccupation with the demise of republican ideals.

By contrast, Bulwer's blend of fashionable novel and social analysis in *Paul Clifford* opens up further possibilities in the multi-faceted representation of social concerns. Above all it is Dickens who offers a symbolic rather than a naturalistic treatment of social issues in the manner of the Godwin school. This is especially

[30] Friedrich Schlegel, 'Athenäum Fragments' [1798], 116, 216, in *Lucinde and the Fragments*, trans. Peter Firchow (Minneapolis, 1971), 175, 190; cf. F. Schlegel, 'On Goethe's *Meister*' [1798], English text in *German Aesthetic and Literary Criticism: The Romantic Ironists and Goethe*, ed. Kathleen M. Wheeler (Cambridge, 1983), 59–73.

evident in the direct line of continuity between *Caleb Williams*, *Paul Clifford*, and Dickens's early works dealing with criminal subject-matter, *Oliver Twist* (1838), *Barnaby Rudge* (1841), and *Martin Chuzzlewit* (1844).[31] With its focus on the wrongly accused child at the centre of an unjust legislative system, *Paul Clifford* provides the starting-point for Dickens's amplification of Godwin's symbolic themes in his portrayal of children and criminals rendered vicious by institutional and parental negligence. Bulwer pressed home the social message of *Paul Clifford* in his Preface to the 1848 edition:

> A child who is cradled in ignominy; whose schoolmaster is the felon;—whose academy is the House of Correction . . . becomes less a responsible and reasonable human being than a wild beast which we suffer to range in the wilderness—till it prowls near our homes, and we kill it in self-defence.
>
> In this sense the Novel of 'Paul Clifford' is a loud cry to society to mend the circumstance—to redeem the victim.[32]

Here Bulwer highlights a recurring nineteenth-century concern with how failures of parental and social responsibility breed vengeful offspring, and thus reaffirms the power of Godwin's distinctive plot to body forth the multiple levels at which individuals experience social change. Equally, however, his preoccupation with practical reform within an entrenched social system marks his distance from Godwin's speculative concern with the possibilities of liberating humankind from legislative restraints.

Given the expansiveness of nineteenth-century fiction, in which bold symbolic patterns are overlaid by detailed observation of material circumstances, there is a loss of the selective, theoretical, and intensely imagined treatment of political issues in the Godwinian first-person narrative. Finally the major significance of the Godwinian novel rests apart from its contribution to mainstream fiction, and may indeed be pitted over and against large concepts of literary tradition. The dispersal and deflection of Godwinian techniques in nineteenth-century fiction only throw into relief the historically specific achievement of the Godwin school.

[31] On Dickens's debt to the plot of *Paul Clifford* in *Oliver Twist*, see Jack Lindsay, *Charles Dickens: A Biographical and Critical Study* (London, 1950), 167, 172.

[32] Bulwer, Preface to *Paul Clifford* (London, 1848), p. ix.

Bibliography

I. MANUSCRIPT SOURCES

Bodleian Library, Oxford. The Abinger Collection, owned by Lord Abinger, includes Godwin's diaries and most of his manuscripts, notes, and letters (all uncatalogued).

Keats House, London. 'The Catalogue of the Curious Library of that Very Eminent and Distinguished Author William Godwin, Esq., . . . which will be sold by Auction, by Mr Sotheby and Son' (1836).

Pforzheimer Library, New York. The collection includes the MS of *Fleetwood*, revisions of *St Leon*, notes, and letters. Available in *Shelley and his Circle: 1773–1822*, 8 vols. to date: i–iv, ed. Kenneth Neill Cameron; v–vi, ed. Donald H. Reiman; vii–viii, ed. Reiman and Doucet Devin Fischer (Cambridge, Mass., 1961–86).

II. CONTEMPORARY BRITISH PERIODICALS

Analytical Review
Blackwood's Edinburgh Magazine
British Critic
British Magazine; or, Miscellany of Polite Literature
Edinburgh Review
Edinburgh [Scots] Magazine
English Review
Fraser's Magazine
Monthly Magazine
Monthly Mirror
Monthly Review
New Monthly Magazine
Panoramic Miscellany
Quarterly Review

III. BOOKS, PAMPHLETS, ARTICLES

ALDINI, JOHN, *An Account of the Late Improvements in Galvanism, with a series of Curious and Interesting Experiments performed before the*

Commissioners of the French National Institute, and repeated lately in the Anatomical Theatres of London (London, 1803).

ALDISS, BRIAN W., *Billion Year Spree: The History of Science Fiction* (London, 1973).

ALLEN, B. SPRAGUE, 'The Reaction against William Godwin', *Modern Philology*, 16 (1918), 57–75.

ALLEN, WALTER, *The English Novel: A Short Critical History* (Harmondsworth, 1954).

ALTICK, R. D., *The English Common Reader: A Social History of the Mass Reading Public, 1800–1900* (Chicago, 1957).

[ANON.], *Mandeville; or, The Last Words of a Maniac! A Tale of the Seventeenth Century in England. By Himself, vol. iv* (London, 1818).

ARENDT, HANNAH, *On Revolution* (New York, 1963, 1965).

—— *Between Past and Future: Six Exercises in Political Thought* (London, 1961).

ASHTON, ROSEMARY, *The German Idea: Four English Writers and the Reception of German Thought, 1800–1860* (Cambridge, 1980).

AUGUSTINE, St, *Concerning the City of God against the Pagans*, trans. Henry Bettenson, ed. David Knowles (Harmondsworth, 1972).

BAGE, ROBERT, *Mount Henneth*, 2 vols. (London, 1782).

—— *Man As He Is*, 4 vols. (London, 1792).

—— *Hermsprong; or, Man As He Is Not* (1796), ed. Peter Faulkner (Oxford, 1985).

BAILLIE, JOANNA, *De Monfort*, in *A Series of Plays: in which it is Attempted to Delineate the Stronger Passions of the Mind*, vol. i (London, 1798).

BAINE, RODNEY M., *Thomas Holcroft and the Revolutionary Novel* (Athens, Ga., 1965).

BAKER, ERNEST A., *The History of the English Novel*, vols. v–vii (London, 1934, 1957).

BAKHTIN, MIKHAIL, *Problems of Dostoevsky's Poetics*, ed. and trans. Caryl Emerson, introd. Wayne C. Booth (Manchester, 1984).

BALDICK, CHRIS, *In Frankenstein's Shadow: Myth, Monstrosity, and Nineteenth-Century Writing* (Oxford, 1987).

BARKER, GERARD A., 'Justice to *Caleb Williams*', *Stud. N* 6 (1974), 377–88.

—— 'Ferdinando Falkland's Fall: Grandison in Disarray', *Papers on Language and Literature*, 16 (1980), 376–86.

BARRUEL, l'Abbé AUGUSTIN, *Memoirs, Illustrating the History of Jacobinism*, trans. Robert Clifford, 4 vols. (London, 1797–8).

BELL, MICHAEL DAVITT, ' "The Double-Tongued Deceiver": Sincerity and Duplicity in the Novels of Charles Brockden Brown', *EAL* 9 (Fall 1974), 143–63.

BERTHOFF, WARNER, 'Charles Brockden Brown's Historical Sketches: A Consideration', *American Literature*, 28 (1956), 147–54.

—— 'Brockden Brown: The Politics of the Man of Letters', *Serif*, 3/4 (Dec. 1966), 3–11.

BETTELHEIM, BRUNO, *The Uses of Enchantment: The Meaning and Importance of Fairy Tales* (1976; Harmondsworth, 1978).

BLACKALL, ERIC A., *The Novels of the German Romantics* (Ithaca, NY, 1983).

[BLAIR, HUGH], *Critical Dissertation on the Poems of Ossian* (London, 1763).

BLOOM, HAROLD, '*Frankenstein*, or the New Prometheus', *Partisan Review*, 32 (1965), 611–18, reprinted in *The Ringers in the Tower* (Chicago, 1971), 119–29.

BLUNDEN, EDMUND, 'Godwin's Library Catalogue', *Keats–Shelley Memorial Bulletin*, 9 (1958), 27–9.

BOULTON, JAMES T., *The Language of Politics in the Age of Wilkes and Burke* (London, 1963).

BRAILSFORD, H. N., *Shelley, Godwin and their Circle* (Oxford, 1913).

BROWN, CEDRIC, C., *John Milton's Aristocratic Entertainments* (Cambridge, 1985).

BROWN, CHARLES BROCKDEN, *The Novels and Related Works of Charles Brockden Brown*, Bicentennial Edition, ed. Sydney J. Krause *et al.*, 6 vols. (Kent, Oh., 1977–86): i, *Wieland; or, The Transformation. An American Tale, with Memoirs of Carwin, the Biloquist* (1977); ii, *Ormond; or, The Secret Witness* (1982); iii, *Arthur Mervyn; or, Memoirs of the Year 1793*, First and Second Parts (1980); iv, *Edgar Huntly; or, Memoirs of a Sleep-Walker* (1984); v, *Clara Howard: In a Series of Letters, with Jane Talbot: A Novel* (1986); vi, *Alcuin: A Dialogue, with Memoirs of Stephen Calvert* (1986).

—— ed., *Monthly Magazine, and American Review*, 3 vols. (New York, 1799–1800), Microfilm USA 17, from original in Library of Congress.

BROWN, DAVID, *Sir Walter Scott and the Historical Imagination* (London, 1979).

BROWN, F. K., *The Life of William Godwin* (London, 1926).

BRYSON, GLADYS, *Man and Society: The Scottish Inquiry of the Eighteenth Century* (Princeton, NY, 1945).

BULWER, EDWARD LYTTON, *Falkland* (London, 1827).

—— *Pelham; or, The Adventures of a Gentleman*, 3 vols. (London, 1828).

—— *The Disowned* (1828), 2 vols. (3rd edn., London, 1835).

—— *Devereux*, 3 vols. (London, 1829).

—— *Paul Clifford*, 3 vols. (London, 1830).

—— 'The Lounger', *New Monthly Magazine*, 28 (1830), Part 1, 361–7.

—— *Eugene Aram*, 3 vols. (London, 1832).

—— 'On Moral Fictions. Miss Martineau's *Illustrations of Political Economy*', *New Monthly Magazine*, 37 (1833), Part 1, 146–51.

—— *England and the English*, 2 vols. (1833), ed. Standish Meacham (Chicago, 1970).

—— *The Works of Sir Edward Lytton Bulwer, Bart*, 10 vols. (London, 1840).

—— trans., *The Poems and Ballads of Schiller*, 2 vols. (London, 1844).

—— *A Word to the Public; containing Hints towards a Critical Essay upon the Artistic Principles and Ethical Designs of Fiction* (London, 1847).

BUNYAN, JOHN, *The Pilgrim's Progress from this World to that which is to Come* (1678, 1684), ed. Roger Sharrock (Harmondsworth, 1965).

BURKE, EDMUND, *The Works and Correspondence of the Right Hon. Edmund Burke*, 8 vols. (London, 1852).

—— *A Philosophical Enquiry into the Origin of our Ideas of the Sublime and Beautiful* (1757), ed. James T. Boulton (1958; rev. edn., Oxford, 1987).

—— *Reflections on the Revolution in France, and on the Proceedings in Certain Societies in London Relative to that Event, In a Letter Intended to have been Sent to a Gentleman in Paris* (1790), ed. Conor Cruise O'Brien (Harmondsworth, 1969).

—— *A Letter from Mr Burke to a Member of the National Assembly; in Answer to some Objections to his Book on French Affairs* (London, 1791).

—— *Letters on the Proposals for Peace with the Regicide Directory of France* (London, 1796).

BUTLER, MARILYN, *Jane Austen and the War of Ideas* (Oxford, 1975; 2nd edn., 1987).

—— *Peacock Displayed: A Satirist in his Context* (London, 1979).

—— *Romantics, Rebels, and Reactionaries: English Literature and its Background, 1760–1830* (Oxford, 1981).

—— 'Godwin, Burke, and *Caleb Williams*', *EIC* 32 (1982), 237–57.

—— (ed.), *Burke, Paine, Godwin, and the Revolution Controversy* (Cambridge, 1984).

—— 'Satire and the Images of Self in the Romantic Period: The Long Tradition of Hazlitt's *Liber Amoris*', *Yearbook of English Studies*, 14 (1984), 209–25.

—— 'Romanticism in England', in Roy Porter and Mikuláš Teich (eds.), *Romanticism in National Context* (Cambridge, 1988), 37–67.

BYRON, GEORGE GORDON, Lord, *Byron: Poetical Works*, ed. Frederick Page, corr. John Jump (Oxford, 1970).

CALLAHAN, PATRICK J., 'Frankenstein, Bacon and the "Two Truths" ', *Extrapolation*, 14/1 (Dec. 1972), 39–48.

CAMERON, KENNETH NEILL, 'A Major Source of *The Revolt of Islam*', *PMLA* 56 (1941), 175–206.

CAMPBELL, THOMAS, *The Complete Poetical Works of Thomas Campbell*, ed. J. Logie Robertson (Oxford, 1907).

CANNING, GEORGE, *The Speeches and Public Addresses of the Right Hon. George Canning, during the election in Liverpool, 1816* (Liverpool, 1816).

CANTOR, PAUL A., *Creature and Creator: Myth-Making and English Romanticism* (Cambridge, 1984).

CARLYLE, THOMAS, *The Collected Works of Thomas Carlyle*, Centenary Edition, 30 vols. (London, 1896–9): i, *Sartor Resartus* [1833–4]; xxvi, 'On the State of German Literature' [1827].

CAZAMIAN, LOUIS, *The Social Novel in England, 1830–50* (1903), trans. from the French by Martin Fido (London, 1973).

CHASE, RICHARD, *The American Novel and its Tradition* (New York, 1957).

CHRISTENSEN, ALLAN CONRAD, *Edward Bulwer-Lytton: The Fiction of New Regions* (Athens, Ga., 1976).

CLARENDON, EDWARD HYDE, 1st Earl of, *History of the Rebellion and Civil Wars in England, begun in the Year 1641* (1702–4), re-ed. W. Dunn Macray, 6 vols. (Oxford, 1888, 1969).

CLARK, DAVID LEE, *Charles Brockden Brown: Pioneer Voice of America* (Durham, NC, 1952).

CLARK, TIMOTHY, *Embodying Revolution: The Figure of the Poet in Shelley* (Oxford, 1989).

CLIFFORD, GAY, '*Caleb Williams* and *Frankenstein*: First Person Narrative and "Things As They Are" ', *Genre*, 10 (1977), 601–17.

COBB, JOAN P., 'Godwin's Novels and *Political Justice*', *Enlightenment Essays*, 4 (1973), 15–28.

COBBAN, ALFRED, *The Debate on the French Revolution, 1789–1800* (London, 1950).

COHAUSEN, JOHANN HEINRICH, *Hermippus Redivivus; or, The Sage's Triumph over Old Age and the Grave. Wherein, a Method is laid down for Prolonging the Life and Vigour of Man*, trans. Dr John Campbell (London, 1744).

COLERIDGE, SAMUEL TAYLOR, *The Complete Poetical Works of Samuel Taylor Coleridge*, ed. E. H. Coleridge, 2 vols. (Oxford, 1912).

—— *The Collected Letters of Samuel Taylor Coleridge*, ed. E. L. Griggs, 6 vols. (Oxford, 1956–71).

—— *The Collected Works of Samuel Taylor Coleridge*, ed. Kathleen Coburn, Bollingen Series 75, 16 vols. in progress (Princeton, NJ, 1969–): i, *Lectures 1795 on Politics and Religion*, ed. Lewis Patton and Peter Mann (1971); vi, *Lay Sermons*, ed. R. J. White (1972);

x, *On the Constitution of the Church and State*, ed. John Colmer (1977).

COLLINS, PHILIP, *Dickens and Crime* (London, 1962, 1964).

COLMER, JOHN, 'Godwin's *Mandeville* and Peacock's *Nightmare Abbey*', *Review of English Studies*, 21 (1970), 331–6.

CONRAD, PETER, *Shandyism: The Character of Romantic Irony* (Oxford, 1978).

CRANSTON, MAURICE, *Philosophers and Pamphleteers: Political Theorists of the Enlightenment* (Oxford, 1986).

CREASER, JOHN, ' "The Present Aid of this Occasion": The Setting of *Comus*', in David Lindley (ed.), *The Court Masque* (Manchester, 1984), 111–34.

CRÈVECOEUR, MICHEL-GUILLAUME JEAN DE, *Letters from an American Farmer* (London, 1782).

CRONIN, JAMES E., 'Elihu Hubbard Smith and the New York Friendly Club, 1795–8', *PMLA* 64 (1949), 471–9.

CRUTWELL, PATRICK, 'On *Caleb Williams*', *Hudson Review*, 11 (1958), 87–95.

DAHL, CURTIS, 'Bulwer-Lytton', in Lionel Stevenson (ed.), *Victorian Fiction: A Guide to Research* (Cambridge, Mass., 1964), 35–43.

—— 'Edward Bulwer-Lytton', in George H. Ford (ed.), *Victorian Criticism: A Second Guide to Research* (New York, 1978), 28–33.

DANTE ALIGHIERI, *The Vision; or, Hell, Purgatory, and Paradise*, trans. Henry Francis Cary, 3 vols. (1814; 2nd edn., corr., with additional notes, London 1819).

DARWIN, ERASMUS, *Zoonomia; or, The Laws of Organic Life*, 2 vols. (London, 1794, 1796).

DAVIS, DAVID BRION, *Homicide in American Fiction, 1789–1860: A Study in Social Values* (Ithaca, NY, 1957).

DAVIS, LENNARD, *Resisting Novels: Ideology and Fiction* (London, 1987).

DAWSON, P. M. S., *The Unacknowledged Legislator: Shelley and Politics* (Oxford, 1980).

DAY, WILLIAM PATRICK, *In the Circles of Fear and Desire: A Study of Gothic Fantasy* (Chicago, 1985).

DEFOE, DANIEL, *The Life and Strange Surprizing Adventures of Robinson Crusoe, of York, Mariner* (1719), ed. J. Donald Crowley (Oxford, 1972).

—— *A Journal of the Plague Year; being Observations or Memorials of the Most Remarkable Occurrences . . . which happened in London during the last Great Visitation in 1665* (1722), ed. Anthony Burgess and Christopher Bristow (Harmondsworth, 1966).

DICKENS, CHARLES, *The Novels of Charles Dickens*, New Oxford

Illustrated Edition, 21 vols. (Oxford, 1947–59): *Oliver Twist* (1838); *Barnaby Rudge* (1841); *Martin Chuzzlewit* (1844); *Dombey and Son* (1846).

DICKENS, CHARLES, *The Letters of Charles Dickens*, Pilgrim Edition, ed. Madeline House *et al.* (Oxford, 1965–), vol. iii.

Dictionary of National Biography (1890).

DISRAELI, BENJAMIN, *Sybil; or, The Two Nations* (1845), ed. Sheila M. Smith (Oxford, 1981).

DOLLEANS, EDOUARD, 'Un Essai de psychologie historique: William Godwin', *Revue de Métaphysique et de Morale*, 23 (1916), 363–95.

DONALDSON, IAN, *The Rapes of Lucretia: A Myth and its Transformations* (Oxford, 1982).

DONOHUE, JOSEPH W., Jr., *Dramatic Character in the English Romantic Age* (Princeton, NJ, 1970).

DUBROW, HEATHER, *Genre*, The Critical Idiom, 42 (London and New York, 1982).

DUFFY, EDWARD, *Rousseau in England: The Context for Shelley's Critique of the Enlightenment* (Berkeley, Calif., 1979).

DUMAS, D. GILBERT, 'Things As They Were: The Original Ending of *Caleb Williams*', *SEL* 6 (1966), 575–97.

DUNLAP, WILLIAM, *Memoirs of Charles Brockden Brown, the American Novelist; with Selections from his Original Letters, and Miscellaneous Writings* (Philadelphia, 1815; London, 1822).

EAGLETON, TERRY, *The Rape of Clarissa* (Oxford, 1982).

EDGEWORTH, MARIA, *Castle Rackrent: An Hibernian Tale* (1800), ed. George Watson (Oxford, 1964, 1969).

EIGNER, EDWIN M., *The Metaphysical Novel in England and America: Dickens, Bulwer, Hawthorne, Melville* (Berkeley, Calif., 1978).

—— and WORTH, GEORGE G., (eds.), *Victorian Criticism of the Novel* (Cambridge, 1985).

ELIAS, NORBERT, *The Court Society*, trans. Edmund Jephcott (Oxford, 1983).

ELIOT, GEORGE, *The Works of George Eliot*, Cabinet Edition, 20 vols. (Edinburgh and London, 1878): *Romola* (1863); *Felix Holt, The Radical* (1866).

ELLIOTT, EMORY, *Revolutionary Writers: Literature and Authority in the New Republic, 1725–1810* (New York, 1982).

ELLIS, KATE, 'Monsters in the Garden: Mary Shelley and the Bourgeois Family', in George Levine and U. C. Knoepflmacher (eds.), *The Endurance of Frankenstein: Essays on Mary Shelley's Novel* (Berkeley, Calif., 1979), 123–42.

ERDMAN, D. V., 'Blake and Godwin', *Notes and Queries*, 198 (1954), 66–7.

Evans, Evan, *Some Specimens of the Poetry of the Antient Welsh Bards, Translated into English* (London, 1764).

Everest, Kelvin, *Coleridge's Secret Ministry: The Context of the Conversation Poems, 1795–1798* (Hassocks, 1979).

—— and Edwards, Gavin, 'William Godwin's *Caleb Williams*: Truth and "Things As They Are" ' in Francis Barker *et al.* (eds.), *1789: Reading, Writing, Revolution. Proceedings of the Essex Conference on the Sociology of Literature* (Colchester, 1982), 129–46.

Farouk, Marion Omar, '*Mandeville: A Tale of the Seventeenth Century*—Historical Novel or Psychological Study?', in Anselm Schlösser *et al.* (eds.), *Essays in Honor of William Gallacher: Life and Literature of the Working Class* (Berlin, 1966), 111–17.

Feaver, William, *The Art of John Martin* (Oxford, 1975).

[Fenwick, John], 'William Godwin', in *Public Characters of 1799–1800*, vol. ii (London 1799), 358–75.

Ferguson, Robert A., 'Literature and Vocation in the Early American Republic: The Example of Charles Brockden Brown', *Modern Philology*, 78 (1980), 139–52.

Fiedler, Leslie A., *Love and Death in the American Novel* (rev. edn., Harmondsworth, 1960, 1982).

Fielding, Henry, *An Apology for the Life of Mrs Shamela Andrews. In which, the many notorious* FALSHOODS *and* MISREPRESENTATIONS *of a Book called Pamela are exposed and refuted* (1741), in *Joseph Andrews and Shamela*, ed. Douglas Brooks-Davies and Martin Battestin (Oxford, 1970, 1989).

—— *The Life of Mr Jonathan Wild the Great* (1743), ed. David Nokes (Harmondsworth, 1982).

—— *The History of Tom Jones, a Foundling* (1749), ed. R. P. C. Mutter (Harmondsworth, 1966).

Flanders, W. A., 'Godwin and Gothicism: *St Leon*', *Texas Studies in Literature and Language*, 7 (1967), 533–45.

Fleck, P. D., 'Mary Shelley's Notes to Shelley's Poems and *Frankenstein*', *SIR* 6 (1967), 226–54.

Fleishman, Avrom, *The English Historical Novel: Walter Scott to Virginia Woolf* (Baltimore, 1971).

Florescu, Radu, *In Search of Frankenstein* (London, 1977).

Foner, Eric A., *Tom Paine and Revolutionary America* (New York, 1976).

Foster, James R., *History of the Pre-Romantic Novel in England* (New York, 1949).

Foucault, Michel, *Madness and Civilisation: A History of Insanity in the Age of Reason* (1961), trans. from the French by Richard Howard (London, 1967).

Foucault, Michel, *The Order of Things: An Archaeology of the Human Sciences* (1966), trans. from the French (London, 1970).

Fowler, Alastair, *Kinds of Literature: An Introduction to the Theory of Genres and Modes* (Oxford, 1982).

Fuller, Margaret, *The Writings of Margaret Fuller*, ed. Mason Wade (New York, 1941, 1973).

Furbank, P. N., 'Godwin's Novels', *EIC* 5 (1955), 214–28.

Frye, Northrop, *Anatomy of Criticism* (Princeton, NJ, 1957).

Garside, Peter D., '*Old Mortality*'s Silent Minority', *Scottish Literary Journal*, 7 (1980), 127–44.

Gaskell, Elizabeth, *Mary Barton: A Tale of Manchester Life* (1848), ed. Stephen Gill (Harmondsworth, 1970).

Gilbert, Sandra M., and Gubar, Susan, *The Madwoman in the Attic: The Woman Writer and the Nineteenth-Century Literary Imagination* (New Haven, Conn., 1979).

Gilfillan, George, 'William Godwin', *A Gallery of Literary Portraits* (Edinburgh, 1845), 15–36.

—— 'Mrs Shelley', *A Second Gallery of Literary Portraits* (Edinburgh, 1850), 283–96.

Gilmore, Michael T., 'Calvinism and Gothicism: The Example of Brown's *Wieland*', *Stud. N* 9 (1977), 107–18.

Godwin, William, *History of the Life of William Pitt, Earl of Chatham* (London, 1783).

—— *A Defence of the Rockingham Party, in their Late Coalition with the Right Honourable Frederic Lord North* (London, 1783).

—— *An Account of the Seminary that will be opened on Monday the Fourth Day of August, at Epsom in Surrey, for the Instruction of Twelve Pupils in the Greek, Latin, French, and English Languages* (London, 1783).

—— *Sketches of History, in Six Sermons* (London, 1784).

—— *The Herald of Literature; or, A Review of the Most Considerable Publications that will be made in the Course of the Ensuing Winter: with extracts* (London, 1784).

—— *Instructions to a Statesman, humbly inscribed to the Right Honourable George Earl Temple* (London, 1784).

—— *Four Early Pamphlets (1783–1784)*, ed. Burton R. Pollin (Gainesville, Fla., 1966).

—— *Damon and Delia: A Tale* (London, 1784).

—— *Italian Letters; or, The History of the Count de St Julian* (1784), ed. Burton R. Pollin (Lincoln, Nebr., 1965).

—— *Imogen: A Pastoral Romance. From the Ancient British* (1784), ed. Jack W. Marken (New York, 1963).

—— Letter 'To the Right Honourable Edmund Burke', signed 'Mucius', *Political Herald, and Review*, 1 (Dec. 1785), 321–9.

—— Letter ii, 'To Mr. Reeves, Chairman of the Society for Protecting Liberty and Property against Republicans and Levellers', signed 'Mucius', *Morning Chronicle*, 8 Feb. 1793.

—— *Cursory Strictures on the Charge Delivered by Lord Chief Justice Eyre to the Grand Jury; 2 October 1794* (London, 1794).

—— *Uncollected Writings (1785–1822)*, ed. Jack W. Marken and Burton R. Pollin (Gainesville, Fla., 1968).

—— *Enquiry Concerning Political Justice, Its Influence on Morals and Happiness*, photographic facsimile of 3rd edn., corr. and ed. with variant readings of 1st and 2nd edns., and with critical introduction and notes by F. E. L. Priestley, 3 vols. (Toronto, 1946).

—— *Enquiry Concerning Political Justice* (1798), ed. Isaac Kramnick (Harmondsworth, 1976).

—— *Things As They Are; or, The Adventures of Caleb Williams*, 3 vols. (London, 1794); 2nd edn., 3 vols. (London, 1796); 3rd edn., 3 vols. (London, 1797); 4th edn., 3 vols. (London, 1816); 5th edn. (London, 1831).

—— *Caleb Williams*, ed. David McCracken (Oxford, 1970).

—— *Caleb Williams*, ed. Maurice Hindle (Harmondsworth, 1988).

—— Letter to the Editor on *Caleb Williams*, 7 June 1795, *British Critic*, 6 (July 1795), 94–5.

—— *The Enquirer: Reflections on Education, Manners and Literature. In a Series of Essays* (London, 1797, 1823).

—— *Memoirs of the Author of A Vindication of the Rights of Woman* (1798), ed. in one vol. with Mary Wollstonecraft, *Letters Written During a Short Residence in Sweden, Norway, and Denmark* (1796), by Richard Holmes (Harmondsworth, 1987).

—— *St Leon: A Tale of the Sixteenth Century*, 4 vols. (London, 1799); 3rd edn. (London, 1831).

—— *Thoughts Occasioned by the Perusal of Dr Parr's Spital Sermon* (London, 1801).

—— *Life of Geoffrey Chaucer, the Early English Poet; including Memoirs of his near Friend and Kinsman John of Gaunt, Duke of Lancaster; with Sketches of the Manners, Opinions, Arts and Literature of England in the Fourteenth Century*, 2 vols. (London, 1803).

—— *Fleetwood; or, The New Man of Feeling*, 3 vols. (London, 1805); 2nd edn. (London, 1832).

—— *Lives of Edward and John Philips, Nephews and Pupils of Milton; including Various Particulars of the Literary and Political History of their Times* (London, 1815).

—— *Mandeville: A Tale of the Seventeenth Century in England*, 3 vols. (Edinburgh, 1817).

GODWIN, WILLIAM, *History of the Commonwealth of England. From its Commencement, to the Restoration of Charles the Second*, 4 vols. (London, 1824–8).

—— *Cloudesley. A Tale*, 3 vols. (London, 1830).

—— *Thoughts on Man, his Nature, Productions and Discoveries. Interpersed with some Particulars respecting the Author* (London, 1831).

—— *Deloraine*, 3 vols. (London, 1833).

—— *Godwin and Mary: Letters of William Godwin and Mary Wollstonecraft*, ed. Ralph M. Wardle (Lawrence, Kan., 1966).

GOETHE, JOHANN WOLFGANG VON, *The Sorrows of Young Werther* (1774), trans. Victor Lange (New York, 1949).

—— *Faust/Part One* (1773–1808), trans. Philip Wayne (Harmondsworth, 1949).

GOLD, ALEX, 'It's Only Love: The Politics of Passion in *Caleb Williams*', *Texas Studies in Literature and Language*, 19 (1977), 135–60.

GOLDBERG, M. A., 'Moral and Myth in Mrs Shelley's *Frankenstein*', *Keats–Shelley Journal*, 8 (1959), 27–38.

GOLDSTEIN, LAURENCE, *Ruins and Empire: The Evolution of a Theme in Augustan and Romantic Literature* (Pittsburgh, 1977).

GOODWIN, ALBERT, *The Friends of Liberty: The English Democratic Movement in the Age of the French Revolution* (London, 1979).

GOSSE, EDMUND, *Silhouettes* (London, 1925).

GOULD, STEPHEN JAY, *Time's Arrow, Time's Cycle: Myth and Metaphor in the Discovery of Geological Time* (1987; Harmondsworth, 1988).

GRABO, NORMAN S., *The Coincidental Art of Charles Brockden Brown* (Chapel Hill, NC, 1981).

GRAY, THOMAS, *The Poems of Gray, Collins and Goldsmith*, ed. Roger Lonsdale, Longman Annotated English Poets (London, 1969).

GREGORY, ALLENE, *The French Revolution and the English Novel* (New York, 1915).

GROB, ALAN, 'Wordsworth and Godwin: A Reassessment', *SIR* 6 (1966), 99–119.

GROSS, HARVEY, 'The Pursuer and the Pursued: A Study of *Caleb Williams*', *Texas Studies in Literature and Language*, 1 (1959), 401–11.

GRYLLS, R. GLYNN, *Mary Shelley: A Biography* (Oxford, 1938).

HALÉVY, ELIE, *A History of the English People in the Nineteenth Century*, 6 vols. (1912–32), trans. from the French by E. I. Watkin and D. A. Barker (London, 1924–34, 1961), i, *England in 1815*; ii, *The Liberal Awakening, 1815–1830*.

—— *The Growth of Philosophic Radicalism* (1928), trans. from the French by Mary Morris with a Preface by John Plamenatz (London, 1972).

HARVEY, A. D., 'The Nightmare of *Caleb Williams*', *EIC* 26 (1976), 236–49.

HAYS, MARY, *Memoirs of Emma Courtney*, 2 vols. (London, 1796).

HAZLITT, WILLIAM, *The Complete Works of William Hazlitt*, ed. P. P. Howe, 21 vols. (London, 1930–4).

HEDGES, WILLIAM L., 'Charles Brockden Brown and the Culture of Contradictions', *EAL* 9 (1974), 107–42.

HILL, CHRISTOPHER, 'Clarissa Harlowe and her Times', *EIC* 5 (1955), 315–40.

—— *Puritanism and Revolution* (1958; Harmondsworth, 1986).

HIRSCH, DAVID H., 'Charles Brockden Brown as a Novelist of Ideas', *Books at Brown*, 20 (1965), 165–84.

HODGART, MATTHEW, 'Politics and Prose Style in the Late Eighteenth Century: The Radicals', *Bulletin of the New York Public Library*, 65 (1962), 464–9.

HOGG, JAMES, *The Private Memoirs and Confessions of a Justified Sinner* (1824), ed. John Carey (Oxford, 1969, 1981).

—— *Memoirs of the Author's Life and Familiar Anecdotes of Sir Walter Scott* (1832, 1834), ed. Douglas S. Mack (Edinburgh, 1972).

HOLCROFT, THOMAS, *Anna St Ives* (1792), ed. Peter Faulkner (Oxford, 1970).

—— Review of *The Castle of Vallery, An Ancient Story* [1792], *Monthly Review* NS 9 (Nov. 1792), 337.

—— *The Adventures of Hugh Trevor* (1794–7), ed. Seamus Deane (Oxford, 1973).

HOLLINGSWORTH, KEITH, *The Newgate Novel, 1830–47: Bulwer, Ainsworth, Dickens and Thackeray* (Detroit, 1963).

HOOK, ANDREW, *Scotland and America: A Study of Cultural Relations, 1750–1835* (Glasgow, 1975).

[HOPE, THOMAS], *Anastasius; or, Memoirs of a Greek: Written at the Close of the Eighteenth Century*, 3 vols. (London, 1819).

HOWE, SUSANNE, *Wilhelm Meister and his English Kinsmen: Apprentices to Life* (New York, 1930).

HUGHES, DEAN, 'The Composition of *Caleb Williams*: Dickens's Misunderstanding', *Dickens Studies Newsletter*, 8/3 (Sept. 1977), 80.

HUME, DAVID, *A Treatise of Human Nature: Being an Attempt to Introduce the Experimental Method of Reasoning into Moral Subjects* (1739–40), ed. L. A. Selby-Bigge, 2nd edn., rev. P. H. Nedditch (Oxford, 1978).

HUME, ROBERT D., 'Gothic Versus Romantic: A Revaluation of the Gothic Novel', *PMLA* 84 (1969), 282–90.

INCHBALD, ELIZABETH, *A Simple Story* (1791), ed. J. M. S. Tompkins (Oxford, 1967).

INCHBALD, ELIZABETH, *Nature and Art*, 2 vols. (London, 1796).

JACKSON, ROSEMARY, *Fantasy: The Literature of Subversion* (London, 1981).

JACOBUS, MARY, 'Is there a Woman in this Text?, *New Literary History*, 14 (1982), 117–41.

JOHNSON, BARBARA, 'My Monster/My Self', *Diacritics*, 12/2 (Summer 1982), 3–11.

JONES, FREDERICK L., 'Introduction' to *The Letters of Mary Wollstonecraft Shelley*, 3 vols. (Norman, Okla., 1944).

JUSTUS, JAMES H., 'Arthur Mervyn, American', *American Literature*, 42 (1970), 304–24.

KEATS, JOHN, *The Letters of John Keats, 1814–1821*, ed. Hyder E. Rollins, 2 vols. (Cambridge, Mass., 1958).

KEEBLE, N. H., *The Literary Culture of Nonconformity in Later Seventeenth-Century England* (Leicester, 1987).

KELLY, GARY, *The English Jacobin Novel, 1780–1805* (Oxford, 1976).

—— 'History and Fiction: Bethlem Gabor in Godwin's *St Leon*', *English Language Notes*, 14 (1976), 117–20.

—— *English Fiction of the Romantic Period, 1789–1830* (London, 1989).

KIELY, ROBERT, *The Romantic Novel in England* (Cambridge, Mass., 1972).

KOVAČEVIĆ, IVANKA, *Fact into Fiction: English Literature and the Industrial Scene, 1750–1850* (Leicester, 1975).

KROPF, C. R., '*Caleb Williams* and the Attack on Romance', *Stud. N* 8 (1976), 81–7.

KUCZYNSKI, INGRID, 'Pastoral Romance and *Political Justice*', in Anselm Schlösser *et al.* (eds.), *Essays in Honor of William Gallacher: Life and Literature of the Working Class* (Berlin, 1966), 101–10.

LAMB, CHARLES, *The Letters of Charles and Mary Anne Lamb*, ed. Edwin J. Marrs, Jr., 3 vols. (Ithaca, NY, 1975–8).

LASKY, MELVIN J., *Utopia and Revolution: On the Origins of a Metaphor* (Chicago, 1976).

LESSENICH, ROLF P., 'Godwin and Shelley: Rhetoric versus Revolution', *Studia Neophilologica*, 47 (1975), 40–52.

LEVINE, GEORGE, *The Realistic Imagination: English Fiction from Frankenstein to Lady Chatterley* (Chicago, 1983).

—— and KNOEPFLMACHER, U. C., eds., *The Endurance of Frankenstein: Essays on Mary Shelley's Novel* (Berkeley, Calif., 1979).

LEWIS, MATTHEW, *The Monk: A Romance* (1796), ed. Howard Anderson (Oxford, 1973).

LINCOLN, A. H., *Some Political and Social Ideas of English Dissent, 1763–1800* (Cambridge, 1938).

LINDSAY, JACK, *Charles Dickens: A Biographical and Critical Study* (London, 1950).

LLOYD, MICHAEL, 'Bulwer-Lytton and the Idealising Principle', *English Miscellany*, 7 (1956), 25–39.

LOCKE, DON, *A Fantasy of Reason: The Life and Thought of William Godwin* (London, 1980).

LOSHE, LILLIE D., *The Early American Novel, 1789–1830* (New York, 1907).

LOUGHREY, BRIAN, ed., *The Pastoral Mode: A Casebook* (London, 1984).

LOVELL, ERNEST J., Jr., *Byron: The Record of a Quest. Studies in a Poet's Concept and Treatment of Nature* (Austin, Tex., 1949).

—— 'Byron and Mary Shelley', *Keats–Shelley Journal*, 2 (1953), 35–49.

LUKÁCS, GEORG, *The Historical Novel* (1937), trans. from the German by Hannah and Stanley Mitchell (1962; Harmondsworth, 1981).

—— *The Theory of the Novel: A Historico-Philosophical Essay on the Forms of Great Epic Literature* (1920), trans. from the German by Anna Bostock (London, 1971).

LYLES, W. H., *Mary Shelley: An Annotated Bibliography* (New York, 1975).

LYTTON, GEORGE EARLE LYTTON BULWER, 1st Baron Lytton of Knebworth. See under BULWER.

LYTTON, VICTOR ALEXANDER, 2nd Earl of, *The Life of Edward Bulwer, First Lord Lytton, by his Grandson*, 2 vols. (London, 1913).

MCCRACKEN, DAVID, 'Godwin's *Caleb Williams*: A Fictional Rebuttal of Burke', *Studies in Burke and his Time*, 11–12 (1969–71), 1442–52.

—— 'Godwin's Literary Theory: The Alliance between Fiction and Political Philosophy', *Philological Quarterly*, 49 (1970), 113–33.

—— 'Godwin's Reading in Burke', *English Language Notes*, 7 (1970), 264–70.

MCDOWELL, TREMAINE, 'Scott on Cooper and Brockden Brown', *Modern Language Notes*, 45 (1930), 18–20.

MCFARLAND, Thomas, *Romanticism and the Forms of Ruin: Wordsworth, Coleridge, and Modalities of Fragmentation* (Princeton, NJ, 1981).

MCGANN, JEROME J., *The Romantic Ideology: A Critical Investigation* (Chicago, 1983).

—— *The Beauty of Inflections: Literary Investigations in Historical Method and Theory* (Oxford, 1985; 2nd edn., 1988).

MACKENZIE, HENRY, *The Man of Feeling* (1771), ed. Brian Vickers (Oxford, 1970).

—— *Anecdotes and Egotisms, 1745–1831*, ed. H. W. Thompson (Oxford, 1927).

MCKEON, MICHAEL, *The Origins of the English Novel, 1600–1740* (Baltimore, 1987).

Mackintosh, James, *Vindiciae Gallicae. Defence of the French Revolution and its English Admirers, against the Accusations of the Right Hon. Edmund Burke* (London, 1791).

—— Review of Godwin, *Lives of Edward and John Philips, Nephews and Pupils of Milton*, *Edinburgh Review*, 25 (1815), 485–91.

McNeill, William H., *Plagues and Peoples* (1976; Harmondsworth, 1979).

McNiece, Gerald, *Shelley and the Revolutionary Idea* (Cambridge, Mass., 1969).

[Macpherson, James], *Fragments of Ancient Poetry, Collected in the Highlands of Scotland, and Translated from the Galic or Erse Language* (Edinburgh, 1760).

—— *The Poems of Ossian*, 2 vols. (London, 1805).

Marchand, Ernest, 'The Literary Opinions of Charles Brockden Brown', *Studies in Philology*, 31 (1934), 541–66.

Marshall, Mrs Julian, *The Life and Letters of Mary Wollstonecraft Shelley*, 2 vols. (London, 1889).

Marshall, Peter, *William Godwin* (New Haven, Conn., 1984).

Martin, Terence, *The Instructed Vision: Scottish Common Sense Philosophy and the Origins of American Fiction* (Bloomington, Ind., 1961).

Masson, David, *British Novelists and their Styles* (Cambridge, 1859).

Maturin, Charles, *Melmoth the Wanderer* (1820), ed. Douglas Grant (Oxford, 1968).

Mellor, Anne K., *Mary Shelley: Her Life, her Fiction, her Monsters* (New York and London, 1988).

Messac, Regis, 'Bulwer Lytton et Dostoïevski: De Paul Clifford à Raskolnikof', *Revue de Littérature Comparée*, 6 (1926), 638–53.

Mill, John Stuart, *Mill on Bentham and Coleridge*, ed. F. R. Leavis (Cambridge, 1950, 1978).

Miller, Jacqueline T., 'The Imperfect Tale: Articulation, Rhetoric and Self in *Caleb Williams*', *Criticism*, 20 (1978), 366–82.

Miller, Samuel, *A Brief Retrospect of the Eighteenth Century*, 2 vols. (New York, 1803).

Milton, John, *Complete Shorter Poems*, ed. John Carey, Longman Annotated English Poets (London, 1968, 1971).

—— *Paradise Lost* (1667), ed. Alastair Fowler, Longman Annotated English Poets (London, 1968, 1971).

—— *Areopagitica: A Speech of Mr John Milton for the Liberty of Unlicenc'd Printing to the Parliament of England* (1644), *The Complete Prose Works of John Milton*, ed. Don M. Wolfe *et al.*, 8 vols. (New Haven, Conn., 1953–82), vol. ii.

MODLESKI, TANIA, *Loving with a Vengeance: Mass-Produced Fantasies for Women* (New York and London, 1982).

MOERS, ELLEN, *The Dandy: Brummell to Beerbohm* (London, 1960).

—— *Literary Women* (New York, 1977).

MONRO, D. H., *Godwin's Moral Philosophy: An Interpretation of William Godwin* (Oxford, 1953).

[MOORE, DR JOHN], *Zeluco: Various Portraits of Human Nature, Taken from Life and Manners, Foreign and Domestic*, 2 vols. (London, 1789).

MOORE, THOMAS, *The Epicurean: A Tale* (London, 1827).

[MORE, HANNAH], *Village Politics, Addressed to All the Mechanics, Journeymen, and Labourers, in Great Britain. By Will Chip, a Country Carpenter* [1793], *The Works of Hannah More*, 8 vols. (London, 1801), vol. i.

MORETTI, FRANCO, *Signs Taken for Wonders: Essays in the Sociology of Literary Forms*, trans. Susan Fischer, David Forgacs, David Miller (London, 1983).

MORGAN, PRYS, *A New History of Wales: The Eighteenth-Century Renaissance* (Llandybie, 1981).

—— 'From a Death to a View: The Hunt for the Welsh Past in the Romantic Period', in Eric Hobsbawm and Terence Ranger (eds.), *The Invention of Tradition* (Cambridge, 1983), 43–100.

MORISON, SAMUEL ELIOT, COMMAGER, HENRY STEELE, and LEUCHTENBURG, WILLIAM H., *The Growth of the American Republic*, 2 vols. (6th edn., New York, 1969).

MURCH, A. E., *The Development of the Detective Novel* (London, 1958).

MURRY, JOHN MIDDLETON, 'The Protestant Dream', in *Heaven—and Earth* (London, 1938), 254–68.

MYERS, MITZI, 'Godwin's Changing Conception of *Caleb Williams*', *SEL* 12 (1972), 591–628.

NEAL, JOHN, *American Writers: A Series of Papers Contributed to Blackwood's Magazine (1824–5)*, ed. Fred Lewis Patee (Durham, NC, 1937).

NELSON, LOWRY, Jr., 'Night Thoughts on the Gothic Novel', *Yale Review*, 52 (1963), 236–57.

NITCHIE, ELIZABETH, *Mary Shelley: Author of Frankenstein* (New Brunswick, NJ, 1953).

NORBROOK, DAVID, *Poetry and Politics in the English Renaissance* (London, 1984).

Nouvelle Biographie Générale (Paris, 1863).

OUSBY, IAN, ' "My Servant Caleb": Godwin's *Caleb Williams* and the Political Trials of the 1790s', *UTQ* 44 (1974), 47–55.

PAINE, THOMAS, *Common Sense* (1776), ed. Isaac Kramnick (Harmondsworth, 1976).

PAINE, THOMAS, *Rights of Man; Being an Answer to Burke's Attack on the French Revolution* (1791–2), ed. Henry Collins (Harmondsworth, 1969).

PALACIO, JEAN DE, 'Godwin et la tentation de l'autobiographie (William Godwin et J. J. Rousseau)', *Études Anglaises*, 27 (1974), 143–57.

—— *William Godwin et son monde intérieur* (Lille, 1980).

PARK, ROY, *Hazlitt and the Spirit of the Age: Abstraction and Critical Theory* (Oxford, 1971).

PARKER, PATRICIA L., *Charles Brockden Brown: A Reference Guide* (London, 1980).

PATTEE, FRED LEWIS, 'Introduction' to Charles Brockden Brown, *Wieland; or, The Transformation, together with Memoirs of Carwin the Biloquist* (New York, 1926).

PAUL, C. KEGAN, *William Godwin: His Friends and Contemporaries*, 2 vols. (London, 1876).

PAULSON, RONALD, 'Gothic Fiction and the French Revolution', *English Literary History*, 48 (1981), 532–54.

—— *Representations of Revolution (1789–1820)* (New Haven, Conn., 1983).

PEACOCK, THOMAS LOVE, *The Works of Thomas Love Peacock*, ed. H. F. B. Brett-Smith and C. E. Jones, Halliford Edition, 10 vols. (London, 1924–34).

PECK, WALTER E., 'Shelley and the Abbé Barruel', *PMLA* 36 (1921), 347–53.

PHILP, MARK, *Godwin's Political Justice* (London, 1986).

PLATO, *The Republic*, trans. A. D. Lindsay, with introduction and notes by Renford Bambrough, Everyman's Library (London, 1976, 1984).

POE, EDGAR ALLAN, 'The Philosophy of Composition' [1846], *The Complete Works of Edgar Allan Poe*, ed. James A. Harrison, 17 vols. (New York, 1965), vol. xiv.

POLLIN, BURTON R., *Education and Enlightenment in the Works of William Godwin* (New York, 1962).

—— 'Primitivism in *Imogen*', *Bulletin of the New York Public Library*, 67 (1963), 186–90, rpt. in *Imogen: A Pastoral Romance*, ed. Jack W. Marken (New York, 1963), 113–17.

—— 'William Godwin's "Fragment of a Romance"', *Comparative Literature*, 16 (1964), 40–54.

—— 'Philosophical and Literary Sources of *Frankenstein*', *Comparative Literature*, 17 (1965), 97–108.

—— *Godwin Criticism: A Synoptic Bibliography* (Toronto, 1967).

POOVEY, MARY, 'Ideology and *The Mysteries of Udolpho*', *Criticism*, 21 (1979), 307–30.

—— '"My Hideous Progeny": Mary Shelley and the Feminization of Romanticism', *PMLA* 95 (1980), 332–47.

—— *The Proper Lady and the Woman Writer: Ideology as Style in the Works of Mary Wollstonecraft, Mary Shelley, and Jane Austen* (Chicago, 1984).

PORTE, JOEL, 'In the Hands of an Angry God: Religious Terror in Gothic Fiction', in G. R. Thompson (ed.), *The Gothic Imagination: Essays in Dark Romanticism* (Pullman, Wash., 1974), 42–64.

PORTER, ROY, *English Society in the Eighteenth Century* (Harmondsworth, 1982; rev. edn., 1990).

—— and TEICH, MIKULÁŠ, ed., *Romanticism in National Context* (Cambridge, 1988).

POWELL, NICHOLAS, *Fuseli: The Nightmare* (London, 1973).

PRICE, RICHARD, *Observations on the Importance of the American Revolution, and the Means of Making it a Benefit to the World* (London, 1785).

—— *A Discourse on the Love of Our Country* (London, 1789).

PRIESTLEY, F. E. L., 'Critical Introduction' to Godwin, *Enquiry Concerning Political Justice*, 3 vols. (Toronto, 1946).

PRIMER, IRWIN, 'Some Implications of Irony', *Bulletin of the New York Public Library*, 67 (1963), 237–40, rpt. in *Imogen: A Pastoral Romance*, ed. Jack W. Marken (New York, 1963), 118–21.

PUNTER, DAVID, *The Literature of Terror: A History of Gothic Fictions from 1765 to the Present Day* (London, 1980).

PUTTENHAM, GEORGE, *The Art of English Poesie* (1589), in *Elizabethan Critical Essays*, ed. G. Gregory Smith, 2 vols. (Oxford, 1903), vol. ii.

RADCLIFFE, ANN, *The Romance of the Forest* (1791), ed. Chloe Chard (Oxford, 1986).

—— *The Mysteries of Udolpho: A Romance* (1794), ed. Bonamy Dobrée and Frederick Garber (Oxford, 1966, 1970).

—— *The Italian; or, The Confessional of the Black Penitents: A Romance* (1797), ed. Frederick Garber (Oxford, 1981).

REEVE, CLARA, *The Progress of Romance, Through Times, Countries and Manners*, 2 vols. (London, 1785), facsimile reprint (New York, 1930).

REID, S. W., 'Brockden Brown in England: Notes on Henry Colburn's 1822 Editions of his Novels', *EAL* 9 (1974), 188–95.

REIMAN, DONALD H., ed., *The Romantics Reviewed: Contemporary Reviews of British Romantic Writers*, 8 vols. (New York, 1972).

RICHARDSON, SAMUEL, *Pamela; or, Virtue Rewarded* (1740), ed. Peter Sabor, introd. Margaret Doody (Harmondsworth, 1980).

—— *Clarissa; or, The History of a Young Lady* (1747–8), ed. Angus Ross (Harmondsworth, 1985).

—— *Selected Letters of Samuel Richardson*, ed. John Carroll (Oxford, 1964).

RICHETTI, J. J., *Popular Fiction Before Richardson* (Oxford, 1969).

RIEGER, JAMES, *The Mutiny Within: The Heresies of Percy Bysshe Shelley* (New York, 1967).

RINGE, DONALD A., 'Charles Brockden Brown', in Everett Emerson (ed.), *Major Writers of Early American Literature* (Madison, Wis., 1972), 273–94.

ROBBINS, CAROLINE, *The Eighteenth-Century Commonwealthman* (Cambridge, Mass., 1959).

ROBERTS, J. M., *The Mythology of the Secret Societies* (London, 1972).

ROBINSON, HENRY CRABB, *Crabb Robinson in Germany, 1800–1805: Extracts from his Correspondence*, ed. Edith J. Morley (Oxford, 1929).

—— *Henry Crabb Robinson on Books and their Writers*, ed. Edith J. Morley, 3 vols. (Oxford, 1938).

ROBISON, JOHN, *Proofs of a Conspiracy against all the Governments of Europe, Carried on in the Secret Meetings of Free Masons, Illuminati and Reading Societies* (Edinburgh, 1797).

ROEMER, DONALD, 'The Achievement of Godwin's *Caleb Williams*: The Proto-Byronic Squire Falkland', *Criticism*, 18 (1976), 81–7.

ROPER, DEREK, *Reviewing before the Edinburgh: 1788–1802* (London, 1978).

ROTHSTEIN, ERIC, 'Allusion and Analogy in the Romance of *Caleb Williams*', *UTQ* 37 (1967), 18–30.

ROUSSEAU, JEAN-JACQUES, *Discourse on the Origins and Foundations of Inequality among Men* (1755), trans. and ed. Maurice Cranston (Harmondsworth, 1984).

—— *The Confessions* (1781), trans. J. M. Cohen (Harmondsworth, 1953).

—— *The Reveries of the Solitary Walker* (1783), trans. and ed. Peter France (Harmondsworth, 1979).

RUBENSTEIN, MARC A., ' "My Accursed Origin": The Search for the Mother in *Frankenstein*', *SIR* 15 (1976), 136–47.

SADLEIR, MICHAEL, *Edward and Rosina, 1803–1836 (A Panorama)* (London, 1931).

—— *XIX Century Fiction: A Bibliographical Record based on his own Collection*, 2 vols. (London and Los Angeles, 1951).

ST CLAIR, WILLIAM, *The Godwins and the Shelleys: The Biography of a Family* (London, 1989).

SAMBROOK, A. J., 'A Romantic Theme: The Last Man', *Forum for Modern Language Studies*, 2 (1966), 25–33.

SCHEUERMANN, MONA, 'From Mind to Society: *Caleb Williams* as Psychological Novel', *Dutch-Quarterly Review of Anglo-American Letters*, 7 (1977), 115–27.

SCHILLER, FRIEDRICH, *The Ghost-Seer; or, Apparitionist* (1789), trans. D. Boileau (London, 1795).

SCHLEGEL, FRIEDRICH, 'On Goethe's *Meister*' (1798), English text in

German Aesthetic and Literary Criticism: The Romantic Ironists and Goethe, ed. Kathleen M. Wheeler (Cambridge, 1983), 59–73.

—— *Lucinde and the Fragments*, trans. Peter Firchow (Minneapolis, 1971).

SCOTT, SIR WALTER, *Waverley Novels*, New Edition with the Author's Notes, 48 vols. (Edinburgh, 1829–33): *Waverley; or, 'Tis Sixty Years Since* (1814); *Guy Mannering; or, The Astrologer* (1815); *The Antiquary* (1816); *Tales of My Landlord: The Black Dwarf/Old Mortality* (1816); *Tales of My Landlord, Second Series: The Heart of Mid-Lothian* (1818); *Tales of My Landlord, Third Series: The Bride of Lammermoor/A Legend of Montrose* (1819); *Redgauntlet* (1824).

—— *The Miscellaneous Prose Works of Sir Walter Scott, Bart*, ed. J. G. Lockhart, 28 vols. (Edinburgh, 1834–6), vols. xvii–xviii.

—— *The Letters of Sir Walter Scott*, Centenary Fiction, ed. H. J. C. Grierson, *et al.*, 12 vols. (London, 1932–7).

—— *Sir Walter Scott on Novelists and Fiction*, ed. Ioan Williams (London, 1968).

SHAKESPEARE, WILLIAM, *Cymbeline*, in *Complete Works*, ed. P. Alexander (London and Glasgow, 1951).

SHARROCK, ROGER, 'Godwin and Milton's Satan', *Notes and Queries*, 207 (1962), 463–5.

SHAW, HARRY E., *The Forms of Historical Fiction: Sir Walter Scott and his Successors* (Ithaca, NY, 1983).

SHELLEY, MARY WOLLSTONECRAFT, *History of A Six Weeks Tour through a Part of France, Switzerland, Germany, and Holland, with Letters descriptive of a Sail round the Lake of Geneva, and of the Glaciers of Chamouni* (London, 1817).

—— *Frankenstein; or, The Modern Prometheus, the 1818 text*, ed. with variant readings, introduction, and notes by James Rieger (1974; Chicago, 1982).

—— *Frankenstein; or, The Modern Prometheus*, ed. James Kinsley and M. K. Joseph (Oxford, 1969, 1980).

—— *Mathilda* [1819], ed. Elizabeth Nitchie (Chapel Hill, NC, 1959).

—— *Valperga; or, The Life and Adventures of Castruccio, Prince of Lucca*, 3 vols. (London, 1823).

—— *The Last Man* (1826), ed. Hugh J. Luke, Jr. (Lincoln, Nebr., 1965).

—— *The Last Man* (1826), introd. Brian Aldiss (London, 1985).

—— *The Fortunes of Perkin Warbeck: A Romance*, 3 vols. (London, 1830).

—— *Collected Tales and Stories*, ed. Charles E. Robinson (Baltimore, 1976).

—— *The Letters of Mary Wollstonecraft Shelley*, ed. Frederick L. Jones, 3 vols. (Norman, Okla., 1944).

SHELLEY, MARY WOLLSTONECRAFT, *The Letters of Mary Wollstonecraft Shelley*, ed. Betty T. Bennett 3 vols. (Baltimore, 1980–8).

—— *The Journals of Mary Wollstonecraft Shelley, 1814–1844*, ed. Paul R. Feldman and Diana Scott-Kilvert, 2 vols. (Oxford, 1987).

SHELLEY, PERCY BYSSHE, *The Complete Works of Percy Bysshe Shelley*, ed. Roger Ingpen and Walter E. Peck, Julian Edition, 10 vols. (London, 1926–30, vols. v–vii: Prose.

—— *Shelley: Poetical Works*, ed. Thomas Hutchinson, corr. G. M. Matthews (Oxford, 1970).

—— *Zastrozzi and St. Irvyne*, ed. Stephen C. Behrendt (Oxford, 1986).

—— *The Letters of Percy Bysshe Shelley*, ed. Frederick L. Jones, 2 vols. (Oxford, 1964).

SHERBURN, GEORGE, 'Godwin's Later Novels', *SIR* 1 (1962), 65–82.

SHKLAR, JUDITH, *After Utopia: The Decline of Political Faith* (Princeton, NJ, 1957).

SICKELS, ELEANOR, 'Shelley and Charles Brockden Brown', *PMLA* 45 (1930), 1116–28.

SMALL, CHRISTOPHER, *Ariel Like a Harpy: Shelley, Mary, and Frankenstein* (London, 1972).

SMITH, CHARLOTTE, *Desmond: A Tale*, 3 vols. (London, 1792).

SMITH, SUSAN HARRIS, '*Frankenstein*: Mary Shelley's Psychic Divisiveness', *Women and Literature*, 5/2 (Fall 1977), 42–53.

SMOLLETT, TOBIAS, *Ferdinand Count Fathom* (1753), ed. Damian Grant (Oxford, 1971).

SNYDER, ROBERT LANCE, 'Apocalypse and Indeterminacy in Mary Shelley's *The Last Man*', *SIR* 17 (1978), 435–52.

SONTAG, SUSAN, *Illness as Metaphor* (New York, 1978).

SOUTHEY, ROBERT, *Sir Thomas More; or, Colloquies on the Progress and Prospects of Society*, 2 vols. (London, 1829).

SPARK, MURIEL, *Child of Light: A Reassessment of Mary Wollstonecraft Shelley* (Hadleigh, 1951), revised as *Mary Shelley* (London, 1988).

SPATT, HARTLEY S., 'Mary Shelley's Last Men: The Truth of Dreams', *Stud. N.* 7 (1975), 526–37.

SPENCER, JANE, *The Rise of the Woman Novelist* (Oxford, 1986).

SPENSER, EDMUND, *The Faerie Queene*, ed. A. C. Hamilton, Longman Annotated English Poets (London, 1977).

SPIVAK, GAYATRI CHAKRAVORTY, 'Three Women's Texts and a Critique of Imperialism', *Critical Inquiry*, 12 (1985), 243–61.

STAFFORD, FIONA, *The Sublime Savage: James Macpherson and the Poems of Ossian* (Edinburgh, 1988).

STANG, RICHARD, *The Theory of the Novel in England, 1850–1870* (London, 1959).

STARR, G. A., *Defoe and Spiritual Autobiography* (Princeton, NJ, 1965).

—— 'Henry Brooke, William Godwin and "Barnabas Tirrell/Tyrrel" ', *Notes and Queries*, 25 (1978), 67–8.

STEPHEN, LESLIE, 'William Godwin's Novels', *Studies of a Biographer*, 2nd ser. (London, 1902), iii. 119–54.

STERRENBURG, LEE, '*The Last Man*: Anatomy of Failed Revolutions', *Nineteenth Century Fiction*, 33 (1978), 324–47.

—— 'Mary Shelley's Monster: Politics and Psyche in *Frankenstein*', in George Levine and U. C. Knoepflmacher (eds.), *The Endurance of Frankenstein: Essays on Mary Shelley's Novel* (Berkeley, Calif., 1979), 143–71.

STORCH, R. F., 'Metaphors of Private Guilt and Social Rebellion in Godwin's *Caleb Williams*', *English Literary History*, 34 (1966), 188–207.

SULEIMAN, SUSAN RUBIN, *Authoritarian Fictions: The Ideological Novel as a Literary Genre* (New York, 1983).

SWINGLE, L. J., 'Frankenstein's Monster and its Romantic Relatives: Problems of Knowledge in English Romanticism', *Texas Studies in Literature and Language*, 15 (1973), 51–65.

TANNENBAUM, LESLIE, 'From Filthy Type to Truth: Miltonic Myth in *Frankenstein*', *Keats–Shelley Journal*, 26 (1977), 101–13.

THOMPSON, E. P., *The Making of the English Working Class* (1963; rev. edn., Harmondsworth, 1968, 1980).

TODD, JANET, M., 'Frankenstein's Daughter: Mary Shelley and Mary Wollstonecraft', *Women and Literature*, 4/2 (Fall 1976), 18–27.

TODOROV, TZVETAN, *The Fantastic: A Structural Approach to a Literary Genre* (1970), trans. from the French by Richard Howard (London, 1973).

TOMALIN, CLAIRE, *The Life and Death of Mary Wollstonecraft* (1974; Harmondsworth, 1977).

TOMPKINS, JANE, *Sensational Designs: The Cultural Work of American Fiction, 1790–1860* (New York, 1985).

TOMPKINS, J. M. S., *The Popular Novel in England, 1770–1800* (London, 1932).

TUCKER, SUSIE I., *Enthusiasm: A Study in Semantic Change* (Cambridge, 1972).

TYMMS, RALPH, *Doubles in Literary Psychology* (Cambridge, Mass., 1949).

TYSDAHL, B. J., *William Godwin as Novelist* (London, 1981).

TYSON, G. P., *Joseph Johnson: A Liberal Publisher* (Des Moines, 1979).

UPHAUS, ROBERT W., '*Caleb Williams*: Godwin's Epoch of Mind', *Stud. N* 9 (1977), 279–96.

VIRGIL, *The Georgics*, trans. with introd. and notes by L. P. Wilkinson (Harmondsworth, 1982).

VOLNEY, CONSTANTIN FRANÇOIS CHASSEBOEUF, Comte de, *The Ruins; or, A Survey of the Revolutions of Empires* (1791), anonymously trans. from the French (London, 1792, 1838).

WALPOLE, HORACE, *The Castle of Otranto* (1764), ed. W. S. Lewis (Oxford, 1964, 1982).

WARD, ROBERT PLUMER, *Tremaine; or, The Man of Refinement*, 3 vols. (London, 1825).

WARFEL, HARRY R., 'Charles Brockden Brown's German Sources', *Modern Language Quarterly*, 1 (1940), 357–65.

—— *Charles Brockden Brown: American Gothic Novelist* (Gainesville, Fla., 1949).

WARTON, JOSEPH, *An Essay on the Writings and Genius of Pope*, vol. i (London, 1756); vol. ii (London, 1782).

WARTON, THOMAS, *The History of English Poetry, From the Close of the Eleventh to the Commencement of the Eighteenth Century*, 4 vols., final vols. never completed (London, 1774–81).

WATT, IAN, *The Rise of the Novel* (London, 1957).

WATT, ROBERT, MD, *Bibliotheca Britannica; or, A General Index to British and Foreign Literature* (London, 1824).

WHITNEY, LOIS, *Primitivism and the Idea of Progress in English Popular Literature of the Eighteenth Century* (Baltimore, 1934).

WILLIAMS, GWYN A., *Artisans and Sans-Culottes: Popular Movements in France and Britain during the French Revolution* (1968; rev. edn., London, 1989).

—— *Madoc: The Making of a Myth* (1979; Oxford, 1987).

—— 'Romanticism in Wales', in Roy Porter and Mikuláš Teich (eds.), *Romanticism in National Context* (Cambridge, 1988), 9–36.

WILLIAMS, IOAN (ed.), *Novel and Romance, 1700–1800: A Documentary Record* (London, 1970).

WILLIAMS, RAYMOND, *Culture and Society, 1780–1850* (1958; Harmondsworth, 1963).

—— *The Long Revolution* (1961; Harmondsworth, 1965).

—— *Keywords: A Vocabulary of Culture and Society* (London, 1976).

—— *Writing in Society* (London, 1983).

WILSON, JOHN, *The City of the Plague and Other Poems* (London, 1816).

WOLLSTONECRAFT, MARY, *Vindication of the Rights of Men, in a Letter to the Right Honourable Edmund Burke* (London, 1790).

—— *Vindication of the Rights of Woman; with Strictures on Political and Moral Subjects* (1792), ed. Miriam Brody Kramnick (Harmondsworth, 1975, 1982).

—— *Mary and The Wrongs of Woman*, ed. James Kinsley and Gary Kelly (Oxford, 1976).

—— *An Historical and Moral View of the Origin and Progress of the*

French Revolution, and the Effect it has Produced in Europe, 1 vol. only (1794), facsimile reprint of 2nd edn. (1795), introd. Janet Todd (New York, 1975).

—— *Letters Written During a Short Residence in Sweden, Norway, and Denmark* (1796), ed. in one volume with William Godwin, *Memoirs of the Author of A Vindication of the Rights of Woman*, by Richard Holmes (Harmondsworth, 1987).

WORDSWORTH, WILLIAM, *The Borderers* (1797–9), ed. Robert Osborn (Ithaca, NY, 1982).

—— *The Excursion, Being a Portion of The Recluse, a Poem* (1814), *The Poetical Works of William Wordsworth*, ed. Ernest de Selincourt and Helen Darbishire, 5 vols. (Oxford, 1942–9), vol. v.

—— *The Prelude* (1805), *The Prelude, 1799, 1805, 1850*, ed. Jonathan Wordsworth, M. H. Abrams, and Stephen Gill (New York and London, 1979).

ZIFF, LARZER, 'A Reading of *Wieland*', *PMLA* 77 (1962), 51–7.

—— ed., *The Literature of America: Colonial Period* (New York, 1970).

Index